1001
Secrets for
WINDOWS NT REGISTRY

D1372085

DUKE COMMUNICATIONS INTERNATIONAL

Loveland, Colorado

Library of Congress Cataloging-in-Publication Data

Daniels, Tim, 1962-
    1001 secrets for Windows NT registry / by Tim Daniels. — 1st ed.
      p.   cm.
    Includes index.
    ISBN 1-882419-68-5
    1. Microsoft Windows NT.   2. Operating systems (Computers)
  I. Title. II. Title: One thousand one secrets for Windows NT
  registry. III. Title: One thousand and one secrets for Windows NT
  registry.
  QA76.76.O63D344 1997
  005.4'469—dc21   97-33918
                                                        CIP

Published by DUKE PRESS
DUKE COMMUNICATIONS INTERNATIONAL
Loveland, Colorado

Copyright © 1998 by Tim Daniels

This book was printed and bound in Canada.

ISBN 1-882419-68-5

1 2 3 4 5 6 7 WL 0 9 8

To George and Mary Louise Daniels. Mom and Dad.
I owe them my past, present and future!

To Jean Daniels, my love, my wife.
Your love makes all things possible!

To Christopher and James Daniels, my sons.
There will never be a better moment in my life than when each of you
was born. I will never be as proud of anything as I am of both of you!

I love all of you!

ACKNOWLEDGMENTS

There are many people that are responsible for this book. I have learned that as capable as we may think we are, nobody can go it alone! I would like to first thank my fellow authors: Dean Porter, who is the most technically gifted person I have ever worked with; Mark Russinovich, whose knowledge of Windows NT, Operating Systems, and vintage mid-80s video arcade games is second to none; and Steve Scoggins, whose exuberance and passion for computing is contagious.

I also want to thank the folks at Duke Press, *Windows NT Magazine*, and Duke Communications. First, Marion Agnew, editor extraordinaire, your incredible patience and diligence is the cornerstone of this book. Mick Gussinde-Duffy, for your faith in me and my idea, I will always be grateful to you. Steve Mitchell, who taught me what a book should be and reminded me when I strayed too far. John Morris-Reihl for taking my ugly HTML and making it beautiful and functional. Lynn Riggs, who made the manuscript look like a book, and Dawn Cyr, who tried to make it consistent. Trish McConnell, who dotted all the i's and crossed all the t's. Dave Duke, who allowed me to work at his wonderful company for over a decade. Much of what I learned about people I learned there. Mark Smith, if you hadn't listened to my silly idea about a magazine when we were both in MIS, I would have never had a chance to write this book. Bob Chronister, for your indomitable spirit and curiosity. Your guidance is and was always appreciated. You are a techie's techie. Spyros Sakellariadis, who warned me about writing a book and then convinced me to do it anyway. TJ Harty and John Bredehoeft — I owe you both a latte. Dennis Agosta, Sue Chastine, Helen Kupelli, Dean Porter, Mathew Potter, Casey Tisue and Cheryl Schamel — the Duke Communications MIS department. Your knowledge, support, and e-mail made it seem like I was onsite instead of miles away. Linda Jenkins, for proving that nice people often finish first instead of last. The readers of *Windows NT Magazine*, you kept me honest and never bored.

Tom Pokryfke, the best friend a person could ever have. The crew at the Starbucks on College & Horsetooth and on Lemay. Your coffee and kindness never failed me. Jerry Tschikof, Ken DeLine, and Richard Keith of Center Partners who allowed me to use their facilities, equipment, and Internet connection. Last but not least, David Geiger, for being about as understanding a boss as anybody could hope to have. Your encouragement, witty repartee and "fastball" helped me through some dark hours. Now that the book is done … in the words of your mentor, "I will enjoy it!"

Tim Daniels
timd@centerpartners.com

TABLE OF CONTENTS AT A GLANCE

TABLE OF CONTENTS

SECTION II HARDWARE 125

SECTION III APPLICATIONS 141

SECTION IV MICROSOFT OFFICE 201

SECTION V SECURITY 265

FOREWORD

In my years supporting NT, I have become certain about one thing: not many things in this computer-crazed world are certain. The new supercharged computer purchased last week is now obsolete, and most ideas started today by our industry leaders will probably be changed tomorrow. All this points to a bit of chaos built into our world. And this chaos extends to Windows NT.

We all recognize that the key to Windows NT is hidden in its poorly understood, undocumented, and somewhat chaotic registry. Users tend to assume that changing settings in the registry will provide an instant fix, whether or not the change is called for. I have seen many instances when registry changes have irreversibly killed an installation of NT. In fact, I have been guilty of playing this game of registry roulette myself. You feel fabulous when you succeed but not so good and embarrassed when you spend the night fixing what never should have happened in the first place. So what are we to do? Continue playing registry roulette until the inevitable happens? Many sources of information out there tell us what the registry is. But until now, no book has told us where to find these undocumented goodies in the registry or given us the information necessary to change these settings.

Tim Daniel's new book is indispensable here. It provides a plethora of registry settings for supporting NT. It is as valuable a tool as all your diskettes, CDs, and screwdrivers taken together. Let's face it, not all IS managers or NT users are registry "He-men" — those brave few who have the time on their hands to charge unknowingly into chaos, hoping to emerge the winner.

This book provides a collection of registry settings that have been tried and shown to work. Many of these settings are undocumented and are, quite frankly, neat to try. This book does not help you understand the registry. We do not need another collection of ethereal concepts. What we need is reality in the form of useful, usable settings, and Tim has come through for us on that score. Do you want to change the number of available critical worker threads? The book shows you how. Want to allow a workstation the same cache characteristics as a server? The book shows you how. The book even shows you how to change font types in Internet Explorer. My list could go on and on but the bottom line is simple: this book is mandatory. All serious users of NT will appreciate the wisdom and utility of this book. You will be able to choose registry settings you never knew existed to obtain the results you desire. IS managers can tell before they leap what certain changes will accomplish. For the first time, the wild, chaotic underpinnings of the registry have been tamed and exposed. I certainly hope that the book does not stop here. Future additions to our knowledge of the registry are always welcome. For now, buy the book. It is a superb addition to your support fundamentals.

Dr. Bob Chronister
Windows NT Magazine's "Tricks & Traps" author

INTRODUCTION

THE REGISTRY

Using the registry can sometimes be a scary thing. We've all read this warning: "Using the registry can render your system useless or unstable. The (insert your favorite vendor here) makes no warranties, explicit or implied." Rubbish! When you use a computer, you can render almost anything useless or unstable!

This book is not a "how to use the registry book," nor is it a programmer's guide to the registry. This book is a practical reference — something a network administrator or an NT user could use to solve problems; a roadmap, if you will.

This book assumes you know how use Regedt32.exe and are comfortable backing up and restoring your system. You should also be familiar with Windows NT Server and Workstation.

IN THE BEGINNING

The registry grew out of ini files that have been around since Windows 1.0. In the beginning, all the variable data was stored in ini files, including data such as interrupt settings for printers and temporary directories for word processing programs. Windows 3.0 included a centralized database for this type of information — the registry. Although it was not used very extensively in Windows 3.0, it was there. Slowly, hardware and software vendors started to use this repository to store important information instead of the widely scattered ini files. With the 3.1 and 3.11 releases of Windows, the registry became more integrated with the system. By the time Windows NT was released, the registry was the repository for most data. Subsequent releases 3.5, 3.51 and 4.0 heavily depended on the registry, and the tools we use to manage the registry improved. The advantages of a centralized database for volatile system information are obvious. No longer do you need to hunt through your entire system or network (have you ever seen an .ini file on a mapped network drive?) for that elusive setting that is keeping your computer from functioning correctly.

For a more complete overview, see the excellent Powerpoint presentation at http://www.igug.org/slides96/systems/505/sld001.htm, which is hosted on the Intergraph Users Group site. Written by James Kanya of Cleaver Ketko Gorlitz Papa and Associates, the overview is an excellent tutorial about the registry and what you can do with it.

Today, the registry still holds all the cards. If you want to tweak your system outside the normal parameters supplied by the hardware or software vendor, the registry is your best bet. If you want to squeeze every ounce of performance out of your system, then regedt32.exe is your best friend. If you want to create custom configurations and apply them to large numbers of end-user systems, the registry is the way and the light.

Briefly, registry keys are made up of the following components.

Hive	HKEY_LOCAL_MACHINE	The hive in which the key resides.
Key	SYSTEM\CurrentControlSet\ Services\Atapi	The actual key in which the parameter to modify resides.
Value Name	Start	The actual value to modify.
Data Type	REG_DWORD	The type of data. The options are REG_BINARY, REG_DWORD, REG_EXPAND_SZ, REG_MULTI-SZ, REG_SZ.
Value	0X0	The actual value. You either need to modify your value to match the one listed or add a new entry with this value.

ABOUT THIS BOOK

The book is divided into six different parts: General System, Hardware, Applications, Microsoft Office, Security, and Performance. You may notice that certain registry keys are listed more than once. Don't worry; this book takes a problem-solving approach rather than indexing individual keys. To figure out how to increase network performance, look in the Performance section for how to set the pulse frequency for PDC to BDC replication. At the same time, if your BDCs don't update the PDC frequently enough, the General System section is the place for this kind of specific troubleshooting information. Both modifications use the same key, but under different circumstances.

GENERAL SYSTEM

This section is the largest section of the book. Here you find information about how to customize your desktop — with these tips, you can radically alter its appearance. You can also find answers to common problems all Windows NT users face, including network protocols, printers, disk drives, and domain controllers. I use this section time and time again. I couldn't even wait for the book — I carry a printout around with me at work.

HARDWARE

In this section, you find registry information pertaining to hardware peripherals, such as network adapters, disk controllers, video cards, scanners and CD-ROMs. Windows NT works with a wide array of hardware. Trying to troubleshoot this collage of hardware can be somewhat trying at times. This section provides a practical road map to common hardware problems that can be solved by registry tweaking.

APPLICATIONS

This section contains registry entries for all types of software, from Microsoft SQL Server to Netscape to Windows NT system information. In this section, you can find the details of customizing software for your particular users' needs. You will also find information that lets you troubleshoot problems that typically occur in a day-to-day IT environment.

MICROSOFT OFFICE

We had so many tips for Microsoft Office, particularly for Office 97, that we gave this topic its own section. Never before has a suite of standard office applications provided so much functionality and become so complex. Dean Porter was the major architect of this section. You can completely customize your Office environment, from the cursors and sounds you use to interact with Word, Excel, PowerPoint and Access to the actors that guide you through the intricacies and nuances of Office 97. I have referred to this section countless times in the past few months. My job calls for a high degree of customization — everything from function to appearance. Dean Porter has given us the building blocks to construct the perfect Office 97 environment.

SECURITY

It has been all over the news and Internet that Windows NT isn't as secure as some would lead you to believe This section contains registry tips that let you secure your system. You can monitor all the activities that users can perform (standard NT doesn't do this) as well as limit who can view sensitive information on your systems (such as event logs and other sensitive system information). This section also gives you default values for permissions on your registry, so that as you explore and modify, you will always have a reference point to which you can return.

PERFORMANCE

Whether you are new to Windows NT or a long-time user, you have no doubt heard of Mark Russinovich. Mark Russinovich is probably the brightest star in the Windows NT internals galaxy today. The amount of knowledge Mark has about NT is truly astounding. Mark has picked out some of his favorite performance-oriented registry modifications to help you squeeze every drop of power from your Windows NT machines. From memory allocation to network performance, you'll find it in this section.

Mark Russinovich and Bryce Cogswell, the authors of REGMON, were gracious enough to let us include this utility on the CD-ROM. If you want to learn about the registry internals, you must look at the source code for this wonderful utility.

APPENDIX A

Steve Scoggins asked the question early on in writing the book, "I think these modifications are great, but what if I need to change the registry on 100 or 1000 machines? Then what?" My answer to Steve was "Excellent question, Steve; when can you have it written up?" Much to my surprise, that was not the last time Steve asked those kinds of questions. Steve Scoggins does an excellent job of showing you how you can manipulate the registry via logon scripts and custom programs. Steve even wrote a utility (included on the CD-ROM with both the compiled and source versions) called REGREM, which shows you how to read remote entries on any machine's registry.

This section also has practical examples that you can use to make the registry do what you want, including C source code showing you how to read registry keys and techniques that let you change registry keys on your users' machines remotely and when they log on.

THE TESTING ENVIRONMENT

My co-authors and I tested all of these registry entries, and Bob Chronister, who also wrote the Foreword for this book, also tested a random sample of the entries. We used a variety of machines, from off-the-shelf configurations of Gateway, Compaq, Hitachi, AST, and Dell to custom configurations made up of standard components like Super Micro motherboards, Seagate hard drives, and Matrox video cards. All these systems had two things in common: They were Intel-based machines and they ran Windows NT version 4.0 with either Service Pack 2 or Service Pack 3.

Most machines were connected to a network via ethernet and almost all machines had a minimum of 32 MB of RAM with some using upwards of 128 MB of RAM (Dr. Bob Chronister has more memory for his personal machine than anyone else I know of — 256 MB and counting). Every registry entry was tested for the desired effect; that is, if the entry was supposed to change a particular characteristic, that change is what we tested. What we didn't test is what happens if one machine had all these registry entries applied to it at the same time. My guess is that the universe would probably implode; certainly the poor machine would cease to function.

All kidding aside, the registry changes things at the core. You can and will cause things in your setup to stop working. The good news is that you are not working without a net; if you properly back up your registry and system, you can recover from anything you may do to your registry. I personally destroyed, obliterated, and otherwise rendered unusable my system dozens of times while researching this book. I never once failed to recover.

THE LESSONS I LEARNED

You can do some amazing things in the registry. Some of these functions cannot be had by any other means, although you can also count on Microsoft and other vendors to expose the majority of those functions through control panel applets and other means, if users cry loud enough.

Although service packs are generally good things, they occasionally wreak havoc on registry settings. I found it very useful to print key registry entries before applying service packs. I also found a fair number of modifications using this technique.

Speaking of techniques, I learned a lot of different ways to go spelunking in the registry. With out a doubt, using REGMON is the most fun! I urge you to try this tool (included on the CD-ROM) and if nothing more, just watch the activity that simple functions generate to the registry (bring up the Control Panel from the Start menu, for example).

I also used Internet search engines extensively. I could probably write a chapter on the pros and cons of each individual search engine out there. I used AltaVista (www. altavista.com) for about a month and then switched to HotBot (www.hotbot.com) almost exclusively. When you search on "HKEY," "Registry," or even "Windows NT Registry," you get tens of thousand of hits. I waded through the vast majority of them and culled what I thought to be useful information. Next, I had to reproduce the purported benefit or change on my test systems. My success rate was something like 30 percent, which for you math wizards means 70 percent of what is on the Internet is either duplicate or flat doesn't work on Windows NT.

I also found a huge number of registry entries in newsgroups and list servers. These resources are inexpensive and, more importantly, invaluable. I had a much higher rate of success duplicating the desired result of these registry entries and modifications (better than 85 percent) on my test machines. I list a number of Web sites, newsgroups and List-Servers on the CD-ROM and later in this introduction. Be sure to check the *1001 Secrets for Windows NT Registry* website (http://www.registrysecrets.com) for an updated list.

Finally, I just went spelunking, and I encourage you to do so, too. Fire up Regedt32.exe, or for searching, use Regedit.exe, and start opening keys. Spelunking is really fun and also very dangerous. From spelunking, I learned how to recover from hosing my system. I even went exploring in the SAM key without any special tools. How, you ask? Dean Porter came up with this gem of a procedure, and the exact details are posted on the Web site. SAM stores some interesting information, but so far I have been unable to verify exactly what we can or should modify.

You can back up your registry in a variety of ways. Microsoft provides Rdisk.exe, which helps you safeguard your information but is a bit cumbersome. Many tools to help you manage the registry are in the Microsoft Resource Kit. By the way, if you don't already own this resource, you should. I used it many times to puzzle out exactly what an NT-specific system or registry entry was trying to do or should do. A list of commercial registry management tools is also available on the book's Web site. This list is dynamic and includes test drives and trial versions of software, so check in frequently.

A list of shareware programs is included on the CD-ROM and the Web site. This list is growing constantly, so be sure to check the site frequently.

YOUR MILEAGE MAY VARY

When we set out to write this book, we wanted it to be an effective tool for Windows NT professionals and aficionados alike. We took a great deal of time and effort to make sure every entry is correct and accurate. However, it is impossible to test these entries on every single combination of software and hardware. The bottom line is this: Back up your system before you try these modifications. I also suggest using a test machine, or at least a test install of Windows NT. You can make a multiboot system and install Windows NT on it more than once. I did this on my laptop and made many a discovery while flying at 35,000 feet! I got some seriously strange looks from my fellow passengers when I started whooping it up after discovering a particularly cool modification.

THE RESOURCES

Like most things, this book was not created in a vacuum. A tremendous wealth of information about the registry is available on the World Wide Web, from news groups, and from mailing lists. It never ceases to amaze me the lengths people will go to solve a problem. I have compiled information from a number of sites as well as picking the brains of the contributing authors. I also used several registry tools (included on the CD-ROM) to go spelunking into the registry itself.

MAILING LISTS

NT Internet Security List — This mailing list is a wealth of security-related Windows NT security issues! To subscribe, send e-mail to majordomo@iss.net with the words "subscribe ntsecurity" (no quotes) in the body of your message.

NEWSGROUPS

These newsgroups are available on the msnews.microsoft.com NNTP server:

- microsoft.public.windowsnt.setup — Everything you always wanted to know about Windows NT setup issues. It has a definite Microsoft bias at times. If you are looking to fix setup problems related to other vendor products, this is a good place to start.
- microsoft.public.windowsnt.apps — All NT applications; an excellent source of registry information for specific applications. This newsgroup is an absolute must!
- microsoft.public.windowsnt.protocol.tcpip — If you want to know about the wacky and weird goings on in TCP/IP, this is the place. Great networking tips and registry entry information.
- microsoft.public.windowsnt.protocol.ipx — If you run IPS, you must read this group.

- microsoft.public.windowsnt.protocol.ras — You have RAS questions? They have RAS answers! Lots of good practical information flows through here daily.
- microsoft.public.windowsnt.protocol.misc — Everything else related to protocols that's not covered in the previous three newsgroups.

The following newsgroups are available from your local NNTP server:

- comp.os.ms-windows.nt.admin.misc — General information about living in a Windows NT environment. Good registry information from time to time.
- comp.os.ms-windows.nt.admin.networking — My personal favorite. Good meat-and-potatoes information about how administer a Windows NT network.
- comp.os.ms-windows.nt.setup.hardware — All the hardware-related hacks are here.
- comp.os.ms-windows.nt.software.backoffice — This group is where you find out about SQL, SMS, and all the other Back Office components — a must-read.
- comp.os.ms-windows.nt.software.services — If you want to know about Windows NT, you need to know about the services that comprise it. Good information, with the occasional registry gem.
- comp.os.ms-windows.nt.setup.misc — Very similar to the Microsoft-sponsored newsgroup, except that the bias is not pro-Microsoft, but rather in support of your own personal favorite.

WEB SITES

- Windows NT Registry Secrets — The website for this book. Completely dedicated to the Windows NT registry, this site contains programs, hacks, and examples of how to do just about anything you can think of with the registry. www.registrysecrets.com
- Jerold Schulman International — Windows NT tips, registry hacks, and more tricks, tips, and configuration using the registry. http://www.jsiinc.com/reghack.htm
- Windows NT Internals — The home of NTRegmon, this site has tons of Windows NT and Windows 95 freeware and shareware utilities, as well as technical information on Windows NT and Windows 95 Internals. Be sure to check out the NT Internals Tips and Trivia section for registry examples, utilities, and other extremely useful information about Windows NT internals. http://www.ntinternals.com
- NONAGS — This site includes tons of Windows-related questions and answers and a good software selection. Although it's not NT-specific, it has helpful, knowledgeable people. I find the discussion forums really useful. http://nonags.com/nonags/forum/
- Microsoft.com — Still one of the best places for Windows NT-specific knowledge, especially registry stuff, the site includes hundreds of Knowledge Base articles, white papers, and other literature that cover almost every aspect of the registry that you could want to explore.

BOOKS/MAGAZINES/ARTICLES

Microsoft Windows NT Workstation Resource Kit, Microsoft Press, ISBN 1-57231-343-9

Microsoft Windows NT Server Resource Kit, Microsoft Press, ISBN 1-57231-344-7

Windows NT Magazine, "Tricks and Traps," by Dr. Bob Chronister , 1995 to present

Microsoft TechNet and Knowledge Base articles

THE TOOLS

REGMON.EXE

What can I say? If you could have only one utility for registry spelunking, this is it! This utility is brought to you by the dynamic duo of Mark Russinovich and Bryce Cogswell.

NTRegmon is a device driver/GUI combination that displays all registry activity taking place on a Windows NT System. You can use the NTRegmon menus to set up process and path filters, toggle on and off hooking, control the scrolling of the listview, and save the listview contents to an ASCII file.

Both process and path filters take expressions similar to those the command prompt takes: you can specify names with asterisks (*) representing wild cards. The Path Include filter represents path names that will be monitored and the Path Exclude filter represents path names that will not be monitored. Where the path names overlap, Path Exclude overrides Path Include. Note that the filters are interpreted in a case-*in*sensitive manner.

For example, if you do not want to see activity to Software subkeys, you can specify *Software* as the Path Exclude filter. If you want to see only activity to the HKLM directory, set HKLM* as the Path Include filter. If you set both filters, all activity to HKLM is logged except activity to subkeys with the name Software in them, such as HKLM\Software. By default, the filters are set up to watch all Registry activity. The process filter is *, the Path Include filter is *, and the Path Exclude filter is empty.

REGEDIT.EXE

This editor comes with Windows 95 and is now provided with Windows NT. I don't use it to make any changes to the registry itself, but it has excellent search capabilities. I have used this utility thousands of times in conjunction with NTRegmon during spelunking expeditions.

REGADMIN

This tool is excellent for administering the registry. It adds the features that Microsoft forgot. It's absolutely necessary if you want to properly add or modify registry key account permissions. If you are locking down your system and need to hunt down and kill the Everyone permission, this tool is simply the best.

REGREM

This utility, written by Steve Scoggins, shows you how to read registry keys on remote systems and display useful information. Regrem displays the following information about your current network configuration:

```
Windows NT Network Adapter
Description: 3Com Etherlink III PCI Bus-Master Adapter (3C590)
Manufacturer: 3Com
Product Name: EL59x
Service Name: EL59x1
Interrupt Number: 12ff8c
IO Base Address: 3
TCP/IP DefaultGateway : 200.200.200.254
TCP/IP IPAddress : 200.200.200.200
TCP/IP Subnet Mask : 255.255.255.0
TCP/IP Domain Name: test.com
TCP/IP Hostname: bigdog
TCP/IP DNS Name Servers:
TCP/IP Domain Name Search List:
Windows NT Computer Name: BIGDOG
Windows NT DomainName: BIGDOG
```

To use this utility, type **regrem** and the IP address of the computer you want to examine. The full annotated source code is included on the CD-ROM that accompanies this book.

THE FUTURE

Books are wonderful ways to convey ideas and to store information; however, they suffer from the fact that they are, for the most part, static entities. With *1001 Secrets for Windows NT Registry*, we hope to provide a practical reference in book form as well as a mechanism to allow for the dynamic nature of the Windows NT registry. Our Web site, http://www.registrysecrets.com, is dedicated to the Windows NT Registry and the things you can do with it. Here, you can sort through new tricks and registry hacks and submit your own tricks to share with the rest of the Windows NT community. In conjunction with *Windows NT Magazine*, we also will be hosting a forum dedicated to the Windows NT Registry. We hope that the Windows NT community in general and the Registry community in particular will think of this forum as their own and use it to further explore the Windows NT Registry.

Future editions of this book will include user-submitted registry modifications. As mentioned, we will provide a mechanism for you to submit your favorite modification. If we like what we see, you can earn t-shirts and other prizes that let the whole world know that you too are a Registry Spelunker. In addition, if we publish any of your tips in subsequent editions of this book, you'll receive an official mention in the book and compensation.

I hope to create a place where people can come when they need information about the registry — a place where you'll never read that silly disclaimer. A place that will become a permanent part of your repertoire of problem-solving methods and tactics.

Thank you for buying this book. I hope it is as helpful to you as compiling it has been to me — it has become an invaluable resource for me and my former colleagues at *Windows NT Magazine*. See you online!

Section 1

GENERAL SYSTEM

This section covers a lot of ground. It includes tips for everything from using services on remote machines to successfully uninstalling software. You can change the way your interface looks, customize your Run command, and ensure that your logon scripts run correctly — and that's just the beginning.

SERVICES

Have you ever needed to start a service on a remote machine? You can use the tools in the resource kit, but they often aren't handy or give curious results. Each service has a corresponding registry key and each key has a start value. Each service can have one of these start values:

0x0   Boot
0x1   System
0x2   Automatic
0x3   Manual
0x4   Disabled

To alter the way a service starts, change the appropriate start value for each service. I give two examples and list common services and their registry keys for a generic Windows NT installation. Many other services are available; I just listed a few of the more common ones. Make sure you have your system backed up or have a spare test system when you go spelunking in here.

I-1

Hive: HKEY_LOCAL_MACHINE
Key: System\CurrentControlSet\Services\Atapi
Value Name: Start
Data Type: REG_DWORD
Value: 0x0

This example starts the Atapi service when the machine boots.

I-2

Hive: HKEY_LOCAL_MACHINE
Key: System\CurrentControlSet\Services\Eventlog
Value Name: Start
Data Type: REG_DWORD
Value: 0x2

This value makes the event log start automatically on the target computer. To change this configuration, run regedt32.exe and select the computer that has the service you wish to alter.

I-3

> **Hive:** HKEY_LOCAL_MACHINE
> **Key:** System\CurrentControlSet\Services\Alerter
> **Value Name:** Start
> **Data Type:** REG_DWORD
> **Value:** 0x3

This example makes the alerter service start manually on the target machine.

I-4

> **Hive:** HKEY_LOCAL_MACHINE
> **Key:** System\CurrentControlSet\Services\Browser
> **Value Name:** Start
> **Data Type:** REG_DWORD
> **Value:** 0x2

This example tells the browser service to start automatically every time Windows NT starts.

I-5

> **Hive:** HKEY_LOCAL_MACHINE
> **Key:** System\CurrentControlSet\Services\Busmouse
> **Value Name:** Start
> **Data Type:** REG_DWORD
> **Value:** 0x4

This example disables the busmouse service.

I-6

> **Hive:** HKEY_LOCAL_MACHINE
> **Key:** System\CurrentControlSet\Services\DHCP
> **Value Name:** Start
> **Data Type:** REG_DWORD
> **Value:** 0x2

This example sets the DHCP client service to automatic startup mode.

I-7

> **Hive:** HKEY_LOCAL_MACHINE
> **Key:** System\CurrentControlSet\Services\Replicator
> **Value Name:** Start
> **Data Type:** REG_DWORD
> **Value:** 0x3

This example sets the directory replication service to manual start.

I-8

Hive: HKEY_LOCAL_MACHINE
Key: System\CurrentControlSet\Services\Messenger
Value Name: Start
Data Type: REG_DWORD
Value: 0x2

This example automatically starts the messenger service so you can send and receive system broadcast messages.

I-9

Hive: HKEY_LOCAL_MACHINE
Key: System\CurrentControlSet\Services\Sermouse
Value Name: Start
Data Type: REG_DWORD
Value: 0x2

This example sets the serial mouse service to start automatically.

I-10

Hive: HKEY_LOCAL_MACHINE
Key: System\CurrentControlSet\Services\UPS
Value Name: Start
Data Type: REG_DWORD
Value: 0x4

This value controls the uninterruptible power supply service.

I-11 Change the value of BootExecute under the Session Manager key to prevent Windows NT from running chkdsk at boot time.

Hive: HKEY_LOCAL_MACHINE
Key: System\CurrentControlSet\Control\Session Manager
Value Name: BootExecute
Data Type: REG_DWORD
Value: autocheck autochk *

This change may be necessary if you have really bad disks (other than the boot disk) and need to disable chkdsk so that you can proceed with the boot procedure. Restart the machine for any changes to take effect.

MICROSOFT FINDFAST 8.0/97

I-12

    Hive: HKEY_LOCAL_MACHINE
     Key: Software\Microsoft\Shared Tools\Find Fast\97
Value Name: Path
 Data Type: REG_SZ
    Value: D:\Program Files\Microsoft Office\Office\Findfast.exe

This path leads to the FindFast executable. Other software can use this key to find the FindFast utility.

I-13

    Hive: HKEY_LOCAL_MACHINE
     Key: Software\Microsoft\Shared Tools\Find Fast\97
Value Name: LogFilePath
 Data Type: REG_SZ
    Value: C:\WINNT\System32\FFASTLOG.TXT

This fully qualified path and filename is where the FindFast utility writes its activity.

I-14

    Hive: HKEY_LOCAL_MACHINE
     Key: Software\Microsoft\Shared Tools\Find Fast\97
Value Name: Update Interval
 Data Type: REG_DWORD
    Value: 10800000 (default is 3 hours, 3*60*60*1000)

This value is the interval (in thousandths of a second) at which the FindFast indexes are updated.

I-15

    Hive: HKEY_LOCAL_MACHINE
     Key: Software\Microsoft\Shared Tools\Find Fast\97
Value Name: IFilterConverter
 Data Type: REG_DWORD
    Value: D:\Program Files\Microsoft Office\Office\Ifilter.cnv

This fully qualified path and filename is where the FindFast utility looks for its index filter.

I-16

      Hive: HKEY_LOCAL_MACHINE
       Key: Software\Microsoft\Shared Tools\Find Fast\97\Index List
   SubKey: Index 00

This SubKey sets where FastFind looks for information on a given index.

I-17

      Hive: HKEY_LOCAL_MACHINE
       Key: Software\Microsoft\Shared Tools\Find Fast\97\Index List\Index 00
Value Name: Automatic
  Data Type: REG_DWORD
     Value: 1

Setting this value to 1 means that NT automatically updates the current index; setting this value to 0 means that the current index is not automatically updated. The value is in binary format.

I-18

      Hive: HKEY_LOCAL_MACHINE
       Key: Software\Microsoft\Shared Tools\Find Fast\97\Index List\Index 00
Value Name: Folder
  Data Type: REG_SZ
     Value: C:\

This fully qualified pathname points to the root of the directory structure to be indexed. All the subfolders from the point specified in this entry are indexed.

I-19

      Hive: HKEY_LOCAL_MACHINE
       Key: Software\Microsoft\Shared Tools\Find Fast\97\Index List\Index 00
Value Name: Additional Folders
  Data Type: REG_SZ
     Value:

This value specifies folders to index in addition to the directory pointed to by the Folder key.

GENERAL SYSTEM

I-20

Hive: HKEY_LOCAL_MACHINE
Key: Software\Microsoft\Shared Tools\Find Fast\97\Index List\Index 00
Value Name: Type
Data Type: REG_DWORD
Value: 0

This value specifies the type of documents to be indexed. Acceptable values are:

0   Microsoft Office documents
1   Microsoft Word documents
2   Microsoft Excel documents
3   Microsoft PowerPoint documents
4   Microsoft Project documents
5   All indexable file types (excludes .exe, etc.)

I-21

Hive: HKEY_LOCAL_MACHINE
Key: Software\Microsoft\Shared Tools\Find Fast\97\Index List\Index 00
Value Name: Index Operation
Data Type: REG_DWORD
Value: 3

This value specifies the type of operation to perform on the current index. Acceptable values are:

1   Create the index
2   Update the index one time only
3   Update the index continuously

I-22

Hive: HKEY_LOCAL_MACHINE
Key: Software\Microsoft\Shared Tools\Find Fast\97\Index List\Index 00
Value Name: Proximity Search
Data Type: REG_DWORD
Value: 0

If this value is enabled, entire phrases and quoted strings are included in the index, thus increasing the size of the index file. If it's disabled, the FindFast utility indexes more quickly and keeps a smaller index file, but searching for phrases takes longer.

I-23

Hive: HKEY_LOCAL_MACHINE
Key: Software\Microsoft\Shared Tools\Find Fast\97\Index List\Index 00
Value Name: Size Limit
Data Type: REG_DWORD
Value: 1,537,456,000

This value limits the maximum size of the current index; it specifies the number of bytes allowed.

I-24

Hive: HKEY_LOCAL_MACHINE
Key: Software\Microsoft\Shared Tools\Find Fast\97\Index List\Index 00
Value Name: Last Update
Data Type: REG_BINARY
Value: 50 ea 9c d9 69 54 bc 01

This value specifies the time and date the current index was last updated.

I-25 If your system occasionally hangs up and the desktop is blank or you are missing icons, you have probably discovered that the only way to recover is to reboot. However, look at this registry entry and make sure it is set to 1; the shell can then automatically restart if it crashes.

Hive: HKEY_LOCAL_MACHINE
Key: Software\Microsoft\WindowsNT\CurrentVersion\Winlogon
Value Name: AutoRestartShell
Data Type: REG_DWORD
Value: 1

A value of 1 automatically restarts the shell after a crash. A value of zero does not.

I-26

Hive: HKEY_LOCAL_MACHINE
Key: System\CurrentControlSet\Control\SessionManager\Memory Management\
Value Name: NonPagedPoolSize
Data Type: REG_DWORD
Value: 0

When this value is set to 0, the system uses the default size. A non-zero value specifies in bytes the amount of memory to use.

I-27   **P**roblem: You are copying files from your NT server to an NT workstation on a Token-Ring network and you get the error "Filemanager cannot copy X. The session was canceled." The copying feature works fine with small files but blows up on large files. This registry entry helps you fix this problem.

> **Hive:** HKEY_LOCAL_MACHINE
> **Key:** System\CurrentControlSet\Services\NETFLX1\Parameters
> **Value Name:** MaxFrameSize
> **Data Type:** REG_DWORD
> **Value:** 0x800

This value sets the maximum framesize to 2 kilobytes. This example assumes you are using a NetFlex network interface card.

I-28   **P**roblem: You are having problems with your network after upgrading to FDDI and running Workstation with Novell servers. On the Novell server, your packet size is 4202, but NT workstation gets an error, generally because it tries to execute a read-only file from the Novell server. Changing this registry entry should fix you right up.

> **Hive:** HKEY_LOCAL_MACHINE
> **Key:** System\CurrentControlSet\Services\Nwrdr\Parameters

Add the following value under the Parameters key:

> **Value Name:** DefaultMaxPacketSize
> **Data Type:** REG_DWORD
> **Value:** 1012

Restart the machine for these changes to take effect.

THE RUN COMMAND

If you want to customize what appears in the drop-down box of the Run command (which you get to by clicking Start and selecting Run), change the following registry entries to add and delete items.

I-29

      Hive: HKEY_CURRENT_USER
      Key: Software\Microsoft\Windows\CurrentVersion\Explorer\
      RunMRU
Value Name: MRUList
  Data Type: REG_SZ
     Value: abcdefg (number of entries to display)

The number of letters in this string determines the number of values you want displayed. For example, specifying abc shows only the first three values, whereas abcdef shows the first six values.

For each of the entries below, the value is the command line that is displayed in the corresponding pisition of the Run command's drop-down box. For example, Value Name "a" corresponds to position 8. A sample value for any of these entries is c:\winnt\notepad.exe.

I-30

      Hive: HKEY_CURRENT_USER
      Key: Software\Microsoft\Windows\CurrentVersion\Explorer\
      RunMRU
Value Name: a
  Data Type: REG_SZ
     Value: <full path and file name>

I-31

Value Name: b
  Data Type: REG_SZ
     Value: <full path and file name>

I-32

Value Name: c
  Data Type: REG_SZ
     Value: <full path and file name>

I-33

Value Name: d
  Data Type: REG_SZ
     Value: <full path and file name>

GENERAL SYSTEM

I-34

Value Name: e
Data Type: REG_SZ
Value: <full path and file name>

I-35

Value Name: f
Data Type: REG_SZ
Value: <full path and file name>

I-36

Value Name: g
Data Type: REG_SZ
Value: <full path and file name>

I-37

Value Name: h
Data Type: REG_SZ
Value: <full path and file name>

I-38

Value Name: i
Data Type: REG_SZ
Value: <full path and file name>

I-39

Value Name: j
Data Type: REG_SZ
Value: <full path and file name>

I-40

Value Name: k
Data Type: REG_SZ
Value: <full path and file name>

I-41

Value Name: l
Data Type: REG_SZ
Value: <full path and file name>

I-42

Value Name: m
Data Type: REG_SZ
Value: <full path and file name>

I-43   **Value Name:** n
           Data Type: REG_SZ
               Value: <full path and file name>

I-44   **Value Name:** o
           Data Type: REG_SZ
               Value: <full path and file name>

I-45   **Value Name:** p
           Data Type: REG_SZ
               Value: <full path and file name>

I-46   **Value Name:** q
           Data Type: REG_SZ
               Value: <full path and file name>

I-47   **Value Name:** r
           Data Type: REG_SZ
               Value: <full path and file name>

I-48   **Value Name:** s
           Data Type: REG_SZ
               Value: <full path and file name>

I-49   **Value Name:** t
           Data Type: REG_SZ
               Value: <full path and file name>

I-50   **Value Name:** u
           Data Type: REG_SZ
               Value: <full path and file name>

I-51   **Value Name:** v
           Data Type: REG_SZ
               Value: <full path and file name>

I-52

Value Name: w
Data Type: REG_SZ
Value: <full path and file name>

I-53

Value Name: x
Data Type: REG_SZ
Value: <full path and file name>

I-54

Value Name: y
Data Type: REG_SZ
Value: <full path and file name>

You can associate an executable with any of the above values. Be sure to enter the corresponding letter in the MRUList value to be able to see the command in the drop down menu. Log out for these changes to take effect.

DESKTOP

I-55

Hive: HKEY_CURRENT_USER
Key: Software\Microsoft\Command Processor\Completion
Value Name: Char
Data Type: REG_DWORD
Value: 9

Setting this value to 9 lets you specify a partial pathname at any command prompt and have it be completed when you press the TAB key. For example, typing **c wind <TAB>** expands to c:\windows.

1-56   Does your desktop seem sloooow? Want to speed it up? Try changing this registry entry. Add the following value under the explorer key.

> **Hive:** HKEY_CURRENT_USER
> **Key:** Software\Microsoft\Windows\CurrentVersion\Explorer
> **Value Name:** Max Cached Icons
> **Data Type:** REG_DWORD
> **Value:** number of icons to cache

This value controls how many icons Windows NT stores in memory and in its cache file %systemroot%\ShellIconCache. You will need to experiment to find the right value for your system. Reboot the machine for these values to take effect.

1-57   Problem: Have you ever wanted to remove the Network Neighborhood Icon from your desktop? Try as you might it can't be done, right? That's what I thought, too, but here is a registry entry that gets rid of it. Add the following value under the Explorer key:

> **Hive:** HKEY _CURRENT _USER
> **Key:** Software\Microsoft\Windows\CurrentVersion\Policies\ Explorer
> **Value Name:** NoNetHood
> **Data Type:** REG_DWORD
> **Value:** 0x1

Reboot the machine or log off and back on, and presto! No Network Neighborhood.

1-58   Do you have drive mappings that you want to reconnect automatically each time you log on? Even though you check the "Reconnect at logon" box, they still disappear. Add this value under the NetworkProvider key.

> **Hive:** HKEY_LOCAL_MACHINE
> **Key:** System\CurrentControlSet\Control\NetworkProvider
> **Value Name:** RestoreConnection
> **Data Type:** REG_DWORD
> **Value:** 0

Setting this value to 1 disables reconnecting when you log on.

I-59 If you don't want your users to have access to the network connect and disconnect functions, add the following key and value to the registry:

Hive: HKEY_CURRENT_USER
Key: Software\Microsoft\Windows\CurrentVersion\Policies\Explorer
Value Name: NoNetConnectDisconnect
Data Type: REG_DWORD
Value: 1

I-60 Do you want to modify the text that appears in the caption bar beside the title of the Begin Logon, Logon Information, Workstation Locked, and Unlock Workstation dialog boxes? This registry entry lets you display any string of up to 256 characters.

Hive: HKEY_LOCAL_MACHINE
Key: Software\Microsoft\WindowsNT\CurrentVersion\Winlogon
Value Name: Welcome
Data Type: REG_SZ
Value: any string

Restart Windows NT for these changes to take effect.

I-61 Are your users having problems seeing the icons on their desktop? Do you need more control than simply choosing between big or small icons? Try these registry settings for total control over your icon sizes.

Hive: HKEY_CURRENT_USER
Key: Control Panel\Desktop\WindowMetrics
Value Name: Shell Icon Size
Data Type: REG_SZ
Value: 32 pixels (increase for larger icons; for example, 48 or even 64)

I-62 Do you want to disable the menu that appears when you right-click over Start or any application button on the taskbar? Change this entry.

Hive: HKEY_CURRENT_USER
Key: Software\Microsoft\Windows\CurrentVersion\Policies\Explorer
Value Name: NoTrayContextMenu
Data Type: REG_DWORD
Value: 0 (default)

Setting this value to 1 disables right-clicking over the task bar. To re-enable this function, set this value to 0 and restart your system. You may need to create part of this key and add this subvalue to the registry.

I-63   You can also disable the menu that appears when you right-click over your desktop or one of the file windows in the Explorer by adding this registry key and value:

> **Hive:** HKEY_CURRENT_USER
> **Key:** Software\Microsoft\Windows\CurrentVersion\Policies\Explorer
> **Value Name:** NoViewContextMenu
> **Data Type:** REG_DWORD
> **Value:** 1

Restart the machine for these changes to take effect.

I-64   This registry entry lets you manipulate the size of the small icons displayed in the Start menu and in the Explorer windows when looking at files with the Small, List, or Details view settings.

> **Hive:** HKEY_CURRENT_USER
> **Key:** Control Panel\Desktop\WindowMetrics
> **Value Name:** Shell Small Icon Size
> **Data Type:** REG_SZ
> **Value:** 16 (increase for larger icons)

Setting these values to something other than the default setting can slow down the Start Menu, desktop updates, and Explorer Window updates. Windows must initially regenerate the icons from their original 32 x 32 size, though it caches the regenerated icons. Restart your machine for this value to take effect.

I-65   If you need to change how many colors your desktop uses to display icons, this registry entry is for you. This entry regulates the number of bits per pixel (BPP) that Windows NT uses to render the icons.

> **Hive:** HKEY_CURRENT_USER
> **Key:** Control Panel\Desktop\WindowMetrics
> **Value Name:** Shell Icon BPP
> **Data Type:** REG_SZ
> **Value:** 4

A value of 4 sets the system to use 16 colors for rendering (default), 8 sets 256 colors, 16 sets 65536 colors, 24 sets 16 million colors, and 32 sets true color. Windows NT can show the icons only at the maximum BPP that your graphics card and monitor can display. If an icon at that color resolution is not available, Windows NT takes the highest color resolution available and renders the icon accordingly. Restart the machine for these changes to take effect.

1-66   Would you like to run something other than the Open With application when you try to open something that Windows NT doesn't recognize? Change this value.

   Hive: HKEY_LOCAL_MACHINE
   Key: Software\Classes\Unknown\Shell\OpenAs\Command
   Value Name: <NoName>
   Data Type: REG_EXPAND_SZ
   Value: <program you want to run>

Change the value for <No Name> to the name of the program that you want to use to handle Unknown applications; add a %1 at the end for the path and filename of the file that you tried to open. For example, %SystemRoot%\system32\notepad.exe%1 starts the notepad. Restart Windows NT for this change to take effect.

1-67   Besides being able to customize the shell, you can also have specialty programs run, such as the NT backup program on a dedicated backup machine. This registry entry lets you specify which program is run as the shell.

   Hive: HKEY_LOCAL_MACHINE
   Key: Software\Microsoft\WindowsNT\CurrentVersion\WinLogon
   Value Name: Shell
   Data Type: REG_SZ
   Data: <drivename:\path\program>

1-68   Do you want to make the control panel or printers available from your desktop — not a shortcut, but the real thing? This registry entry lets you do just that.

   Hive: HKEY_CLASSES_ROOT
   Key: CLSID\{21EC2020-3AEA-1069-A2DD-08002B30309D}
   Value Name: Default
   Data Type: REG_SZ
   Value: Control Panel

I use Regedit for this one so that I can use the copy key function.

   After you copy the control panel object's CLSID (class ID) value to the clipboard, you need to

1. Right-click on your desktop and add a new folder.
2. Rename the new folder Control Panel. Be sure to add the period after Control Panel.
3. Press Ctrl + V to paste the Control Panel's CLSID into the folder's name.
4. Edit the folder so that it appears as follows: Control Panel.{21EC2020-3AEA-1069-A2DD-08002B30309D}

You now have the control panel on the desktop.

I-69   The same procedure applies for the printer control.

> **Hive:** HKEY_CLASSES_ROOT
> **Key:** {2227A280-3AEA-1069-A2DE-08002B30309D}
> **Value Name:** Default
> **Data Type:** REG_SZ
> **Value:** Printers

After you have copied the printer object's CLSID value to the clipboard, you need to

1. Right-click on your desktop and add a new folder.
2. Rename the new folder Printers. Be sure to add the period after Printers.
3. Press Ctrl + V to paste the printer's CLSID into the folder's name.
4. Edit the folder so that it appears as follows: Printers.{2227A280-3AEA-1069-A2DE-08002B30309D}

You now have the Printers on the desktop.

I-70   Would you like to modify or disable the task switcher (Alt-Tab, also known as the cool switch)? These registry entries show you how.

> **Hive:** HKEY_CURRENT_USER
> **Key:** Control Panel\Desktop
> **Value Name:** Coolswitch
> **Data Type:** REG_ SZ
> **Value:** 1

The default value is 1, which enables the task switcher. A value of 0 disables the task switcher.

I-71   You can also change the number of columns that the cool switch displays by changing the value below.

> **Hive:** HKEY_CURRENT_USER
> **Key:** Control Panel\Desktop
> **Value Name:** CoolSwitchColumns
> **Data Type:** REG_ SZ
> **Value:** 7

The default value is 7; change the value to the number of columns you want it to display.

GENERAL SYSTEM

I-72 You can also change the number of rows the cool switch displays.

Hive: HKEY_CURRENT_USER
Key: Control Panel\Desktop
Value Name: CoolSwitchRows
Data Type: REG_ SZ
Value: 3

The default value is 3; change the value to the number of rows you want to display.

I made mine tall and skinny by changing the values to 2 for CoolSwitch-Columns and 4 for CoolSwitchRows.

The following registry values affect the way the Display Properties Control Panel command (right-click on the desktop) works. Add the System key under the Policies key, and add the following values under the System key.

I-73

Hive: HKEY_CURRENT_USER
Key: Software\Microsoft\Windows\CurrentVersion\Policies\System
Value Name: DisableTaskMgr
Data Type: REG_ DWORD
Value: 00

This value disables the Task Manager.

I-74

Value Name: NoDispCPL
Data Type: REG_DWORD
Value: 1

This value removes the Control Panel.

I-75

Value Name: NoDispBackgroundPage
Data Type: REG_DWORD
Value: 1

This value removes the Background tab.

I-76

Value Name: NoDispAppearancePage
Data Type: REG_DWORD
Value: 1

This value removes the Appearance tab.

I-77

> **Value Name:** NoDispScrSavPage
> **Data Type:** REG_DWORD
> **Value:** 1

This value removes the Screen Saver tab.

I-78

> **Value Name:** NoDispSettingsPage
> **Data Type:** REG_DWORD
> **Value:** 1

This value removes the Settings tab from the Display Properties Control Panel command (right-click on the desktop).

I-79

> **Value Name:** DisableTaskManager
> **Data Type:** REG_DWORD
> **Value:** 1

This value disables the Task Manager. You must have installed Service Pack 2 or later for this change to take effect. The default value is 0, which enables the feature.

I-80 Are users logging into your system with roaming profiles and cluttering everything up? Do you want to delete the profile cache after they log out? Try adding the following value under the WinLogin key.

> **Hive:** HKEY_LOCAL_MACHINE
> **Key:** Software\Microsoft\WindowsNT\CurrentVersion\WinLogin
> **Value Name:** DeleteRoamingCache
> **Data Type:** REG_ DWORD
> **Value:** 1

Reboot your system for these changes to take effect.

I-81 Do you want to change the timeout value some of the informative dialog boxes use when logging in? For example, when you log in with a roaming profile and your system can't find the system where your roaming profile is stored, you see an error dialog box. This registry entry is useful for both disabling the timeout feature and speeding up the timeout value.

> **Hive:** HKEY_CURRENT_USER
> **Key:** Software\Microsoft\WindowsNT\CurrentVersion\WinLogin
> **Value Name:** ProfileDlgTimeOut
> **Data Type:** REG_ DWORD
> **Value:** n

The value is the time in seconds before the dialog box times out.

I-82 You don't like Explorer and you want to run Program Manager or another alternate shell in its place. Change the following value for Shell from explorer.exe to progman.exe.

> **Hive:** HKEY_LOCAL_MACHINE
> **Key:** Software\Microsoft\WindowsNT\CurrentVersion\Winlogon
> **Value Name:** Shell
> **Data Type:** REG_SZ
> **Value:** explorer.exe

I-83 If you plan to use Program Manager instead of the Explorer, you may also want to set this registry value. This entry lets you specify whether progman.exe waits for your logon scripts to complete before it loads into memory.

Note that this value entry also appears in HKEY_CURRENT_USER\Software\Microsoft\WindowsNT\CurrentVersion\Winlogon. The HKEY_LOCAL_MACHINE value applies to all users. The HKEY_CURRENT_USER value applies only to the current user. You can use the System Policy Editor to change this value.

> **Hive:** HKEY_LOCAL_MACHINE
> **Key:** Software\Microsoft\WindowsNT\CurrentVersion\Winlogon
> **Value Name:** RunLogonScriptSync
> **Data Type:** REG_DWORD
> **Value:** 1

I-84

             Hive: HKEY_CURRENT_USER
             Key: Software\Microsoft\WindowsNT\CurrentVersion\Winlogon
Value Name: RunLogonScriptSync
  Data Type: REG_DWORD
      Value: 1

A value of 1 tells Windows NT to wait until the logon script is finished before loading. A value of 0 indicates that the logon script and progman.exe can run concurrently. Restart Windows NT for these changes to take effect.

I-85 Are you tired of people changing the way your folders look? You get them set up just right, arranged by date with full details, then someone borrows your machine and messes it up. This registry modification prevents the system from saving changes made during the current session. Add the following value under the explorer key.

             Hive: HKEY_CURRENT_USER
             Key: Software\Microsoft\Windows\CurrentVersion\Policies\Explorer
Value Name: NoSaveSettings
  Data Type: Reg_Dword
      Value: 1

I-86 If you are trying to restrict what users can do on their systems, you probably want to disable their ability to right-click the Start button, which normally opens the program folder and Explorer and lets the user run Find. This registry modification disables all these features. Delete the following entries under the shell keys.

             Hive: HKEY_CLASSES_ROOT
             Key: Directory\shell
Value Name: Find

I-87

             Hive: HKEY_CLASSES_ROOT
             Key: Folder\shell
Value Name: Find

Now when a user right-clicks Start, nothing happens.

I-88 Do you need to see how your users have set up their screen savers? Or maybe a user secured the screen saver but forgot the password. To access screen savers remotely, fire up Regedt32.exe and open the registry remotely. These registry values give you everything you want to know about the screen saver.

> **Hive:** HKEY_CURRENT_USER
> **Key:** Control Panel\Desktop
> **Value Name:** ScreenSaveActive
> **Data Type:** REG_SZ
> **Value:** 0

A value of 0 specifies that the current screen saver is disabled; set the value to 1 to enable the current screen saver.

I-89

> **Hive:** HKEY_CURRENT_USER
> **Key:** Control Panel\Desktop
> **Value Name:** ScreenSaveIsSecure
> **Data Type:** REG_SZ
> **Value:** 0

A value of 0 means the screen saver requires no password to deactivate it. Set the value to 1 to enable password protection.

I-90

> **Hive:** HKEY_CURRENT_USER
> **Key:** Control Panel\Desktop
> **Value Name:** ScreenSaveTimeOut
> **Data Type:** REG_SZ
> **Value:** 300

The number represents the time in seconds before the screen saver is activated.

I-91

> **Hive:** HKEY_CURRENT_USER
> **Key:** Control Panel\Desktop
> **Value Name:** Scrnsave.exe
> **Data Type:** REG_SZ
> **Value:** <drivename:\path\program>

This value is the fully qualified path to the program you want to execute when the screen saver is activated.

I-92   **P**roblem: You're tired of looking at the same the Control Panel icons. To change the icons to a custom set, change the following registry entry.

Hive: HKEY_LOCAL_MACHINE
Key: Software\Classes\CLSID\{21EC2020-3AEA-1069-A2DD-08002B30309D}\DefaultIcon
Value Name: <No Name>
Data Type: REG_EXPAND_SZ
Value: C:\Program Files\Plus!\Themes\Ancient Pathways Recycle Full.ico,2

The number 2 is the number of the icon in the file you want displayed. In this case, 2 specifies the third icon because the first icon in a file is numbered 0. If no number is used, the default is 0.

I-93   **P**roblem: You're tired of looking at the same the Printer icons in the start menu and want to change them to a custom set. The following registry entry lets you do so.

Hive: HKEY_LOCAL_MACHINE
Key: Software\Classes\CLSID\{2227A280-3AEA-1069-A2DE-08002B30309D}\DefaultIcon
Value Name: <No Name>
Data Type: REG_EXPAND_SZ
Value: C:\Program Files\Plus!\Themes\Ancient Pathways Printer.ico,2

The number 2 is the number of the icon in the file you want displayed. In this case, 2 specifies the third icon because the first icon in a file is numbered 0. If no number is used, the default is 0.

I-94   **P**roblem: You're tired of looking at the same the dialup networking icon in the start menu and want to change it to a custom icon. The following registry entry lets you do so.

Hive: HKEY_LOCAL_MACHINE
Key: Software\Classes\CLSID\{a4d92740-67cd-11cf-96f2-00aa00a11dd9}\DefaultIcon
Value Name: <No Name>
Data Type: REG_EXPAND_SZ
Value: C:\Program Files\Plus!\Themes\Ancient Pathways Network.ico,2

The number 2 is the number of the icon in the file you want displayed. In this case, 2 specifies the third icon because the first icon in a file is numbered 0. If no number is used, the default is 0.

I-95 **P**roblem: You are tired of looking at the same the MS Office Binder icon in the start menu. To change it to a custom icon, change the following registry entry.

> **Hive:** HKEY_LOCAL_MACHINE
> **Key:** Software\Classes\CLSID\{59850400-6664-101B-B21C-00AA004BA90B}\DefaultIcon
> **Value Name:** <No Name>
> **Data Type:** REG_EXPAND_SZ
> **Value:** C:\Program Files\Plus!\Themes\Ancient Pathways Office.ico,2

The number 2 is the number of the icon in the file you want displayed. In this case, 2 specifies the third icon, because the first icon in a file is numbered 0. If no number is used, the default is 0.

I-96 **P**roblem: You want to rename the Recycle Bin. You right-click on the Recycle Bin icon, but renaming it isn't an option. Modify the following key under ShellFolder.

> **Hive:** HKEY_CLASSES_ROOT
> **Key:** CLSID\{645FF040-5081-101B-9F08-00AA002F954E}\ShellFolder
> **Value Name:** Attributes
> **Data Type:** REG_BINARY
> **Value:** 50010020

Now right-click the Recycle Bin, and you can rename the icon.

I-97 **P**roblem: You want to delete the Recycle Bin Icon. Right-clicking on the icon brings up the menu, but it has no delete option. Modify the following key under ShellFolder.

> **Hive:** HKEY_CLASSES_ROOT
> **Key:** CLSID\{645FF040-5081-101B-9F08-00AA002F954E}\ShellFolder
> **Value Name:** Attributes
> **Data Type:** REG_BINARY
> **Value:** 60010020

Now right-click the Recycle Bin, and you can delete the icon.

I-98   Problem: You have deleted the Recycle Bin and now you want it back. Modify this registry entry and everything will be back as it was.

> **Hive:** HKEY_LOCAL_MACHINE
> **Key:** Software\Microsoft\Windows\CurrentVersion\Explorer\
> Desktop\NameSpace

Add the following key:

> **Key:** {645FF040-5081-101B-9F08-00AA002F954E}
> **Value Name:**
> **Data Type:** REG_SZ
> **Value:** Recycle Bin

Press F5 to refresh the key, and there's the recycle bin.

I-99   Problem: You want to rename the Inbox. You right-click the Inbox icon, but renaming it isn't an option. Try this registry modification.

> **Hive:** HKEY_CLASSES_ROOT
> **Key:** CLSID\{00020D75-0000-0000-C000-000000000046}\ShellFolder

Modify the following value under ShellFolder:

> **Value Name:** Attributes
> **Data Type:** REG_BINARY
> **Value:** 50000000

Now right-click the Inbox, and you can rename the icon.

I-100   Problem: You want to delete the Inbox Icon. Right-clicking on the icon brings up the menu, but deleting it isn't an option. Try this registry modification.

> **Hive:** HKEY_CLASSES_ROOT
> **Key:** CLSID\{00020D75-0000-0000-C000-000000000046}\ShellFolder

Modify the following value under ShellFolder:

> **Value Name:** Attributes
> **Data Type:** REG_BINARY
> **Value:** 60000000

Now right-click the Inbox, and you can delete the icon.

I-101   Problem: You have deleted the Inbox and now you want it back. Modify this registry entry and everything will be back as it was.

> **Hive:** HKEY_LOCAL_MACHINE
> **Key:** Software\Microsoft\Windows\CurrentVersion\Explorer\Desktop\NameSpace

Add the following key:

> **Key:** {00020D75-0000-0000-C000-000000000046}

Under the key you just added, add this value:

Value Name:
Data Type: REG_SZ
Value: Inbox

Press F5 to refresh the key, and there's the Inbox.

I-102   Problem: Users keep accidentally deleting the Internet icon from the desktop. You can fix this problem by removing the Delete option from the icon menu. Modify the following key under ShellFolder.

> **Hive:** HKEY_CLASSES_ROOT
> **Key:** CLSID\{FBF23B42-E3F0-101B-8488-00AA003E56F8}\ShellFolder

Value Name: Attributes
Data Type: REG_BINARY
Value: 40000000

Right-click the Internet icon, and the delete option is removed.

I-103   Problem: You're tired of looking at those little arrows on shortcuts. This registry modification lets you do away with the arrows, leaving the original icon. Delete the following value from the LNKFILE key.

> **Hive:** HKEY_CLASSES_ROOT
> **Key:** LNKFILE
> **Value Name:** IsShortcut

Restart your machine for these new values to take effect.

I-104 Problem: You have a machine that different people use at different times. You have recently had complaints that people can see what others were working on and that it is a potential security problem. You can manually remove these file entries, but this registry modification automatically deletes the files for you. Modify the following value under User Shell Folders.

> **Hive:** HKEY_CURRENT_USER
> **Key:** Software\Microsoft\Windows\CurrentVersion\Policies\
> Explorer\User Shell Folders
> **Value Name:** Recent
> **Data Type:** REG_DWORD
> **Value:** C:\Recycle

Set your recycle bin to automatically delete files. Log off and then log back on. Now the Document menu option always reads empty.

I-105 Problem: The Explorer interface seems a little slow on some of the older computers in your installation. Here is a neat little trick to turn off animated or so-called "exploding" windows. Add the following value under the explorer key:

> **Hive:** HKEY_CURRENT_USER
> **Key:** Control Panel\Desktop\WindowsMetrics
> **Value Name:** MinAnimate
> **Data Type:** REG_DWORD
> **Value:** 0

I-106 Problem: When you select an option from the Start menu and that menu option has multiple options, a window displays the additional menu selections — but sometimes these additional menus seem slow or delayed. You can really speed things up with the following registry modification. The lower the number, the faster the menus are displayed. The default value on my system was 400. Change the following value under the Desktop key.

> **Hive:** HKEY_CURRENT_USER
> **Key:** Control Panel\Desktop
> **Value Name:** MenuShowDelay
> **Data Type:** REG_SZ
> **Value:** 1

Now choose the Programs option from the Start menu. The submenus are displayed instantly! No delay.

I-107 Problem: You want to restrict access to network drives and local drives from the Explorer interface. This registry modification lets you do just that. To disable all drives, add the following value under the Explorer key:

>   **Hive:** HKEY_CURRENT_USER
>   **Key:** Software\Microsoft\Windows\CurrentVersion\Policies\
>   Explorer
> **Value Name:** NoDrives
>   **Data Type:** REG_DWORD
>   **Value:** 03FFFFFF

This value is a bit field, where each bit corresponds to a letter in the alphabet, as shown below.

```
   3    F    F    F    F    F    F
0011 1111 1111 1111 1111 1111 1111
  zy xwvu tsrq ponm lkji hgfe dcba
```

If the bit is on (value of 1), access to the drive from Explorer is disabled. If the bit is off (value of 0), access to the drive is enabled. To disable everything but the A, B, C, and D drives, just set this value to 03FFFFF0:

```
   3    F    F    F    F    F    0
0011 1111 1111 1111 1111 1111 0000
  zy xwvu tsrq ponm lkji hgfe dcba
```

You must log off for these new values to take effect. Note that this change does not disable access to the drives; it just disables their appearance in the Explorer interface.

I-108 Problem: You have a corporate standard for the way users are supposed to configure their systems. Yet you have a pesky user — you know the one — who knows enough to mess up everything, but not quite enough to fix it. To disable users' ability to save settings on their computers, add the following value under the Explorer key:

>   **Hive:** HKEY_CURRENT_USER
>   **Key:** Software\Microsoft\Windows\CurrentVersion\Policies\
>   Explorer
> **Value Name:** NoSaveSettings
>   **Data Type:** REG_DWORD
>   **Value:** 1

Restart your machine for these new values to take effect.

I-109 Problem: You want to keep users from running programs from the Start menu. This registry entry disables the Run command. Add the following value under the Explorer key:

> **Hive:** HKEY_CURRENT_USER
> **Key:** Software\Microsoft\Windows\CurrentVersion\Policies\ Explorer
> **Value Name:** NoRun
> **Data Type:** REG_DWORD
> **Value:** 1

Restart your machine for these new values to take effect.

I-110 Problem: Users continually clutter their desktops with icons, then they can't figure out what they've done and you have to come fix it. This registry entry lets you hide all icons on the desktop. That way users can run programs only from their respective program groups. Add the following value under the explorer key:

> **Hive:** HKEY_CURRENT_USER
> **Key:** Software\Microsoft\Windows\CurrentVersion\Policies\ Explorer
> **Value Name:** NoDesktop
> **Data Type:** REG_DWORD
> **Value:** 1

Restart your machine for these new values to take effect.

I-111 Problem: You want to keep users from using the Find command in the Start menu. This registry entry lets you disable the Find command. Add the following value under the explorer key:

> **Hive:** HKEY_CURRENT_USER
> **Key:** Software\Microsoft\Windows\CurrentVersion\Policies\ Explorer
> **Value Name:** NoFind
> **Data Type:** REG_DWORD
> **Value:** 1

Restart your machine for these new values to take effect.

I-112 Problem: Windows NT selects the location of default folders in the following manner. Each user has a default location where Windows NT stores files — for example, the Favorites folder. This folder points to a directory stored in the HKEY_CURRENT_USER\Software\Microsoft\Windows\CurrentVersion\Explorer\ Shell Folders key. The default value is %USERPROFILE%\<app type>. For example, Favorites would be stored under %USERPROFILE%\Favorites. You can change the value in any of the thirteen keys to reflect a different directory than the default value.

> **Hive:** HKEY_CURRENT_USER
> **Key:** Software\Microsoft\Windows\CurrentVersion\Explorer\ Shell Folders
> **Value Name:** Favorites
> **Data Type:** REG_SZ
> **Value:** <fully qualified path name> example: c:\winnt\profiles\ timd\Favorites

This value gives the path name to which the Favorites button in Word points. Shortcuts you create in Internet Explorer are also stored here.

I-113

> **Value Name:** Application Data
> **Data Type:** REG__SZ
> **Value:** <fully qualified path name> example: c:\winnt\profiles\ timd\App Data

This value sets where application datafiles reside, on a per-user basis. You could also use this value to point many users to one set of files.

I-114

> **Value Name:** Desktop
> **Data Type:** REG_SZ
> **Value:** <fully qualified path name> example: c:\winnt\profiles\ timd\otherdesktop

This value sets where Windows NT stores the files or shortcuts that appear on your desktop. This information is stored on a per-user basis.

I-115
   Value Name: Fonts
   Data Type: REG_ SZ
      Value: <fully qualified path name> example: c:\winnt\profiles\ timd\AppData

This value sets where Windows NT stores the fonts available on the system. This path generally points to a common directory for all users, but it could be modified for different users.

I-116
   Value Name: NetHood
   Data Type: REG_SZ
      Value: <fully qualified path name> example: c:\winnt\profiles\ timd\newnethood

This value sets where the folders, files, and shortcuts you see when you click on the Network Neighborhood icon are stored. Values are stored on a per-user basis.

I-117
   Value Name: Personal
   Data Type: REG_ SZ
      Value: <fully qualified path name> example: c:\winnt\profiles\ timd\mystuff

This directory is for personal data. When you store files in Word to your personal directory, this value sets the location.

I-118
   Value Name: PrintHood
   Data Type: REG_SZ
      Value: <fully qualified path name> example: c:\winnt\profiles\ timd\myprintstuff

This value sets data storage for the folders, files, and shortcuts you see when you click Printers in the Start Menu. PrintHood values are stored on a per-user basis.

I-119
   Value Name: Programs
   Data Type: REG_ SZ
      Value: <fully qualified path name> example C:\winnt\profiles\ timd\startmenu\junk

This path sets data storage for data shown when you click Programs in the Start menu.

I-120

> **Value Name:** Recent
> **Data Type:** REG_SZ
> **Value:** <fully qualified path name> example: c:\winnt\profiles\ timd\things

This value sets storage for the folders, files, and shortcuts you see when you click Documents in the Start menu. Document values are stored on a per-user basis.

I-121

> **Value Name:** SendTo
> **Data Type:** REG_ SZ
> **Value:** <fully qualified path name> example C:\winnt\profiles\ timd\Sendto

This value sets what you see when you right-click an object and choose Send To. The default values are 3½ floppy, Mail Recipient, and Briefcase. You can also add more options.

I-122

> **Value Name:** StartMenu
> **Data Type:** REG_SZ
> **Value:** <fully qualified path name> example: c:\winnt\profiles\ timd\AltStrtMenu

This value sets where all the files, shortcuts, and folders that appear under the Start menu are located.

I-123

> **Value Name:** StartUp
> **Data Type:** REG_ SZ
> **Value:** <fully qualified path name> example C:\winnt\profiles\ timd\startmenu\programs\Startup

This directory houses the data that appears in the startup menu, which you find by selecting Programs from the Start menu and then selecting Startup.

I-124

> **Value Name:** Templates
> **Data Type:** REG_ SZ
> **Value:** <fully qualified path name> example C:\winnt\ShellNew

This directory stores template files for various programs. The default files in the directory are amipro, excel, excel4, lotus, powerpnt, presenta, quattro, winword, winword2 and wordpfct.

The next six registry values affect the way the default logon screen looks. Remember, when you work with the HKEY_USERS hive, your changes affect all users for the system.

I-125

> **Hive:** HKEY_USERS
> **Key:** Default\Control Panel\Desktop
> **Value Name:** Wallpaper
> **Data Type:** REG_SZ
> **Value:** <your wallpaper file>

This value sets the background on the logon screen. You must provide the fully qualified path and file name. These files are case sensitive, so be sure to type the path and file name correctly. Log off and back on for changes to take effect.

I-126

> **Hive:** HKEY_USERS
> **Key:** Default\Control Panel\Desktop
> **Value Name:** TileWallpaper
> **Data Type:** REG_SZ
> **Value:** 1

This value determines whether the default background graphic is tiled. A value of 1 means you want the graphic tiled. A value of 0 centers the graphic. Log off for changes to take effect.

I-127 These registry values determine the behavior of the default screen saver for the logon screen.

> **Hive:** HKEY_USERS
> **Key:** Default\Control Panel\Desktop
> **Value Name:** Scrnsave.exe
> **Data Type:** REG_SZ
> **Value:** <screen saver file name>

This value is the fully qualified path to the screen saver executable. The default is logon.scr (boring). Log off and back on for any changes to take effect.

I-128

> **Hive:** HKEY_USERS
> **Key:** Default\Control Panel\Desktop
> **Value Name:** ScreenSaveTimeout
> **Data Type:** REG_SZ
> **Value:** <timeout value in seconds>

This value controls how long Windows NT waits before invoking the screen saver. The value is stored in seconds.

I-129

Hive: HKEY_USERS
Key: Default\Control Panel\Desktop
Value Name: ScreenSaveActive
Data Type: REG_SZ
Value: 1

This registry entry determines whether the screen saver specified in the Scrnsave.exe value is currently active. Setting this value to 0 temporarily disables the current screen saver.

I-130

Hive: HKEY_USERS
Key: Default\Control Panel\Desktop
Value Name: ScreenSaveIsSecure
Data Type: REG_SZ
Value: 0

This value determines whether the screen saver prompts for a password before allowing you access to the system. Since this value specifies the screensaver for the main logon screen, enabling this value is redundant. However, those of you who want double security measures can set this value to 1 (password security enabled). Log off for this value to take effect.

INSTALLATION

I-131 **P**roblem: You install Windows NT from a local drive, either a floppy or CD-ROM. When you update or add components, Windows NT first looks for these components in the original location you installed from. If you installed an Intel version of Windows NT from the local drive e:\i386, that's where NT looks first. Instead of having to lug the diskettes or CD with you, you can create a directory on your network and copy the pertinent directories from the installation disk.

For example, if you have only Intel-based machines, you may want to copy only the i386 directory to your network drive. Now when you update NT, you can access the installation files from the network. The problem is that NT still looks for your installation files from the original source (e:\i386). You can change the location in the dialog box, but you have to change it every time. Here is a way to update the registry to reflect the new home of your installation files.

> **Hive:** HKEY_LOCAL_MACHINE
> **Key:** Software\Microsoft\WindowsNT\CurrentVersion
> **Value Name:** SourcePath
> **Data Type:** REG_SZ
> **Value:** drive:\directory

I-132 **I**f you have trouble installing software with Windows NT or if you are constantly prompted to insert your diskette into non-existent drives, consider making these changes. These registry entries let you specify which installation drives are defaults.

> **Hive:** HKEY_LOCAL_MACHINE
> **Key:** Software\Microsoft\WindowsNT\CurrentVersion
> **Value Name:** SourcePath
> **Data Type:** REG_SZ
> **Value:** E:\i386\

This value is the drive that Windows NT was installed from.

I-133

> **Hive:** HKEY_LOCAL_MACHINE
> **Key:** Software\Microsoft\WindowsNT\CurrentVersion
> **Value Name:** PathName
> **Data Type:** REG_SZ
> **Value:** C:\Winnt40

This value is the current directory of the OS.

GENERAL SYSTEM

I-134

> **Hive:** HKEY_LOCAL_MACHINE
> **Key:** Software\Microsoft\WindowsNT\CurrentVersion
> **Value Name:** SystemRoot
> **Data Type:** REG_SZ
> **Value:** C:\Winnt40

This value is the same as PathName; it's the directory in which Windows NT was installed.

I-135 These entries are for older applications — 16 bit and the like.

> **Hive:** HKEY_LOCAL_MACHINE
> **Key:** Software\Microsoft\Windows\CurrentVersion\Setup
> **Value Name:** BootDir
> **Data Type:** REG_SZ
> **Value:** C:\

I-136

> **Hive:** HKEY_LOCAL_MACHINE
> **Key:** Software\Microsoft\Windows\CurrentVersion\Setup
> **Value Name:** Installation Sources
> **Data Type:** REG_MULTI_SZ
> **Value:** A:\

I-137

> **Hive:** HKEY_LOCAL_MACHINE
> **Key:** Software\Microsoft\Windows\CurrentVersion\Setup
> **Value Name:** SourcePath
> **Data Type:** REG_SZ
> **Value:** A:\

I-138 Are you having problems uninstalling software? Even though you uninstall the software according to the manufacturer's directions, it just won't go away from the Add/Remove list. Try this registry key and its associated value to fix your problem. You can also just remove the key for the specific application and it will no longer appear on the Add/Remove programs list.

These entries are useful if you have deleted some applications from your hard drive without using the control panel applet.

        Hive: HKEY_LOCAL_MACHINE
         Key: Software\Microsoft\Windows\CurrentVersion\Uninstall\
         [appname]
  Value Name: DisplayName
    Data Type: REG_SZ
       Value: <Name displayed in the uninstall application>

I-139

        Hive: HKEY_LOCAL_MACHINE
         Key: Software\Microsoft\Windows\CurrentVersion\Uninstall\
         [appname]
  Value Name: UninstallString
    Data Type: REG_SZ
       Value: <Uninstall program and parameters to uninstall the application>

This information is very useful. Sometimes what the uninstall programs actually need to run and what is stored in the registry differ. If you need to, you can manually correct this value.

Restart the machine for the new values to take effect. Next time you need to install something from the installation disk, you can use your new settings.

CONTROL PANEL

Do you need to customize what the Control Panel displays to your users? These registry entries let you limit what is displayed.

I-140

        Hive: HKEY_CURRENT_USER
        Key: Control Panel

Add the following key under the control panel key:
        Key: Don't Load
Value Name: Console.cpl
  Data Type: REG_SZ
      Value: yes

This value tells the Control Panel not to load the Console.cpl control panel applet, which controls the console functions and configuration. A value of "yes" prohibits the loading of the .cpl file. A blank value allows the file to be loaded and displayed.

I-141

Value Name: Liccpa.cpl
  Data Type: REG_SZ
      Value: yes

This value tells the Control Panel not to load the Liccpa.cpl control panel applet, which controls the licensing functions and configuration.

I-142

Value Name: Access.cpl
  Data Type: REG_SZ
      Value: yes

This value tells the Control Panel not to load the Access.cpl control panel applet, which controls the accessibility functions and configuration.

I-143

Value Name: Appwiz.cpl
  Data Type: REG_SZ
      Value: yes

This value tells the Control Panel not to load the Appwiz.cpl control panel applet, which controls the Add and Remove applications functions and configuration.

I-144
Value Name: Bhcontrol.cpl
Data Type: REG_SZ
Value: yes

This value tells the Control Panel not to load the Bhcontrol.cpl control panel applet, which controls the network monitor function and configuration.

I-145
Value Name: Desk.cpl
Data Type: REG_SZ
Value: yes

This value tells the Control Panel not to load the Desk.cpl control panel applet, which controls the display functions and configuration.

I-146
Value Name: Devapps.cpl
Data Type: REG_SZ
Value: yes

This value tells the Control Panel not to load the Devapps.cpl control panel applet, which controls the PC card, SCSI, and Tape device functions and configuration.

I-147
Value Name: Findfast.cpl
Data Type: REG_SZ
Value: yes

This value tells the Control Panel not to load the Findfast.cpl control panel applet, which controls the FindFast functions and configuration.

I-148
Value Name: Inetcpl.cpl
Data Type: REG_SZ
Value: yes

This value tells the Control Panel not to load the Inetcpl.cpl control panel applet, which controls the Internet functions and configuration.

I-149
Value Name: Intl.cpl
Data Type: REG_SZ
Value: yes

This value tells the Control Panel not to load the Intl.cpl control panel applet, which controls the regional settings functions and configuration.

I-150

Value Name: Main.cpl
Data Type: REG_SZ
Value: yes

This value tells the Control Panel not to load the Main.cpl control panel applet, which controls the mouse, keyboard, fonts, and printer functions and configuration.

I-151

Value Name: Joy.cpl
Data Type: REG_SZ
Value: yes

This value tells the Control Panel not to load the Joy.cpl control panel applet, which controls the joystick functions and configuration.

I-152

Value Name: Mlcfg32.cpl
Data Type: REG_SZ
Value: yes

This value tells the Control Panel not to load the Mlcfg32.cpl control panel applet, which controls the mail and fax functions and configuration.

I-153

Value Name: Mmsys.cpl
Data Type: REG_SZ
Value: yes

This value tells the Control Panel not to load the Mmsys.cpl control panel applet, which controls the multimedia and sound functions and configuration.

I-154

Value Name: Modem.cpl
Data Type: REG_SZ
Value: yes

This value tells the Control Panel not to load the Modem.cpl control panel applet, which controls the modem functions and configuration.

I-155

Value Name: Ncpa.cpl
Data Type: REG_SZ
Value: yes

This value tells the Control Panel not to load the Ncpa.cpl control panel applet, which controls the network functions and configuration.

I-156

Value Name: Nwc.cpl
Data Type: REG_SZ
Value: yes

This value tells the Control Panel not to load the Nwc.cpl control panel applet, which controls the Gateway Services for Novell functions and configuration.

I-157

Value Name: Odbccp32.cpl
Data Type: REG_SZ
Value: yes

This value tells the Control Panel not to load the Odbccp32.cpl control panel applet, which controls the ODBC functions and configuration.

I-158

Value Name: Ports.cpl
Data Type: REG_SZ
Value: yes

This value tells the Control Panel not to load the Ports.cpl control panel applet, which controls the ports functions and configuration.

I-159

Value Name: Rascpl.cpl
Data Type: REG_SZ
Value: yes

This value tells the Control Panel not to load the Rascpl.cpl control panel applet, which controls the RAS functions and configuration.

I-160

Value Name: Sfmmgr.cpl
Data Type: REG_SZ
Value: yes

This value tells the Control Panel not to load the Sfmmgr.cpl control panel applet, which controls the MacFile functions and configuration.

I-161

Value Name: Srvmgr.cpl
Data Type: REG_SZ
Value: yes

This value tells the Control Panel not to load the Srvmgr.cpl control panel applet, which controls the devices, server, and services functions and configuration.

I-162

Value Name: Sysdm.cpl
Data Type: REG_SZ
Value: yes

This value tells the Control Panel not to load the Sysdm.cpl control panel applet, which controls the System functions and configuration.

I-163

Value Name: Telephon.cpl
Data Type: REG_SZ
Value: yes

This value tells the Control Panel not to load the Telephon.cpl control panel applet, which controls the telephony functions and configuration.

I-164

Value Name: Themes.cpl
Data Type: REG_SZ
Value: yes

This value tells the Control Panel not to load the Themes.cpl control panel applet, which controls the Desktop Themes functions and configuration.

I-165

Value Name: Ups.cpl
Data Type: REG_SZ
Value: yes

This value tells the Control Panel not to load the Ups.cpl control panel applet, which controls the UPS functions and configuration.

I-166

Value Name: Datetime.cpl
Data Type: REG_SZ
Value: yes

This value tells the Control Panel not to load the Datetime.cpl control panel applet, which controls the date and time configurations and functions.

I-167

Value Name: Wgpocpl.cpl
Data Type: REG_SZ
Value: yes

This value tells the Control Panel not to load the Wgpocpl.cpl control panel applet, which controls the Microsoft Mail Post Office functions and configuration.

ICONS

I-168 When you click My Computer, the default setup is to display all your drives. How about having My Computer come up in Explorer view instead? Change this registry entry.

> **Hive:** HKEY_CLASS_ROOT
>
> **Key:** CLSID\\{20D04FEO-3AEA-1069-A2D8-08002B30309D}\\Shell

Add the following key under the shell key.

> **Key:** Open

Add the following key under the new Open key.

> **Key:** command

Add the following value under the Command key.

> **Value Name:** <NoName>
>
> **Data Type:** Reg_SZ
>
> **Value:** Explorer.exe

I-169 You can do the same thing to the Network Neighborhood by modifying the following registry key:

> **Hive:** HKEY_CLASS_ROOT
>
> **Key:** CLSID\\{208D2C60-3AEA-1069-A2D7-08002B30309D}\\Shell

As before, add the following key under the shell key.

> **Key:** Open

Add the following key under the new Open key.

> **Key:** command

Add the following value under the Command key.

> **Value Name:** <NoName>
>
> **Data Type:** Reg_SZ
>
> **Value:** Explorer.exe

You can also add this feature to these following objects by changing these keys:

I-170   **Recycle Bin** CLSID\\{645FF040-5081-101B-9F08-00AA002F954E}

I-171   **My Briefcase** CLSID\\{85BBD920-42A0-1069-A2E4-08002B30309D}

Follow the same procedure you did with My Computer.

I-172 Next, we look at customizing various icons on your system. Each example works for a specific icon. In each case, the number after the comma in the value is the particular icon that you wish to display from a file. In most examples, we use the number 2 to indicate the third icon, because the first icon in a file is numbered 0. If no number is used, the default is 0.

Hive: HKEY_LOCAL_MACHINE
Key: Software\Classes\CLSID\{85BBD920-42A0-1069-A2E4-08002B30309D}
Value Name: DefaultIcon
Data Type: REG_EXPAND_SZ
Value: C:\Program Files\Plus!\Themes\Ancient Pathways Briefcase.ico,2

This entry modifies the briefcase icon on the desktop.

I-173 This entry modifies the Internet Explorer icon on the desktop.

Hive: HKEY_LOCAL_MACHINE
Key: Software\Classes\CLSID\{FBF23B42-E3F0-101B-8488-00AA003E56F8}
Value Name: DefaultIcon
Data Type: REG_EXPAND_SZ
Value: C:\Program Files\Plus!\Microsoft Internet\Iexplore.exe,0

I-174 The next three entries affect the recycle bin icon.

Hive: HKEY_LOCAL_MACHINE
Key: Software\Classes\CLSID\{645FF040-5081-1018-9F08-00AA002F954E}
Value Name: DefaultIcon
Data Type: REG_EXPAND_SZ
Value: C:\Program Files\Plus!\Themes\Ancient Pathways Recycle Full.ico,2

I-175

Value Name: Empty
Data Type: REG_EXPAND_SZ
Value: C:\Program Files\Plus!\Themes\Ancient Pathways Recycle Full.ico,2

I-176	**Value Name:**	Full
	Data Type:	REG_EXPAND_SZ
	Value:	C:\Program Files\Plus!\Themes\Ancient Pathways Recycle Full.ico,2

I-177 This registry entry is for the Network Neighborhood icon.

Hive: HKEY_LOCAL_MACHINE
Key: Software\Classes\CLSID\{208D2C60-3AEA-1069-A2D7-08002B30309D}
Value Name: DefaultIcon
Data Type: REG_EXPAND_SZ
Value: C:\Program Files\Plus!\Themes\Ancient Pathways Network.ico,2

I-178 This entry modifies the My Computer icon.

Hive: HKEY_LOCAL_MACHINE
Key: Software\Classes\CLSID\{20D04FE0-3AEA-1069-A2D8-08002B30309D}
Value Name: DefaultIcon
Data Type: REG_EXPAND_SZ
Value: C:\Program Files\Plus!\Themes\Ancient Pathways Computer.ico,2

PRINTER SERVICE

I-179 NT doesn't use DOS-style interrupts in printing. If this feature causes you problems, enable them with this change.

Hive: HKEY_CURRENT_USER
Key: Software\Microsoft\WindowsNT\CurrentVersion\Windows

Change the following value under the Windows key.

Value Name: DosPrint
Data Type: REG_SZ
Value: No

Reboot for this change to take effect.

I-180 Your network contains a few Novell servers and you think printing is a pretty good job for them. The problem is that every time you print on that printer, you get a pop-up message telling you about your print job. To turn off the message, change the following registry entry.

> **Hive:** HKEY_LOCAL_MACHINE
> **Key:** System\CurrentControlSet\Control\Print\Providers
> **Value Name:** NetPopup
> **Data Type:** REG_DWORD
> **Value:** 0

Change the NetPopup value to 0; you may have to add it under the Providers key if it doesn't exist. Reboot the machine for the changes to take effect.

I-181 During installation, NT opted to use a slow drive for your print spooling. You have recently installed a bigger and faster drive and want to change the drive NT uses for print spooling By default, NT uses the %systemroot%\system32\spool folder. The following registry entry lets you specify an alternate path for all printers. Change the value for Default-SpoolDirectory under the Printers key to your new path and directory.

> **Hive:** HKEY_LOCAL_MACHINE
> **Key:** System\CurrentControlSet\Control\Print\Printers
> **Value Name:** DefaultSpoolDirectory
> **Data Type:** REG_SZ
> **Value:** <path>

SECURITY

I-182 Are you worried that someone will see who logged into a system last? This registry entry disables that feature.

> **Hive:** HKEY_LOCAL_MACHINE
> **Key:** Software\Microsoft\WindowsNT\CurrentVersion\WinLogin

Add the following value under the WinLogin

> **Value Name:** DontDisplayLastUserName
> **Data Type:** REG_DWORD
> **Value:** 1

Make sure you restart the machine for these changes to take effect.

I-183   You want to add a corporate message or disclaimer before people log on to their machines. The next two registry entries let you display a message before the user logs on.

> **Hive:** HKEY_LOCAL_MACHINE
> **Key:** Software\Microsoft\WindowsNT\CurrentVersion\Winlogon

Change the following values under the Winlogon key.

> **Value Name:** LegalNoticeText
> **Data Type:** REG_SZ
> **Value:** "Text you want displayed before the user logs on"

I-184
> **Value Name:** LegalNoticeCaption
> **Data Type:** REG_SZ
> **Value:** "Text you want displayed on the title bar of the dialog box"

I-185   If you have a Windows NT machine and you don't really care about security, you can have the system log on for you automatically by modifying or adding the following registry entries. Set the DefaultDomain and the DefaultUserName to the domain and user name that you want the system to use to log on.

> **Hive:** HKEY_LOCAL_MACHINE
> **Key:** Software\Microsoft\WindowsNT\CurrentVersion\WinLogin
> **Value Name:** DefaultDomainName
> **Data Type:** REG_SZ
> **Value:** <domain name>

> **Hive:** HKEY_LOCAL_MACHINE
> **Key:** Software\Microsoft\WindowsNT\CurrentVersion\WinLogin
> **Value Name:** DefaultUserName
> **Data Type:** REG_SZ
> **Value:** <username>

Next, add these two values:

> **Hive:** HKEY_LOCAL_MACHINE
> **Key:** Software\Microsoft\WindowsNT\CurrentVersion\WinLogin
> **Value Name:** DefaultPassword
> **Data Type:** REG_SZ
> **Value:** <password>

> **Hive:** HKEY_LOCAL_MACHINE
> **Key:** Software\Microsoft\WindowsNT\CurrentVersion\WinLogin
> **Value Name:** AutoAdminLogon
> **Data Type:** REG_SZ
> **Value:** 1

Be sure to set the AutoAdminLogon value to 1. Remember, your system is now quite insecure. Anyone with access to the registry can read the password.

NOVELL 4.0

1-186 If you have NetWare 4.0 servers on a network with Windows NT servers and you're trying to synchronize user accounts via the Directory Service Manager for NetWare (DSMN), you may run into problems. First, make sure your Net-Ware 4.0 server is running in bindery emulation mode, then add the following registry value:

> **Hive:** HKEY_LOCAL_MACHINE
> **Key:** System\CurrentControlSet\Services\MSSYNC\parameters
> **Value Name:** Allow4X
> **Data Type:** REG_DWORD
> **Value:** 1

Restart the machine for this change to take effect.

LOGON SCRIPTS

I-187   If your logon scripts aren't working correctly, you may want to verify the following value on your server — it's the fully qualified path to the directory where the Logon Scripts are stored.

> **Hive:** HKEY_LOCAL_MACHINE
> **Key:** System\CurrentControlSet\Services\NetLogon\Parameters
> **Value Name:** Scripts
> **Data Type:** REG_MULTI_SZ
> **Value:** <fully qualified pathname>

DOMAIN CONTROLLERS

I-188   If you need to verify the list of trusted domains on a machine from a remote location, look at the following registry value.

> **Hive:** HKEY_LOCAL_MACHINE
> **Key:** System\CurrentControlSet\Services\NetLogon\Parameters
> **Value Name:** TrustedDomainList
> **Data Type:** REG_MULTI_SZ
> **Value:** <any list of valid domain names>

I-189   If you are having database problems with your primary domain controllers (PDCs), you may want them to completely synchronize every time they boot. This value lets you control the behavior of individual domain controllers. Change the Update value to Yes.

> **Hive:** HKEY_LOCAL_MACHINE
> **Key:** System\CurrentControlSet\Services\Netlogon\Parameters
> **Value Name:** Update
> **Data Type:** REG_SZ
> **Value:** Yes

`I-190` If you apply large-scale changes to your domain user accounts all at once, you can cause network congestion. Tuning the following parameters can help reduce that congestion.

> **Hive:** HKEY_LOCAL_MACHINE
> **Key:** System\CurrentControlSet\Services\Netlogon\Parameters

Add the ChangeLogSize value.

> **Value Name:** ChangeLogSize
> **Data Type:** REG_SZ
> **Value:** 0x4000000

This value defines the size of the Change Log (%systemroot%\Netlogon.chg). The default value is 64K. Changing this value to the maximum 4 MB helps congestion on systems that are very volatile or frequently have large changes. In testing this value, we noted little impact on overall system performance.

`I-191`

> **Hive:** HKEY_LOCAL_MACHINE
> **Key:** System\CurrentControlSet\Services\Netlogon\Parameters

Add the Pulse value.

> **Value Name:** Pulse
> **Data Type:** REG_DWORD
> **Value:** 300

The pulse value defines how often (in seconds) a pulse is sent to a backup domain controller (BDC) that needs to be updated with SAM or LSA changes. By default, the NetLogon service determines the optimal frequency for pulses. If you are doing lots of updates, you may need to increase this value. Frequent updates clog the network, and decreasing the value would reduce clog. However, decreasing the value means you could lose more data if your system crashes, because it's been longer since a backup. The range is 60 to 172,800. Restart the server for this value to take effect.

`I-192`

> **Hive:** HKEY_LOCAL_MACHINE
> **Key:** System\CurrentControlSet\Services\Netlogon\Parameters

Add the PulseConcurrency value.

> **Value Name:** PulseConcurrency
> **Data Type:** REG_DWORD
> **Value:** 20

This value determines the maximum number of concurrent pulses the PDC sends to BDCs. This value lets you control how many BDCs are being updated at any one time, which can reduce network traffic.

I-193   This value determines the absolute longest interval that a BDC goes without receiving a request for update (pulse), even if the BDC is up-to-date.

>   **Hive:** HKEY_LOCAL_MACHINE
>   **Key:** System\CurrentControlSet\Services\Netlogon\Parameters

Add the PulseMaximum value.

>   **Value Name:** PulseMaximum
>   **Data Type:** REG_DWORD
>   **Value:** 7200

The default is 7200 seconds (2 hours). Reboot the machine for any changes to take effect.

I-194

>   **Hive:** HKEY_LOCAL_MACHINE
>   **Key:** System\CurrentControlSet\Services\Netlogon\Parameters

Add the PulseTimeout1 value.

>   **Value Name:** PulseTimeout1
>   **Data Type:** REG_DWORD
>   **Value:** 5

This value tells the PDC how long to wait before giving up on a BDC that has failed to respond. Once a PDC sends a pulse to a BDC, the BDC must respond within this time frame; if it doesn't, it is considered unavailable. The PDC then sends a pulse to another BDC. If this value is set very high and you have many BDCs on your network, network updates can take a long time. However, if you have a heavily congested network, setting this value too low causes the PDC to give up on the BDC prematurely. The default value is 5 seconds, and the range is 1 to 120 seconds.

I-195

>   **Hive:** HKEY_LOCAL_MACHINE
>   **Key:** System\CurrentControlSet\Services\Netlogon\Parameters

Add the PulseTimeout2 value.

>   **Value Name:** PulseTimeout2
>   **Data Type:** REG_DWORD
>   **Value:** 300

This value determines how long a PDC waits for a BDC to finish replication. Even if a BDC has responded correctly to a pulse, it is still possible for BDCs to have problems during replication. If the PDC doesn't hear from the BDC in the interval specified by PulseTimeout2, the PDC determines that the BDC is having trouble. The default is 300 seconds, and the valid range is 60 to 300 seconds.

I-196

Hive: HKEY_LOCAL_MACHINE
Key: System\CurrentControlSet\Services\Netlogon\Parameters
Value Name: Randomize
Data Type: REG_DWORD
Value: 1

When the BDC receives a pulse, it waits the number of seconds specified in the Randomize value before answering. You should keep this value small. If you tune the value in PulseTimeout1, remember to set the Randomize value smaller. If this value is not in the registry, Netlogon figures out the best value depending on server load. Restart the machine for any changes to take effect.

I-197

Hive: HKEY_LOCAL_MACHINE
Key: System\CurrentControlSet\Services\Netlogon\Parameters
Value Name: ReplicationGovernor
Data Type: REG_DWORD
Value: 100

This value sets the frequency with which the PDC transfers data to the BDC and the amount of data it sends at a time. If the replication governor is set to 50, the BDC has a replication call pending only 50 percent of the time and uses a 64K buffer instead of the 128K buffer it uses for a 100 setting. A value of 0 causes Netlogon to never replicate, which gets the databases on the PDC and BDC completely out of sync.

ENVIRONMENT VARIABLES

I-198 If you want to set certain environment variables for all the users on a particular machine, try this registry entry.

Hive: HKEY_LOCAL_MACHINE
Key: System\CurrentControlSet\Control\Session Manager\Environment

Here you will find some environment variables such as ComSpec and Path. You can add more variables or change existing ones.

Value Name: Path
Data Type: REG_SZ
Value: any valid path statement

You must restart the machine for any changes to take effect.

I-199   The default system font NT uses is not very readable on high-resolution displays. You can change the system fonts by editing the following registry values. You can substitute any .fon file from your %systemroot%\SYSTEM directory for the default fonts.

          Hive: HKEY_LOCAL_MACHINE
           Key: Software\Microsoft\WindowsNT\CurrentVersion\
                     GRE_Initialize
Value Name: Fixedfon.fon
   Data Type: REG_SZ
       Value: vgafix.fon

I-200

          Hive: HKEY_LOCAL_MACHINE
           Key: Software\Microsoft\WindowsNT\CurrentVersion\
                     GRE_Initialize
Value Name: Fonts.fon
   Data Type: REG_SZ
       Value: vgasys.fon

I-201

          Hive: HKEY_LOCAL_MACHINE
           Key: Software\Microsoft\WindowsNT\CurrentVersion\
                     GRE_Initialize
Value Name: Oemfont.fon
   Data Type: REG_SZ
       Value: vgaoem.fon

Restart your system for these values to take effect.

I-202   When you reboot your Windows NT system, you sometimes get popup warning messages. Most of the time, these messages are very helpful and point to potential problems. However, when you are debugging a system, you often don't need to be reminded each time. This registry entry disables these messages, including event errors.

          Hive: HKEY_LOCAL_MACHINE
           Key: Software\Microsoft\WindowsNT\CurrentVersion\Winlogon
Value Name: NoPopupsOnBoot
   Data Type: REG_SZ
       Value: 1

I-203 When you're debugging a server problem or configuring new systems, it is often expedient to have the system complete its boot process as quickly as possible. This registry entry lets you reboot the system without going through all the BIOS checks (i.e., perform a warm boot).

Hive: HKEY_LOCAL_MACHINE
Key: Software\Microsoft\WindowsNT\CurrentVersion\Winlogon
Value Name: EnableQuickReboot
Data Type: REG_SZ
Value: 1

Reboot your machine for these changes to take effect.

I-204 Holding down the shift key when Windows NT boots keeps any programs located in the Startup folders from executing. As an administrator, you may want these programs to execute for a variety of reasons. This registry entry lets you disable the option of holding down the shift key during the boot process.

Hive: HKEY_LOCAL_MACHINE
Key: Software\Microsoft\WindowsNT\CurrentVersion\Winlogon
Value Name: IgnoreShiftOveride
Data Type: REG_SZ
Value: 1

A value of 1 enables the shift override mechanism. The default is 0.

I-205 Do you want to disable the Autorun feature of the CD-ROM? Does it annoy you that every time you insert a CD, it runs its little splash screen and install program? This registry disables the Autorun feature.

Hive: HKEY_LOCAL_MACHINE
Key: System\CurrentControlSet\Services\CDROM
Value Name: AutoRun
Data Type: REG_DWORD
Value: 0

Restart Windows NT for this change to take effect.

I-206

Hive:	HKEY_LOCAL_MACHINE
Key:	Software\Microsoft\WindowsNT\CurrentVersion\Winlogon
Value Name:	ReportBootOk
Data Type:	REG_SZ
Value:	1

When this value is set to 0, it disables the automatic startup acceptance. This registry entry is used in conjunction with the Bootvrfy.exe program, which lets you verify the startup of a system from a remote system. To correctly implement the procedure, change the following keys and values as well. See the Windows NT Resource Kit for more information on this procedure.

I-207

Hive:	HKEY_LOCAL_MACHINE
Key:	System\CurrentControlSet\Services\BootVerification
Value Name:	ErrorControl
Data Type:	REG_DWORD
Value:	1

I-208

Value Name:	ImagePath
Data Type:	REG_EXPAND_SZ
Value:	bootvrfy.exe

I-209

Value Name:	ObjectName
Data Type:	REG_SZ
Value:	LocalSystem

I-210

Value Name:	Start
Data Type:	REG_DWORD
Value:	0x3

I-211

Value Name:	Type
Data Type:	REG_DWORD
Value:	0x2

Restart Windows NT for these changes to take effect.

I-212 Do you need to reinstall Windows NT, but you've lost your CD Key? This registry entry stores the value.

> **Hive:** HKEY_LOCAL_MACHINE
> **Key:** Software\Microsoft\WindowsNT\CurrentVersion
> **Value Name:** ProductID
> **Data Type:** REG_SZ
> **Value:** <machine dependent>

Ignore the first five numbers. The next ten are your CD Key. Ignore the last five numbers, too.

I-213 If you don't want your users to have access to Task Manager for security reasons, change these entries:

> **Hive:** HKEY_CURRENT_USER
> **Key:** Software\Microsoft\Windows\CurrentVersion\Policies\System
> **Value Name:** DisableTaskMgr
> **Data Type:** REG_BINARY
> **Value:** 01 hexadecimal

The default value is 00 hexadecimal, which enables the Task Manager. Changing this value to 01 hex disables Task Manager, and you should see a message that your administrator has disabled the Task Manager.

I-214 Do you need to have all your 16-bit applications run in separate virtual DOS machines? This registry lets you specify this setup as the default for running 16-bit applications.

> **Hive:** HKEY_LOCAL_MACHINE
> **Key:** System\CurrentControlSet\Control\WOW
> **Value Name:** DefaultSeperateVDM
> **Data Type:** REG_SZ
> **Value:** YES

Reboot for this change to take effect.

I-215   **P**roblem: you want to open a command prompt and switch to a directory that is nested deep within your directory structure without typing a long **chdir** pathname. These registry keys allow you to start a command prompt in the folder or drive of your choice by simply right-clicking over the folder in which you want to open a command prompt.

Hive: HKEY_CLASSES_ROOT
Key: Directory\Shell\DosHere
Value Name: <No Name>
Data Type: REG_SZ
Value: Command Prompt Here

This value is the text that appears on the popup menu when you right-click a directory.

I-216

Hive: HKEY_CLASSES_ROOT
Key: Directory\Shell\DosHere\Command
Value Name: <No Name>
Data Type: REG_SZ
Value: (system directory)\System32\cmd.exe /k cd "%1"

This value is the command that is executed when you select the "Command Prompt Here" item you set for the popup menu in the entry above.

I-217

Hive: HKEY_CLASSES_ROOT
Key: Drive\Shell\DosHere
Value Name: <No Name>
Data Type: REG_SZ
Value: Command Prompt Here

This value sets the text that appears on the popup menu when you right-click a drive.

I-218

Hive: HKEY_CLASSES_ROOT
Key: Drive\Shell\DosHere\Command
Value Name: <No Name>
Data Type: REG_SZ
Value: (system directory)\System32\cmd.exe /k cd "%1"

This value sets the command that is executed when you select the "Command Prompt Here" item you set for the popup menu in the entry above.

1-219 Does your system support Auto Powerdown? Do you want to enable it on NT? This registry entry does the trick.

> **Hive:** HKEY_LOCAL_MACHINE
> **Key:** Software\Microsoft\WindowsNT\CurrentVersion\Winlogon
> **Value Name:** PowerDownAfterShutDown
> **Data Type:** REG_SZ
> **Value:** 1

Reboot for this change to take effect.

1-220 If your system takes too long to shut down, you may want to adjust the next three registry entries.

> **Hive:** HKEY_CURRENT_USER
> **Key:** Control Panel\Desktop
> **Value Name:** HungAppTimeout
> **Data Type:** REG_DWORD
> **Value:** time in milliseconds

This value governs how long the system waits after you try to close an application before displaying the Wait, End Task, and Close dialog box.

1-221

> **Hive:** HKEY_CURRENT_USER
> **Key:** Control Panel\Desktop
> **Value Name:** WaitToKillAppTimeout
> **Data Type:** REG_DWORD
> **Value:** time in milliseconds

This value governs how long the system waits after the Log Off or Shutdown command was given to an application before it displays the Wait, End Task, and Close dialog box.

1-222 To have the system automatically shut down all hung applications, change the following registry value.

> **Hive:** HKEY_CURRENT_USER
> **Key:** Control Panel\Desktop
> **Value Name:** AutoEndTasks
> **Data Type:** REG_DWORD
> **Value:** 1

By default, this value is 0, which shows the Wait, End Task, and Close dialog box; changing the value to 1 automatically shuts down all hung applications.

I-223 If you need to specify which executables Windows NT runs at logon, the next two registry entries show you the default executables and let you add a few of your own. These executables run in the User context.

        Hive: HKEY_LOCAL_MACHINE
         Key: Software\Microsoft\WindowsNT\CurrentVersion\Winlogon
Value Name: Userinit
  Data Type: REG_SZ
      Value: Userinit,Nddeagnt.exe

I-224 These executables run in the System context.

        Hive: HKEY_LOCAL_MACHINE
         Key: Software\Microsoft\WindowsNT\CurrentVersion\Winlogon
Value Name: System
  Data Type: REG_SZ
      Value: LSASS.exe

These values are the defaults. You can add your own by editing the string, being sure to include commas. Restart Windows NT for these changes to take effect.

I-225 Tired of having to log on just to power down? Try this registry entry.

        Hive: HKEY_LOCAL_MACHINE
         Key: Software\Microsoft\WindowsNT\CurrentVersion\Winlogon
Value Name: ShutDownWithOutLogon
  Data Type: REG_SZ
      Value: 1

Reboot for this change to take effect.

I-226 Do you get those annoying "insufficient memory" messages for the server service when you know you have plenty of disk and memory? These registry parameters control the server service, and tweaking them can help you avoid these messages.

        Hive: HKEY_LOCAL_MACHINE
         Key: System\CurrentControlSet\Services\LanmanServer\
             Parameters\
Value Name: MinFreeConnections
  Data Type: REG_DWORD
      Value: 3

This parameter specifies the number of free connection blocks maintained at each system in the connection. Acceptable values can range from 2 to 5.

I-227

> **Hive:** HKEY_LOCAL_MACHINE
> **Key:** System\CurrentControlSet\Services\LanmanServer\
> Parameters\
> **Value Name:** MinFreeWorkItems
> **Data Type:** REG_DWORD
> **Value:** 2

This value specifies the minimum number of available work items that the server receives before it starts processing a potential multiblock SMB request. Increasing this value increases the probability that work items are available for nonblocking requests. The downside of increasing the value is that the likelihood of rejecting blocking requests goes up. The default value is 2; any value between 0 and 10 is acceptable.

I-228

> **Hive:** HKEY_LOCAL_MACHINE
> **Key:** System\CurrentControlSet\Services\LanmanServer\
> Parameters\
> **Value Name:** MinKeepSearch
> **Data Type:** REG_DWORD
> **Value:** 480

This parameter specifies the minimum time in seconds the server keeps incomplete MS-DOS searches. You should not have to tweak this unless you are approaching the maximum number of open searches. The default is 480; values can range between 5 and 5000.

I-229

> **Hive:** HKEY_LOCAL_MACHINE
> **Key:** System\CurrentControlSet\Services\LanmanServer\
> Parameters\
> **Value Name:** MinLinkThroughPut
> **Data Type:** REG_DWORD
> **Value:** 0

This value specifies the minimum throughput the server allows before it disables certain locks for a given connection. Increasing this value helps tune for network congestion. The default is 0; values can range from 0 to infinity.

I-230

Hive: HKEY_LOCAL_MACHINE
Key: System\CurrentControlSet\Services\LanmanServer\Parameters\
Value Name: MinRcvQueues
Data Type: REG_DWORD
Value: 3

This parameter specifies the minimum number of free receive work items the server needs before it allocates more Receive Queues. The value can range from 0 to 10.

I-231 If you simply want to stop the insufficient memory messages, the following series usually does the trick.

Hive: HKEY_LOCAL_MACHINE
Key: System\CurrentControlSet\Services\LanmanServer\Parameters\
Value Name: MinFreeConnections
Data Type: REG_DWORD
Value: 5

Start Control Panel and go to the network icon. Highlight Services and choose the Server service. Select Properties and then select Maximize Throughput for File Sharing. These changes should solve the problem.

I-232 Are you tired of having error messages popping up and slowing down your system? This registry entry shows you how to eliminate them.

Hive: HKEY_CURRENT_USER
Key: Software\Microsoft\WindowsNT\CurrentVersion\Windows

Add the following value under the Windows key.

Value Name: ErrorMode
Data Type: REG_DWORD
Value: 0

You have a choice of three values for this value. A value of 0 serializes errors and waits for a response. A value of 1 excludes system errors the system writes to the event log. Normal errors still show up. A value of 2 logs the error to the Event Log and suppresses the message box. The default is 0; to turn off pop-up messages, set this value to 2. Reboot for these changes to take effect.

I-233 If you ever wondered where the Performance Monitor messages are stored, look at this registry entry.

> **Hive:** HKEY_LOCAL_MACHINE
> **Key:** Software\Microsoft\WindowsNT\CurrentVersion\Perflib\009
> **Value Name:** Help
> **Data Type:** REG_MULTI_SZ
> **Value:**

See this book's Website for a complete list of the valid values for this registry entry.

I-234 This registry entry sets the %Server environment variable on a server.

> **Hive:** HKEY_LOCAL_MACHINE
> **Key:** System\CurrentControlSet\Control\SessionManager\ Environment

Add the following value under the Environment key.

> **Value Name:** Servername
> **Data Type:** REG_SZ
> **Value:** <server_name>

I-235 You upgraded to Windows NT 4.0, and you need to have a HPFS file system on the server. But NT 4.0 doesn't support HPFS. Bummer. This registry modification lets you get around that problem.

> **Hive:** HKEY_LOCAL_MACHINE
> **Key:** System\CurentControlSet\Services\Pinball

Add the following values under the Pinball Key.

> **Value Name:** ErrorControl
> **Data Type:** REG_DWORD
> **Value:** 0x1

I-236

> **Value Name:** Group
> **Data Type:** REG_SZ
> **Value:** Boot File System

I-237

> **Value Name:** Start
> **Data Type:** REG_DWORD
> **Value:** 0x1

I-238

        Value Name: Type
          Data Type: REG_DWORD
            Value: 0x2

Copy Pinball.sys from the NT 3.51 distribution CD to your servers' %system-root%\system32\drivers directory. You must reboot your machine for these changes to take effect.

I-239 You want to let a user schedule jobs, but the user doesn't have administrator rights. This registry entry shows you how.
           Hive: HKEY_LOCAL_MACHINE
            Key: System\CurrentControlSet\Control\LSA

Add the following value under the Parameters key.
        Value Name: SubmitControl
          Data Type: REG_DWORD
            Value: 00000001

The value is in hexadecimal. Reboot your system for the changes to take effect. If changing this key doesn't work, you may need to change the following entry as well.

I-240

           Hive: HKEY_LOCAL_MACHINE
            Key: System\CurrentControlSet\Services\Schedule

On the subkey for the accounts you want to grant access, choose Full Control for Permissions Access Type Stop and restart the scheduler service in the control panel applet.

I-241 To set a server on your network to act as the domain time source server, change this entry.
           Hive: HKEY_LOCAL_MACHINE
            Key: System\CurrentControlSet\Services\LanManServer\
                 Parameters

Add the following value under the Parameters key.
        Value Name: TimeSource
          Data Type: REG_DWORD
            Value: 1

Restart Windows NT for these changes to take effect.

I-242 You want to limit the use of command extensions for any .cmd file. This registry entry does just that.

> **Hive:** HKEY_CURRENT_USER
> **Key:** Software\Microsoft\Command Processor
> **Value Name:** EnableExtensions
> **Data Type:** REG_DWORD
> **Value:** 0

When the value is set to 0, the .cmd files do not run. Reboot your machine for these values to take effect.

I-243 Your computer locks up when you are using the drag-and-drop method to move files to your floppy drive. The only way out is a reboot. Try this registry entry to help solve the problem.

> **Hive:** HKEY_LOCAL_MACHINE
> **Key:** System\CurrentControlSet\Control\GraphicsDrivers\

Add the following key under the GraphicsDrivers Key:

> **Key:** DisableUSWC

When you add this key, you tell Windows NT not to use Uncache Speculative Write Combining on the video cards. No value is needed under the DisableUSWC key. Reboot the machine for this change to take effect.

I-244 Modifying the registry entries below lets you disable the Long File Names feature in Windows NT. Note this change doesn't change any disk structures; it only affects the way Windows NT behaves from the time you make the change.

> **Hive:** HKEY_LOCAL_MACHINE
> **Key:** System\CurrentControlSet\Control\FileSystem
> **Value Name:** Win31FileSystem
> **Data Type:** REG_DWORD
> **Value:** 1

Reboot your system for these changes to take effect.

I-245

> **Hive:** HKEY_LOCAL_MACHINE
> **Key:** System\CurrentControlSet\Control\FileSystem
> **Value Name:** NtfsDisable8dot3NameCreation
> **Data Type:** REG_DWORD
> **Value:** 1

This change prohibits Windows NT from creating an 8.3 twin for the long filenames you create.

I-246 Problem: In a previous version of NT, you were notified by a message that NT saw your 16550N UART chip. For some reason, that notification has stopped and you wish to enable it again. This registry modification makes NT notify you when it recognizes the 16550N UART.

> **Hive:** HKEY_LOCAL_MACHINE
> **Key:** System\CurrentControlSet\Services\Serial

Make sure the following values are present. If any are missing, add them.

> **Value Name:** ForceFIFOEnable
> **Data Type:** REG_DWORD
> **Value:** 1

I-247
> **Value Name:** LogFIFO
> **Data Type:** REG_DWORD
> **Value:** 1

I-248
> **Value Name:** PermitShare
> **Data Type:** REG_DWORD
> **Value:** 1

I-249
> **Value Name:** RxFIFO
> **Data Type:** REG_DWORD
> **Value:** 0x8

I-250
> **Value Name:** TxFIFO
> **Data Type:** REG_DWORD
> **Value:** 0x1

Reboot the system for these changes to take effect. The event log now reports "While validating that COM1 was really a serial port, a FIFO was detected. The FIFO will be used."

I-251 Problem: You want to change the registered owner or organization to something other than the one you used during the installation. Change one of these values.

> **Hive:** HKEY_LOCAL_MACHINE
> **Key:** Software\Microsoft\WindowsNT\CurrentVersion
> **Value Name:** RegisteredOwner
> **Data Type:** REG_SZ
> **Value:** <registered owner>

I-252

    Value Name: RegisteredOrganization
      Data Type: REG_SZ
         Value: <registered organization>

I-253 **P**roblem: You want to have a program run every time Windows NT loads, but you don't want to put it in the startup folder where people can tinker with it. This registry modification lets you set a program to execute every time Windows NT loads.
         Hive: HKEY_LOCAL_MACHINE
         Key: Software\Microsoft\Windows\CurrentVersion\Run

Add the following value under the Run key:
    Value Name: <any name>
      Data Type: REG_SZ
         Value: <fully qualified path and name of the program you want
                 to run>

I-254 **I**f you want the program to run only one time, use this registry entry.
         Hive: HKEY_LOCAL_MACHINE
         Key: Software\Microsoft\Windows\CurrentVersion\RunOnce

Add the following value under the RunOnce key:
    Value Name: <any name>
      Data Type: REG_SZ
         Value: fully qualified path and name of the program you want to run

---

I-255 **W**e all know that Windows NT lets programs register themselves for later removal. If you ever want to remove a program from the list (and not actually remove the program), this registry entry is for you.
         Hive: HKEY_LOCAL_MACHINE
         Key: Software\Microsoft\Windows\CurrentVersion\Uninstall

The programs that are registered show under the uninstall key. I use the example of Internet Information Server, but you can substitute any program.
      SubKey: MSIIS
    Value Name: DisplayName
      Data Type: REG_SZ
         Value: Microsoft Internet Information Server

I-256
          Value Name: UninstallString
              Data Type: REG_SZ
                  Value: C:\NTS40\System32\Inetsrv\Setup.exe

I-257 **P**roblem: On your dual-boot system, the DOS variables are set up when you boot Windows NT. This setup is causing problems, and you want to eliminate it. Changing this registry entry does the trick.

                 Hive: HKEY_CURRENT_USER
                  Key: Software\Microsoft\WindowsNT\CurrentVersion\WinLogon
      Value Name: ParseAutoexec
          Data Type: REG_SZ
              Value: 0

The default value is 1. Remember, you need to disable autoexec parsing for each user separately.

DIAL-UP

I-258 **T**o enable or disable autodialing for remote connections for individual users, try the following registry entry.

                 Hive: HKEY_CURRENT_USER
                  Key: Software\Microsoft\RAS Autodial\Control
      Value Name: DisableConnectionQuery
          Data Type: REG_DWORD
              Value: 0

Setting this value to 0 requires NT to prompt you before it autodials. Restart the machine for these values to take effect.

SYSTEM RECOVERY

I-259 If you have ever lost the administrative password on a Domain controller, you probably thought it was impossible to recover your system. However, if you follow these steps and use the registry, it is possible to regain control of your system.

1. Power down the primary domain controller.
2. Using the Windows NT installation disks, install Windows NT to a different directory than you're currently using. For example, if the current installation uses c:\winnt, install this version into c:\winntA.
3. Copy SrvAny.exe from the resource kit to C:\Temp.
4. Using Regedt32.exe, open the HKEY_LOCAL_MACHINE hive and highlight the root.
5. Select the Load Hive option and type the following line: **C:\WINNT\SYSTEM32\CONFIG\SYSTEM.** (You must include the period.)
6. Now click Open and type **domain controller** at the key name prompt.
7. Go to the following key and record its value:

> **Hive:** HKEY_LOCAL_MACHINE
> **Key:** DomainSystem\ControlSet001\Services\Spooler\ImagePath
> **Value Name:** ImagePath
> **Data Type:** REG_SZ
> **Value:** c:\Temp\Srvany.exe

The default value is %SystemRoot%\System32\Spoolss.exe.

8. Go the following key and add this key:

> **Hive:** HKEY_LOCAL_MACHINE
> **Key:** DomainController\ControlSet001\Services\Spooler\Parameters

Add the following two values:

> **Value Name:** Application
> **Data Type:** REG_SZ
> **Value:** C:\WinNT\System32\Net.exe

> **Value Name:** AppParameters
> **Data Type:** REG_SZ
> **Value:** user Administrator forgotten

This value sets the administrator password to "forgotten." You can, of course, substitute any password of your liking. Power down the system and reboot using the original configuration (c:\winnt). After the logon screen comes up, wait a few minutes and log on as the domain admin.

9. Using Regedt32.exe, remove the values you added. Remove the following keys:

Hive: HKEY_LOCAL_MACHINE
Key: SYSTEM\CurrentControlSet\Services\Spooler\Parameters

Delete the following two values:

Value Name: Application
Data Type: REG_SZ
Value: C:\Winnt\System32\Net.exe

Value Name: AppParameters
Data Type: REG_SZ
Value: user Administrator forgotten

10. Now change the ImagePath key back to its original value:

Hive: HKEY_LOCAL_MACHINE
Key: DomainController\ControlSet001\Services\Spooler\ImagePath

Change the value to c:\Temp\Srvany.exe
Value Name: ImagePath
Data Type: REG_SZ
Value: %SystemRoot%\system32\spoolss.exe

You can now edit the Boot.ini file and remove the reference to the c:\winntA installation of Windows NT. When you reboot your machine, all is as it was before, except now you know the Domain administrator password again.

UNINSTALLATION

I-260   Have you ever installed some trial software and removed it at the end of the demo period, only to be plagued by the annoying message "Cannot find file C:\filename" (or one of its components)? Try this registry entry to correct the problem.

Hive: HKEY_CURRENT_USER
Key: Software\Microsoft\Windows\CurrentVersion
Value Name: Run
Data Type: REG_SZ
Value: <filename>

REGISTRY

I-261 Problem: Windows NT 4.0 Server requires that people who can remotely access the registry on a given machine belong to the Administrator group. However, someone is still tampering with your registry. To change the permissions, modify this registry entry.

       Hive: HKEY_LOCAL_MACHINE
        Key: System\CurrentControlSet\Control\SecurePipeServers\winreg

Change the permissions on this key to whomever you wish to give access to. The default is Administrators Full Control.

I-262 In Windows NT Workstation, the Winreg key is not in the registry by default. If you add this key to the registry, you must also add the subkey Allowedpaths. Here is the AllowedPaths key under a clean install of Windows NT Server 4.0

       Hive: HKEY_LOCAL_MACHINE
        Key: System\CurrentControlSet\Control\SecurePipeServers\winreg\
           AllowedPaths
Value Name: Machine
  DataType: REG_MULTI_SZ
     Value: System\CurrentControlSet\Control\ProductOptions

I-263   **Value:** System\CurrentControlSet\Control\Print\Printers

I-264   **Value:** System\CurrentControlSet\Services\Eventlog

I-265   **Value:** Software\Microsoft\Windows NT\CurrentVersion

Restart your machine for these new values to take effect.

I-266 Did you ever wonder where the registry files are stored? Well, where else would you expect to find the answer but in the registry itself?

       Hive: HKEY_LOCAL_MACHINE
        Key: System\CurrentControlSet\Control\Hivelist
Value Name: Registry\Machine\Clone
 Data Type: REG_SZ
     Value:

This registry entry stores the clone hive information.

I-267   **Value Name:** Registry\Machine\Hardware
              Data Type: REG_SZ
              Value:

This registry entry stores hardware hive information.

I-268   **Value Name:** Registry\Machine\SAM
              Data Type: REG_SZ
                   Value: Device\Harddisk0\Partition1\NTS40\System32\Config\SAM

This registry entry stores all the SAM information.

I-269   **Value Name:** Registry\Machine\Security
              Data Type: REG_SZ
                   Value: Device\Harddisk0\Partition1\NTS40\System32\Config\Security

This file stores information for the grayed-out Security hive.

I-270   **Value Name:** Registry\Machine\Software
              Data Type: REG_SZ
                   Value: Device\Harddisk0\Partition1\NTS40\System32\Config\
                              Software

This file contains the value for the Software hive.

I-271   **Value Name:** Registry\Machine\System
              Data Type: REG_SZ
                   Value: Device\Harddisk0\Partition1\NTS40\System32\Config\System

This entry shows where the System hive is stored.

I-272   **Value Name:** Registry\User\Default
              Data Type: REG_SZ
                   Value: Device\Harddisk0\Partition1\NTS40\System32\Config\Default

This entry shows where the default values for the user hive are stored.

I-273	

Value Name: Registry\User\<big long user id number>
Data Type: REG_SZ
Value: Device\Harddisk0\Partition1\NTS40\Profiles\<username>\ Ntuser.dat

This entry shows the user data for the current logged-on user.

DEFAULT SECURITY PERMISSIONS

You can use many combinations of Windows NT security measures. These entries represent the default permissions on a brand-new installation. They are helpful when you need to reset your registry.

I-274	

Hive: HKEY_CURRENT_USER
User: Guest
Permissions: Full Control

User: Administrator
Permissions: Full Control

User: System
Permissions: Full Control

I-275	

Hive: HKEY_USERS
User: Guest
Permissions: Read-Only

User: Administrator
Permissions: Full Control

User: System
Permissions: Full Control

I-276

      Hive: HKEY_CLASSES_ROOT
      User: Guest
Permissions: Full Control

      User: Administrator
Permissions: Full Control

      User: System
Permissions: Full Control

I-277

      Hive: HKEY_LOCAL_MACHINE
      Key: Security
      User: Guest
Permissions: None

      User: Administrator
Permissions: Special Access

      User: System
Permissions: Full Control

I-278

      Hive: HKEY_LOCAL_MACHINE
      Key: SAM
      User: Guest
Permissions: None

      User: Administrator
Permissions: None

I-279

      Hive: HKEY_LOCAL_MACHINE
      Key: System
      User: Guest
Permissions: Read-Only

      User: Administrator
Permissions: Full Control

I-280

    Hive: HKEY_LOCAL_MACHINE
    Key: Software
    User: Guest
Permissions: Full Control

    User: Administrator
Permissions: Full Control

I-281

    Hive: HKEY_LOCAL_MACHINE
    Key: Software\Secure
    User: Guest
Permissions: Read-only

    User: Administrator
Permissions: Full Control

I-282

    Hive: HKEY_LOCAL_MACHINE
    Key: Software\Microsoft\Secure
    User: Guest
Permissions: Full Control

    User: Administrator
Permissions: Full Control

I-283

    Hive: HKEY_LOCAL_MACHINE
    Key: Software\Microsoft\WindowsNT
    User: Guest
Permissions: Creation Only

    User: Administrator
Permissions: Full Control

`I-284`

      Hive: HKEY_LOCAL_MACHINE
      Key: Software\Microsoft\ProgramGroup
      User: Guest
Permissions: Read-Only

      User: Administrator
Permissions: Full Control

`I-285`

      Hive: HKEY_LOCAL_MACHINE
      Key: Software\Microsoft\Windows
      User: Guest
Permissions: Full Control

      User: Administrator
Permissions: Full Control

GENERAL NETWORKING

`I-286` Windows NT automatically disconnects idle sessions after a set number of minutes. To disable this feature (or at least set it to a ridiculously high number of minutes), use the following registry setting.
      Hive: HKEY_LOCAL_MACHINE
      Key: System\CurrentControlSet\Services\LanmanServer\
      Parameters

Add the following value
    Value Name: Autodisconnect
      Data Type: REG_DWORD
        Value: 0xffffffff

Restart the system for this value to take effect.

I-287 If you continually get the dreaded error 3013, "The redirector has timed out to Servername," in your system log, fix this problem with this registry entry.

> **Hive:** HKEY_LOCAL_MACHINE
> **Key:** System\CurrentControlSet\Services\LanmanWorkstation\
> Parameters

Increase the following value under the Parameters key or add it if it doesn't already exist.

> **Value Name:** SessTimeOut
> **Data Type:** REG_DWORD
> **Value:** 1

I-288 Your 3COM fast Ethernet card is hanging when you perform a soft reset, and the event log says something about bus mastering. This registry entry fixes your problem.

> **Hive:** HKEY_LOCAL_MACHINE
> **Key:** System\CurrentControlSet\Services\EL59X1\Parameters

Add the following value under the Parameters key.

> **Value Name:** BusMaster
> **Data Type:** REG_SZ
> **Value:** no

This change disables bus mastering on the network card. Restart the machine for these changes to take effect.

I-289 If your Windows NT workstation maintains a browser list and you want to disable this feature, change this registry entry.

> **Hive:** HKEY_LOCAL_MACHINE
> **Key:** System\CurrentControlSet\Services\Browser\Parameters

Add the following value under the Parameters key.

> **Value Name:** MaintainServerList
> **Data Type:** REG_SZ
> **Value:** no

1-290 **P**roblem: You receive the following error repeatedly in the Server event log:
Event ID: 2022
Source: srv
Detail: The server was unable to find free connection *xx* times in the last *xx* seconds.

The actual number represented by *xx* varies depending on your circumstances. Changing this registry entry helps you work around the problem.

> **Hive:** HKEY_LOCAL_MACHINE
> **Key:** System\CurrentControlSet\Services\LanmanServer\Parameters

1. Add the following two values under the Parameters key.

> **Value Name:** MaxFreeConnections
> **Data Type:** REG_DWORD
> **Value:** 8

> **Value Name:** MaxWorkItems
> **Data Type:** REG_DWORD
> **Value:** 255

2. Next, modify this registry parameter to turn off AutoDisconnect.

> **Hive:** HKEY_LOCAL_MACHINE
> **Key:** System\CurrentControlSet\Services\LanmanServer\Parameters

Add the following value under the Parameters key:

> **Value Name:** AutoDisconnect
> **Data Type:** REG_DWORD
> **Value:** FFFFFFFF

Reboot your system for these changes to take effect.

1-291 **Y**ou're trying to set up a connection to your ISP so that your workstation lets other computers on the network access the Internet. The problem is that you can see your machine but nothing else. Try this registry modification to solve the problem.

> **Hive:** HKEY_LOCAL_MACHINE
> **Key:** System\CurrentControlSet\Services\RASARP\Parameters

Add the following value under the Parameters key:

> **Value Name:** DisableOtherSourcePackets
> **Data Type:** REG_DWORD
> **Value:** 0

I-292 Are you tired of your server flooding you with alert messages? You don't want to turn them off; you just don't want them sent as frequently. This registry entry lets you specify how often Windows NT checks alert conditions and sends appropriate messages.

> **Hive:** HKEY_LOCAL_MACHINE
>
> **Key:** System\CurrentControlSet\Services\LanmanServer\Parameters

Add the following value:

> **Value Name:** AlertSched
>
> **Data Type:** REG_DWORD
>
> **Value:** 5

Valid values are from 1 to 65,535, and they are in minutes. The default is 5 minutes. Restart your machine for these values to take effect.

I-293 Are your users leaving open connections to the server and using up resources you don't have? To disconnect idle users after a certain length of time, change this registry entry.

> **Hive:** HKEY_LOCAL_MACHINE
>
> **Key:** System\CurrentControlSet\Services\LanmanServer\Parameters
>
> **Value Name:** AutoDisconnect
>
> **Data Type:** REG_DWORD
>
> **Value:** 15

Valid numbers are from 0 to 0xFFFFFFFF in minutes. The default is 15 minutes. Restart your machine for these values to take effect.

I-294 If you have lots of servers on your network and your users get confused, use this registry entry to specify a comment that is displayed with the server name.

> **Hive:** HKEY_LOCAL_MACHINE
>
> **Key:** System\CurrentControlSet\Services\LanmanServer\Parameters
>
> **Value Name:** Srvcomment
>
> **Data Type:** REG_SZ
>
> **Value:** <new message>

The default is no message. Restart the computer for this change to take effect.

I-295 Are you tired of slow connections making you wait to access your roaming profiles? Do you want to speed things up? These registry entries let you set the time NT waits before timing out and letting you use a local profile.

Hive: HKEY_LOCAL_MACHINE
Key: Software\Microsoft\Windows NT\CurrentVersion\Winlogon
Value Name: SlowLinkDetectEnabled
Data Type: REG_DWORD
Value: 1

I-296

Hive: HKEY_LOCAL_MACHINE
Key: Software\Microsoft\Windows NT\CurrentVersion\Winlogon
Value Name SlowLinkTimeOut
Data Type: REG_DWORD
Value: 2000

If SlowLinkDetectEnabled is set to 1, the value in SlowLinkTimeOut determines how long in milliseconds until users are prompted to choose between Local or Server-based profiles. The default value is 2000 milliseconds.

I-297 To keep your server from showing up in the Network Neighborhood listings, change this registry entry.

Hive: HKEY_LOCAL_MACHINE
Key: System\CurrentControlSet\Services\LanmanServer\
Parameters
Value Name: Hidden
Data Type: REG_BINARY
Value: 1

The default is 0. Restart the computer for this change to take effect.

I-298 You must also have the following registry entry set to 1 for the Hidden and Srvcomment value to be active.

Hive: HKEY_LOCAL_MACHINE
Key: System\CurrentControlSet\Services\LanmanServer\
Parameters
Value Name: Lmannounce
Data Type: REG_DWORD
Value: 1

The default is 0. Restart the computer for this change to take effect.

I-299 Are some of your Word for Windows clients that are running IPX having problems connecting to your Windows NT server? Try adding this registry parameter.

Hive: HKEY_LOCAL_MACHINE
Key: System\CurrentControlSet\Services\LanmanServer\
Parameters
Value Name: EnableWFW311DirectIpx
Data Type: REG_DWORD
Value: True

The default value is False. Restart the computer for this change to take effect.

I-300 If you have older clients running direct-hosted IPX, you may want to add this registry value. It governs how long a client can be idle before it is disconnected, even if it has open files or pipes.

Hive: HKEY_LOCAL_MACHINE
Key: System\CurrentControlSet\Services\LanmanServer\
Parameters
Value Name: ConnectionlessAutoDisc
Data Type: REG_DWORD
Value: 15

Valid entries, in minutes, are 15 to infinity; the default value is 15. Restart the computer for this change to take effect.

I-301 Do you want the server to let you know when the total percentage of network errors is greater than a certain value? This registry entry lets you specify a threshold and force the server to send an alert message that the threshold is exceeded.

Hive: HKEY_LOCAL_MACHINE
Key: System\CurrentControlSet\Services\LanmanServer\Parameters
Value Name: NetworkErrorThreshold
Data Type: REG_DWORD
Value: 5

Valid entries are 1 to 100 percent. The default value is 5. Restart machine for this value to take effect.

I-302 Do you want to change the default string that users see when they are prompted to log on to your server? Try this registry entry.

> **Hive:** HKEY_LOCAL_MACHINE
> **Key:** Software\Microsoft\Windows NT\CurrentVersion\Winlogon
> **Value Name:** LogonPrompt
> **Data Type:** REG_SZ
> **Value:** Enter a user name and password that is valid for this system.

The message shown is the default. Replace it with anything you like; you have up to 256 characters.

I-303 Do you want to change how far in advance your users are warned that their passwords will expire? This registry entry controls the number of days before expiration that Windows NT warns your users.

> **Hive:** HKEY_LOCAL_MACHINE
> **Key:** Software\Microsoft\Windows NT\CurrentVersion\Winlogon
> **Value Name:** PasswordExpiryWarning
> **Data Type:** REG_DWORD
> **Value:** 14

I-304 Are your users experiencing slow response time when performing routine file activities? This parameter lets you allocate more resources by specifying the maximum number of active searches that can run concurrently on your server.

> **Hive:** HKEY_LOCAL_MACHINE
> **Key:** System\CurrentControlSet\Services\LanmanServer\Parameters
> **Value Name:** MaxGlobalOpenSearch
> **Data Type:** REG_DWORD
> **Value:** 4096

Valid values are 1 to infinity. A higher value allows more searches on the server to be active at one time and also uses more resources. A lower value saves resources but can cause clients to experience poor performance.

GENERAL SYSTEM

I-305 Have you ever wanted to set the threshold that triggers the administrative alert for disk space? This registry entry lets you set the value from 0 to 99 percent of remaining free disk space.

> **Hive:** HKEY_LOCAL_MACHINE
> **Key:** System\CurrentControlSet\Services\LanmanServer\Parameters
> **Value Name:** DiskSpaceThreshold
> **Data Type:** REG_DWORD
> **Value:** 10

Values can range from 0 - 99; the default is 10. Restart your system for these values to take effect.

MAILSLOTS

Mailslot controls are part of tweaking your General Networking values.

I-306

> **Hive:** HKEY_LOCAL_MACHINE
> **Key:** System\CurrentControlSet\Services\Netlogon\Parameters

Add the MaximumMailslotMessages value.

> **Value Name:** MaximumMailslotMessages
> **Data Type:** REG_DWORD
> **Value:** 500

This value governs how much space Netlogon sets aside to buffer incoming Mailslot messages. Under normal circumstances, Mailslot messages are serviced as they arrive; however, if you have a particularly busy network, these messages can back up. Each Mailslot message takes up roughly 1500 bytes of nonpaged pool memory until it is removed from the buffer. Altering this value gives you additional control over how much nonpaged pool memory is used.

I-307

> **Hive:** HKEY_LOCAL_MACHINE
>> **Key:** System\CurrentControlSet\Services\Netlogon\Parameters

Add the MaximumMailslotTimeout value.
> **Value Name:** MaximumMailslotTimeout
>> **Data Type:** REG_DWORD
>> **Value:** 10

This value determines how long, in seconds, a Mailslot message is valid. If Netlogon processes a message that is older than the value set in Maximum-MailslotTimeout, it simply discards it. Ideally, Windows NT services incoming Mailslot requests in subsecond time; however, if your system is overloaded or the network congested, you may need to increase this value.

I-308 This number dictates how long NetLogon ignores duplicate Mailslot messages. Netlogon compares previous Mailslot messages with current Mailslot messages. If Netlogon receives the same message as one it has already received in the number of seconds specified by MailslotDuplicateTimeout, it discards the second message.

> **Hive:** HKEY_LOCAL_MACHINE
>> **Key:** System\CurrentControlSet\Services\Netlogon\Parameters

Add the MailslotDuplicateTimeout value.
> **Value Name:** MailslotDuplicateTimeout
>> **Data Type:** REG_DWORD
>> **Value:** 2

TCP/IP

I-309 **P**roblem: when you try to connect to Web servers or FTP sites, you often time out or must retry many times before you finally connect. The problem may be that your time to live (TTL) is too small. TTL is a TCP/IP parameter that controls how many "hops" or routers your packet can go through before it is discarded by the network. Every time the packet goes through a router, its value is decremented by 1. When the value reaches zero, the packet is discarded. With the proliferation of servers and routers on the network, a value that was once a reasonable TTL is now not practical. To modify the TTL, change this entry.

> **Hive:** HKEY_LOCAL_MACHINE
> **Key:** System\CurrentControlSet\Services\Tcpip\Parameters

Add the following value under the Parameters key:

> **Value Name:** DefaultTTL
> **Data Type:** REG_DWORD
> **Value:** 255

Restart your machine for these new values to take effect.

I-310 **S**ometimes it isn't possible to check all the static routes of a remote machine. You can, however, see which persistent routes a particular system has set up. Use the following registry key and its associated values to see these routes.

> **Hive:** HKEY_LOCAL_MACHINE
> **Key:** System\CurrentControlSet\Services\Tcpip\Parameters\
> PersistentRoutes

Add the following value

> **Value Name:** 204.56.55.100,255.255.255.255,127.0.0.1,1
> **Data Type:** REG_SZ
> **Value:**

The value name is the actual route. The format is destination address,subnet mask,source address,metric. You must then make it a REG_SZ entry with a blank value. If you add or delete entries here, you must exit Regedt32.exe for them to take effect on the remote machine.

I-311 TCP/IP on Windows NT uses a lot of different files for its information. These files are located in the following registry key.

> **Hive:** HKEY_LOCAL_MACHINE
> **Key:** System\CurrentControlSet\Services\Tcpip\Parameters
> **Value Name:** DatabasePath
> **Data Type:** REG_EXPAND_SZ
> **Value:** %SystemRoot%\system32\drivers\etc

The actual files stored there are Hosts, Lmhosts, Networks, Protocols, and Services. By altering the directory where these files point, it is possible to have a central location or to have several different working sets of these files.

I-312 If you have trouble with PPTP connections timing out on particularly slow connections, try increasing the following registry parameter:

> **Hive:** HKEY_LOCAL_MACHINE
> **Key:** System\CurrentControlSet\Services\Tcpip\Parameters
> **Value Name:** PPTPTcpMaxDataRetransmissions
> **Data Type:** REG_DWORD
> **Value:** 9

Increasing the default value gives PPTP packets a better chance of getting through on heavily congested networks or particularly slow links. Restart your machine for this value to take effect.

I-313 If you have a mixed network and need your broadcast packets to be the 0-style broadcasts packets (that is, 0.0.0.0 instead of the default 1-style, or 255.255.255.255), change this registry value:

> **Hive:** HKEY_LOCAL_MACHINE
> **Key:** System\CurrentControlSet\Services\Tcpip\Parameters
> **Value Name:** UseZeroBroadcast
> **Data Type:** REG_DWORD
> **Value:** 1

I-314 If you have intermittent problems with your gateways (and who doesn't?), you probably have already established a set of alternate gateways. Use this registry entry to have Windows NT automatically switch to the backup gateway if the current gateway is not responding.

> **Hive:** HKEY_LOCAL_MACHINE
> **Key:** System\CurrentControlSet\Services\Tcpip\Parameters
> **Value Name:** EnableDeadGWDetect
> **Data Type:** REG_DWORD
> **Value:** 1

The default value is 1, which enables the feature. Setting this value to 0 disables the detection. Restart your machine for this value to take effect.

I-315 By default, Windows NT tries to discover the maximum transmission unit (MTU) over a given path to a remote host. By finding the largest packet size it can send, Windows NT maintains a good throughput. Setting this value to 0 causes the MTU to be set to 576 bytes for all connections other than hosts or local subnet destinations.

> **Hive:** HKEY_LOCAL_MACHINE
> **Key:** System\CurrentControlSet\Services\Tcpip\Parameters
> **Value Name:** EnablePMTUDiscovery
> **Data Type:** REG_DWORD
> **Value:** 1

Restart your machine for these values to take effect.

I-316 If you use a RAS connection to route IP packets and are suffering from poor network performance, these registry entries can help you squeeze a little more performance out of your connection.

> **Hive:** HKEY_LOCAL_MACHINE
> **Key:** System\CurrentControlSet\Services\<adapter name>\
> Parameters\Tcpip
> **Value Name:** MaxForwardPending
> **Data Type:** REG_DWORD
> **Value:** 20

The MaxForwardPending value governs how many packets Windows NT forwards to a particular network interface at a given time. If you have a slow connection, changing this value really helps performance. The default value is 20. Restart the machine for any changes to take effect.

I-317 If your Windows NT machine seems to be suffering from lost IP packet syndrome, these registry entries can help you tweak your system for maximum throughput.

> **Hive:** HKEY_LOCAL_MACHINE
> **Key:** System\CurrentControlSet\Services\Tcpip\Parameters
> **Value Name:** ForwardBufferMemory
> **Data Type:** REG_DWORD
> **Value:** 7420

The ForwardBufferMemory value controls how much memory Windows NT sets aside to store packet data in the packet data queue. Each packet buffer is 256 bytes, so the ForwardBufferMemory value should be a multiple of 256. When the packet data queue is full, Windows NT randomly discards packets.

I-318

> **Hive:** HKEY_LOCAL_MACHINE
> **Key:** System\CurrentControlSet\Services\<adapter name>\
> Parameters\Tcpip
> **Value Name:** MaxForwardBufferMemory
> **Data Type:** REG_DWORD
> **Value:** 0xFFFFFFFF

The MaxForwardBufferMemory value governs the total amount of memory Windows NT sets aside to store packet data in the router packet queue. This value must be greater than or equal to the ForwardBufferMemory value. If you don't have IP routing enabled, this registry value is ignored.

I-319

> **Hive:** HKEY_LOCAL_MACHINE
> **Key:** System\CurrentControlSet\Services\<adapter name>\
> Parameters\Tcpip
> **Value Name:** NumForwardPackets
> **Data Type:** REG_DWORD
> **Value:** 50

This value governs the number of IP packet headers that can be stored in the router packet queue. This value should be at least as large as the ForwardBufferMemory divided by 256.

I-320

> **Hive:** HKEY_LOCAL_MACHINE
> **Key:** System\CurrentControlSet\Services\<adapter name>\
> Parameters\Tcpip
> **Value Name:** MaxNumForwardPackets
> **Data Type:** REG_DWORD
> **Value:** 0xFFFFFFFF

This value sets the total number of IP packet headers that can be stored in the router packet queue at a given time. This value needs to be at least as big as NumForwardPackets, if not larger. Restart your machine for any changes to take effect.

I-321 If you need to control the level at which your Windows NT machine supports the Internet Group Management Protocol (IGMP), then this registry entry is for you.

> **Hive:** HKEY_LOCAL_MACHINE
> **Key:** System\CurrentControlSet\Services\Tcpip\Parameters
> **Value Name:** IGMPLevel
> **Data Type:** REG_DWORD
> **Value:** 2

A value of 0 prohibits all multicast support. A value of 1 lets the system send IP multicast packets. The default value of 2 lets the Windows NT machine send and fully participate in receiving IP multicast packets. Restart your machine for any changes to take effect.

I-322 If your aborted sessions aren't properly cleaned up or if your idle but live sessions are dropped inadvertently, you may need to adjust these two registry parameters.

> **Hive:** HKEY_LOCAL_MACHINE
> **Key:** System\CurrentControlSet\Services\Tcpip\Parameters
> **Value Name:** KeepAliveTime
> **Data Type:** REG_DWORD
> **Value:** 7,200,000

I-323

Hive: HKEY_LOCAL_MACHINE
Key: System\CurrentControlSet\Services\Tcpip\Parameters
Value Name: KeepAliveInterval
Data Type: REG_DWORD
Value: 1000

Both values are in milliseconds. The default value for KeepAliveTime is 7,200,000, or 2 hours, and the default for KeepAliveInterval is 1000, or 1 second. KeepAliveTime governs how often Windows NT sends a keep alive packet. A specific application can request that keep-alive packets be sent. If the target system is able, it responds with an acknowledgment. The KeepAliveInterval works with the KeepAliveTime and governs how often keep-alive packets are sent until an acknowledgment is received. If the target machine doesn't respond and the number of retries exceeds the value of TCPMaxDataRetransmissions, the connection is terminated. Restart your machine for any changes to take effect.

I-324 If you need to limit the number of application-requested user ports that Windows NT dynamically assigns, change this registry value.

Hive: HKEY_LOCAL_MACHINE
Key: System\CurrentControlSet\Services\Tcpip\Parameters
Value Name: MaxUserPort
Data Type: REG_DWORD
Value: 0x1388

This value is in hexadecimal. The default value is 1388 hex, or 5000 decimal. Restart the machine for any changes to take effect.

I-325 If your systems are prone to SYN attacks (Unix hackers love that trick), you may want to change this registry entry.

Hive: HKEY_LOCAL_MACHINE
Key: System\CurrentControlSet\Services\Tcpip\Parameters
Value Name: TcpMaxConnectRetransmissions
Data Type: REG_DWORD
Value: 3

This value limits the number of times Windows NT lets someone try to connect during a given connect session. The default value is 3.

I-326   If you have remote users with unreliable connections, you can reduce network congestion by adjusting this registry value.

> **Hive:** HKEY_LOCAL_MACHINE
> **Key:** System\CurrentControlSet\Services\Tcpip\Parameters
> **Value Name:** TcpMaxDataRetransmissions
> **Data Type:** REG_DWORD
> **Value:** 5

This value controls how many times a given data segment is retransmitted. Initially, this value is set according to the length of the round-trip time for a particular connection.

I-327   Do you have too many people connecting to your system with TCP/IP, or are you connecting to more machines than is necessary? You can set a hard limit for the number of connections that TCP/IP can have open at a time.

> **Hive:** HKEY_LOCAL_MACHINE
> **Key:** System\CurrentControlSet\Services\Tcpip\Parameters
> **Value Name:** TcpNumConnections
> **Data Type:** REG_DWORD
> **Value:** 0xffffffe

The default value is 0xffffffe. Restart your system for any changes to take effect.

I-328   If you need strict control over the kind of information that comes into your network, these registry parameters let you specify what your network does and doesn't accept.

> **Hive:** HKEY_LOCAL_MACHINE
> **Key:** System\CurrentControlSet\Services\Tcpip\Parameters
> **Value Name:** EnableSecurityFilters
> **Data Type:** REG_DWORD
> **Value:** 1

When this registry value is set to 1, all incoming raw IP datagrams are filtered. This feature must be enabled before you can use the RawIpAllowedProtocols, TcpAllowedPorts, or UdpAllowedPorts values.

I-329

Hive: HKEY_LOCAL_MACHINE
Key: System\CurrentControlSet\Services\<adapter name>\ Parameters\Tcpip
Value Name: RawIpAllowedProtocols
Data Type: REG_DWORD
Value: 0 <protocol number>

This value determines which IP datagrams are accepted by the transport. A value of 0 indicates that all values are valid. If this value is missing from the registry for a particular interface, all values are accepted.

I-330

Hive: HKEY_LOCAL_MACHINE
Key: System\CurrentControlSet\Services\<adapter name>\ Parameters\Tcpip
Value Name: TcpAllowedPorts
Data Type: REG_DWORD
Value: 0 <port number>

These values control which TCP ports accept SYN requests. A value of 0 indicates that all values are valid. If this value is missing from the registry for a particular interface, all values are accepted.

I-331

Hive: HKEY_LOCAL_MACHINE
Key: System\CurrentControlSet\Services\<adapter name>\ Parameters\Tcpip
Value Name: UdpAllowedPorts
Data Type: REG_DWORD
Value: 0 <port number>

This value determines which ports accept incoming UDP datagrams. A value of 0 indicates that all values are valid. If this value is missing from the registry for a particular interface, all values are accepted.

I-332 If you are using your Windows NT server as a dial-up server on the Internet and can't see all the computers on your network, you may be suffering from multiple default routes. To fix this problem, you must add the following key for each LAN adapter that is not connected to the Internet.

> **Hive:** HKEY_LOCAL_MACHINE
> **Key:** System\Services\<adapter>\Parameters\Tcpip

Add the following value under the Parameters key:

> **Value Name:** DontAddDefaultGateway
> **Data Type:** REG_DWORD
> **Value:** 1

Then use the route command to add persistent routes for the LAN that the other LAN adapters referenced.

I-333 If you are troubleshooting clients running TCP/IP and you aren't using DHCP (shame on you), you often need to adjust particular settings. Using the remote capabilities of Regedt32, you are just a few registry entries away from tweaking TCP/IP to your heart's content. These registry entries store most of the standard TCP/IP information.

> **Hive:** HKEY_LOCAL_MACHINE
> **Key:** System\CurrentControlSet\Services\Tcpip\Parameters
> **Value Name:** Hostname
> **Data Type:** REG_SZ
> **Value:** <computer name> Example: BigDog

This value is the DNS name of your computer. When users issue a "ping -a 200.200.200.1" command, your system returns this value.

I-334

> **Hive:** HKEY_LOCAL_MACHINE
> **Key:** System\CurrentControlSet\Services\Tcpip\Parameters
> **Value Name:** IPAddress
> **Data Type:** REG_MULTI_SZ
> **Value:** any valid IP address. Example: 200.200.200.1

This value is the IP address of a particular machine. Issuing a "ping -a <hostname>" command returns this value.

I-335

Hive: HKEY_LOCAL_MACHINE
Key: System\CurrentControlSet\Services\Tcpip\Parameters
Value Name: SearchList
Data Type: REG_SZ
Value: any valid list of DNS suffixes. Examples: .com .org .edu

When your system tries to resolve a <machine name> via DNS, it applies this list of suffixes to the generic <machine name>. If you specify bigdog.win-ntmag, the first suffix applied to this request is .com. The resultant query then searches for bigdog.winntmag.com.

I-336

Hive: HKEY_LOCAL_MACHINE
Key: System\CurrentControlSet\Services\<adapter name>\
Parameters\Tcpip
Value Name: SubnetMask
Data Type: REG_MULTI_SZ
Value: any valid list of IP addresses

Windows NT uses this value when it applies the subnet mask to a particular IP interface bound to an adapter.

DHCP

I-337 To enable the DHCP client service on a remote system, you can use the Select Computer option in Regedt32.exe to remotely change this registry entry. It tells Windows NT to configure the first IP interface on the machine using DHCP.

Hive: HKEY_LOCAL_MACHINE
Key: System\CurrentControlSet\Services\<adapter name>\
Parameters\Tcpip
Value Name: EnableDhcp
Data Type: REG_DWORD
Value: 1

You need to restart the client for these changes to take effect.

I-338 Ever since you installed DHCP, your network traffic has gone up. This registry parameter helps reduce network broadcast traffic.

> **Hive:** HKEY_LOCAL_MACHINE
> **Key:** System\CurrentControlSet\Services\DhcpServer\Parameters

Add the following value under the Parameters key:

> **Value Name:** IgnoreBroadcastFlag
> **Data Type:** REG_DWORD
> **Value:** 0

This registry modification works only on homogenous Ethernet networks or same-subnet Token-Ring networks. If your network has a router that translates MAC-level addresses, do not modify this registry entry.

I-339 If you need to find out DHCP information about a particular client but don't have access to the DHCP admin tool, you can still get the information by viewing these registry entries remotely.

> **Hive:** HKEY_LOCAL_MACHINE
> **Key:** System\CurrentControlSet\Services\<adapter name>\
>   Parameters\Tcpip
> **Value Name:** DhcpDefaultGateway
> **Data Type:** REG_MULTI_SZ
> **Value:** any valid IP address

This value specifies the default gateway list assigned to the client by the DHCP server.

I-340

> **Hive:** HKEY_LOCAL_MACHINE
> **Key:** System\CurrentControlSet\Services\<adapter name>\
>   Parameters\Tcpip
> **Value Name:** DhcpIPAddress
> **Data Type:** REG_SZ
> **Value:** any valid IP address

This value is the IP address assigned to the user via the DHCP server. If the first value is anything other than 0.0.0.0, that value will override the DHCP-assigned value.

I-341

Hive: HKEY_LOCAL_MACHINE
Key: System\CurrentControlSet\Services\<adapter name>\
Parameters\Tcpip
Value Name: DhcpNameServer
Data Type: REG_SZ
Value: any set of valid IP addresses

This value is the set of name servers that your system uses to resolve DNS queries.

I-342

Hive: HKEY_LOCAL_MACHINE
Key: System\CurrentControlSet\Services\<adapter name>\
Parameters\Tcpip
Value Name: DhcpServer
Data Type: REG_SZ
Value: any valid IP address

This value is the IP address of the DHCP server that granted your client the IP address that's stored in the DhcpIPAddress registry value.

I-343

Hive: HKEY_LOCAL_MACHINE
Key: System\CurrentControlSet\Services\<adapter name>\
Parameters\Tcpip
Value Name: DhcpSubnetMask
Data Type: REG_SZ
Value: any valid subnet mask for the current IP address space

This value is the DHCP Server-assigned subnet mask.

I-344

Hive: HKEY_LOCAL_MACHINE
Key: System\CurrentControlSet\Services\<adapter name>\
Parameters\Tcpip
Value Name: Lease
Data Type: REG_SZ
Value: <time in seconds>

This value is the number of seconds that the current lease is valid for a given client.

I-345

Hive: HKEY_LOCAL_MACHINE
Key: System\CurrentControlSet\Services\<adapter name>\Parameters\Tcpip
Value Name: LeaseObtainedTime
Data Type: REG_SZ
Value: number of seconds since 1/1/70

This value is the time in seconds since the current lease was obtained. You need to convert this number to do anything meaningful with it. Several programs available on the Web can convert it for you.

I-346

Hive: HKEY_LOCAL_MACHINE
Key: System\CurrentControlSet\Services\<adapter name>\Parameters\Tcpip
Value Name: LeaseTerminatesTime
Data Type: REG_SZ
Value: number of seconds since 1/1/70

This value is the time when the current lease will expire, stored in form of the number of seconds since 1/1/70. Using the remote viewing capabilities of Regedt32.exe, you can view this information on any machine you have access to via the network.

I-347 If you need to see what a client's DHCP parameters were before the most recent changes, you can find them in the following registry entries. Note that you find this out by looking at the ControlSet001 value, which is different from the CurrentControlSet value. To go back one more revision, you can look at ControlSet002 value.

Hive: HKEY_LOCAL_MACHINE
Key: System\ControlSet001\Services\<adapter name>\Parameters\Tcpip

The following list of DHCP values is available under the Tcpip key:
Value Name: DefaultGateway
Data Type: REG_MULTI_SZ
Value: 0.0.0.0

I-348

Value Name: EnableDHCP
Data Type: REG_DWORD
Value: 0x1

I-349   **Value Name:** IPAddress
             Data Type: REG_MULTI_SZ
             Value: 0.0.0.0

I-350   **Value Name:** PPTPFiltering
             Data Type: REG_DWORD
             Value: 0

I-351   **Value Name:** SubnetMask
             Data Type: REG_MULTI_SZ
             Value: 0.0.0.0

I-352   **Value Name:** UseZeroBroadcast
             Data Type: REG_DWORD
             Value: 0

You can edit any of these values. Reboot the machine for changes to take effect.

NETBIOS OVER TCP (NETBT)

I-353 If a client is having trouble with its NetBT configuration on Windows NT (see the Appendix for instructions for Windows 95) and you want to change or verify some of the settings, you can use the remote capability of Regedt32.exe. Using the Select Computer option, choose the computer you need to access and use these registry keys to view NetBT-related information. Generally, you set these with the Network Control Panel Application; however, it is very useful to be able to view these values remotely.

                Hive: HKEY_LOCAL_MACHINE
                 Key: System\CurrentControlSet\Services\NetBt\Parameters
          Value Name: EnableLmhosts
            Data Type: REG_DWORD
                Value: 1

When this registry entry is set to 1, NetBT uses the LMHOSTS file to resolve any outstanding queries that couldn't be resolved using WINS or broadcasts.

I-354

Hive: HKEY_LOCAL_MACHINE
Key: System\CurrentControlSet\Services\LanmanServer\Parameters

Add the following value under the Parameters key:
Value Name: OptionalNames
Data Type: REG_SZ
Value: < any name you want as an alias>

You can then use this alias for any command that requires a server, such as Net Use.

I-355

Hive: HKEY_LOCAL_MACHINE
Key: System\CurrentControlSet\Services\NetBt\Parameters
Value Name: EnableDns
Data Type: REG_DWORD
Value: 0

When this registry entry is set to 1, NetBT uses DNS to resolve queries that it could not resolve with WINS, broadcast, or the LMHOSTS file.

I-356

Hive: HKEY_LOCAL_MACHINE
Key: System\CurrentControlSet\Services\NetBt\Parameters
Value Name: EnableProxy
Data Type: REG_DWORD
Value: 0

When this registry entry is set to 1, the machine acts as a proxy name server for networks that are bound to NetBT. A proxy name server answers other clients' name queries for system names it has resolved via WINS.

I-357

Hive: HKEY_LOCAL_MACHINE
Key: System\CurrentControlSet\Services\NetBt\Parameters
Value Name: NameServer
Data Type: REG_DWORD
Value: <any valid IP address>

This value is the address of the machine that the client machine uses for WINS queries. The default value is blank.

I-358

Hive: HKEY_LOCAL_MACHINE
Key: System\CurrentControlSet\Services\NetBt\Parameters
Value Name: NameServerBackup
Data Type: REG_DWORD
Value: <any valid IP address>

This is the address of the secondary WINS server. If the machine whose value is stored in NameServer cannot be reached, the machine at this address is queried.

I-359

Hive: HKEY_LOCAL_MACHINE
Key: System\CurrentControlSet\Services\NetBt\Parameters
Value Name: ScopeID
Data Type: REG_DWORD
Value: <any valid DNS domain name> Example: Winntmag.com

This value governs the NetBios name scope. Any valid DNS domain name automatically overrides the DHCP-assigned equivalent.

I-360 If you have a lot of memory and a fairly busy network, you can specify the maximum amount of memory NetBT allocates to store all outgoing datagrams. If you fill up the allocated memory, any other attempt to send fails.

Hive: HKEY_LOCAL_MACHINE
Key: System\CurrentControlSet\Services\NetBt\Parameters
Value Name: MaxDgramBuffering
Data Type: REG_DWORD
Value: 0x20000

The default is 128K. Restart the machine for any changes to take effect.

I-361 If you have broadcast storms on your network or just are looking for ways to reduce network traffic, try changing these registry entries:

Hive: HKEY_LOCAL_MACHINE
Key: System\CurrentControlSet\Services\NetBt\Parameters
Value Name: BcastNameQueryCount
Data Type: REG_DWORD
Value: 3

I-362

> **Hive:** HKEY_LOCAL_MACHINE
> **Key:** System\CurrentControlSet\Services\NetBt\Parameters
> **Value Name:** NodeType
> **Data Type:** REG_DWORD
> **Value:** 1 or 8 (default)

This value determines the way NetBT registers and resolves names. Valid values and their meanings are listed below.

Value	Node-Type	Description
1	b-node	Uses broadcasts only
2	p-node	Uses point-to-point name queries to a WINS server
4	m-node	Broadcasts first, then queries the name server
8	h-node	Queries the name server first, then broadcasts

Restart your system for any changes to take effect.

I-363 This value limits the number of times NetBT broadcasts a query for a name without receiving a response. Adjusting this value can have a significant effect on the number of broadcasts on your system.

> **Hive:** HKEY_LOCAL_MACHINE
> **Key:** System\CurrentControlSet\Services\NetBt\Parameters
> **Value Name:** BcastQueryTimeout
> **Data Type:** REG_DWORD
> **Value:** 0x2ee

This value is the interval in milliseconds between broadcasts. The default value is 0x2ee, or 750 decimal. If you make any changes to these values, restart your computer.

I-364 If you have a particularly large Lmhosts file and your DNS requests take too long, you can speed up your Lmhosts requests by changing this registry value.

> **Hive:** HKEY_LOCAL_MACHINE
> **Key:** System\CurrentControlSet\Services\NetBt\Parameters
> **Value Name:** LmhostsTimeout
> **Data Type:** REG_DWORD
> **Value:** 6000

The value is the time, in milliseconds, that elapses before a DNS query of Lmhosts times out.

I-365

> **Hive:** HKEY_LOCAL_MACHINE
> **Key:** System\CurrentControlSet\Services\NetBt\Parameters
> **Value Name:** CacheTimeout
> **Data Type:** REG_DWORD
> **Value:** 0x927c0

This value is the time, in milliseconds, that names are cached in the remote name table. The default is 0x927c0 milliseconds, or 600,000 decimal.

I-366 If you use WINS and have problems changing IP addresses for certain machines, you may want to check the following registry value.

> **Hive:** HKEY_LOCAL_MACHINE
> **Key:** System\CurrentControlSet\Services\NetBt\Parameters
> **Value Name:** EnableProxyRegCheck
> **Data Type:** REG_DWORD
> **Value:** 0 (default)

Setting this value to 1 tells the proxy name server to send a negative response to any broadcast name registration when that name is already registered with WINS or is in the proxy's local name cache with a different IP address. Setting this value back to 0 lets you change IP addresses again.

I-367 If you use a service other than WINS to give you name service information, you can tell NetBT to use it instead of WINS. This registry entry specifies which port NetBT uses. The default is 89, which is the port that the Microsoft WINS Server listens on.

> **Hive:** HKEY_LOCAL_MACHINE
> **Key:** System\CurrentControlSet\Services\NetBt\Parameters
> **Value Name:** NameServerPort
> **Data Type:** REG_DWORD
> **Value:** 0x89

Restart your machine for any changes to take effect.

I-368 If WINS name registration takes too long, use this registry value to speed up the interval at which WINS name registration takes place. When it initially registers names, WINS calculates 1/8th of this value and contacts the name server then. After a name is successfully registered, WINS sends a response to the client with the new refresh interval.

Hive: HKEY_LOCAL_MACHINE
Key: System\CurrentControlSet\Services\NetBt\Parameters
Value Name: InitialRefreshTimeout
Data Type: REG_DWORD
Value: 960000

Restart WINS for any changes to take effect.

I-369 If you are having problems with your network since you installed WINS, you can tweak the following registry entries to help improve performance.

Hive: HKEY_LOCAL_MACHINE
Key: System\CurrentControlSet\Services\NetBt\Parameters
Value Name: NameSrvQueryCount
Data Type: REG_DWORD
Value: 3

This value sets the number of times that NetBT queries the WINS server before receiving a response.

I-370

Hive: HKEY_LOCAL_MACHINE
Key: System\CurrentControlSet\Services\NetBt\Parameters
Value Name: Timeout
Data Type: REG_DWORD
Value: 1500

This value is the time, in milliseconds, NetBT waits before sending the next query in a series of successive queries.

I-371

Hive: HKEY_LOCAL_MACHINE
Key: System\CurrentControlSet\Services\NetBt\Parameters
Value Name: SessionKeepAlive
Data Type: REG_DWORD
Value: 3,600,000

This value is the interval, in milliseconds, that NetBT waits between sending keep-alive packets for a particular session.

I-372

Hive: HKEY_LOCAL_MACHINE
Key: System\CurrentControlSet\Services\NetBt\Parameters
Value Name: SizeSmall/Medium/Large
Data Type: REG_DWORD
Value: 1

This value regulates the size of the name table, which stores local and remote names. Valid values are 1 = small (16 entries), 2 = medium (128 entries) and 3 = large (256 entries).

PPTP

You just installed PPTP and are afraid that you may have exposed your network to unwanted attacks. Well, no network is 100 percent secure, but these registry entries let you add a little more security to PPTP.

I-373

Hive: HKEY_LOCAL_MACHINE
Key: System\CurrentControlSet\Services\RasPPTPE\Parameters\ Configuration
Value Name: AuthenticateIncomingCalls
Data Type: REG_DWORD
Value: 1

I-374

Hive: HKEY_LOCAL_MACHINE
Key: System\CurrentControlSet\Services\RasPPTPE\Parameters\ Configuration
Value Name: PeerClientIPAdresses
Data Type: REG_MULTI_SZ
Value: <valid IP addresses>

Using these two values, you can effectively control who can access your network via PPTP. If the AuthenticateIncomingCalls value is set to 0, only the clients whose IP addresses match values stored in the PeerClientIPAdresses value are allowed access. If the AuthenticateIncomingCalls value is enabled and no values are contained in the PeerClientIPAddress value, nobody can access your network via PPTP.

NWNBLINK

I-375 NWNBLink provides many extensions to the Novell NetBios protocol. If you use this protocol in a Microsoft-only shop, you can really speed things up with a few registry parameters.

> **Hive:** HKEY_LOCAL_MACHINE
> **Key:** System\CurrentControlSet\Services\NWNBLink\Parameters
> **Value Name:** Extensions
> **Data Type:** REG_DWORD
> **Value:** 1

Changing this parameter tells NWNBLink to use the Microsoft extensions. If NWBLink is communicating with a client using standard Novell NetBIOS protocol, it falls back to the standard version in favor of the extended version.

I-376

> **Hive:** HKEY_LOCAL_MACHINE
> **Key:** System\CurrentControlSet\Services\NWNBLink\Parameters
> **Value Name:** AckDelayTime
> **Data Type:** REG_DWORD
> **Value:** 250

Windows NT uses this value, which is in milliseconds, when it sends a delayed acknowledgment. You can use this value in conjunction with the AckWindow value, below, to adjust the frequency at which Windows NT must acknowledge frames it is sent. The default value is 250 milliseconds; the value can range from 0 to 65535.

I-377

> **Hive:** HKEY_LOCAL_MACHINE
> **Key:** System\CurrentControlSet\Services\NWNBLink\Parameters
> **Value Name:** AckWindow
> **Data Type:** REG_DWORD
> **Value:** 2

This value controls the number of frames that are received before an acknowledgment is sent. If you have two computers, one on a fast network and the other on a slow link, adjusting this value can increase throughput. Conversely, if both computers are on a fast link, you can turn off this function by setting the value to 0. You can also let Windows NT determine this value dynamically using the AckWindowThreshold value, below. The default value is 2 and represents the number of frames. The range is 0 to 65535.

I-378

Hive: HKEY_LOCAL_MACHINE
Key: System\CurrentControlSet\Services\NWNBLink\Parameters
Value Name: AckWindowThreshold
Data Type: REG_DWORD:
Value: 500

This value, in milliseconds, dynamically determines whether it is necessary to send automatic acknowledgments. The determination is based on round-trip time. If this value is set to 0, the NWNBLink uses the AckWindows entry. The default is 500 milliseconds; the range is 0 to 65535.

I-379

Hive: HKEY_LOCAL_MACHINE
Key: System\CurrentControlSet\Services\NWNBLink\Parameters
Value Name: EnablePiggyBackAck
Data Type: REG_DWORD
Value: 1

Enabling NWNBLink's ability to piggyback acknowledgments can increase your overall network performance if you participate in two-way NetBIOS traffic on your network. If you set this value to 1, NWNBLink can piggyback acknowledgments when it detects the end of a message. If this value is set to 0, NWNBLink waits the number of milliseconds set in the AckDelayTime before it sends an acknowledgment.

I-380

Hive: HKEY_LOCAL_MACHINE
Key: System\CurrentControlSet\Services\NWNBLink\Parameters
Value Name: RcvWindowMax
Data Type: REG_DWORD
Value: 4

This value determines how many frames the receiver handles at one time. This value is generally set at session initialization to tell the sender the limit of frames it can send at a time. Altering this value can increase throughput and performance.

I-381 In addition to Microsoft extensions to NetBIOS, additional parameters can help improve network performance and work with either standard Novell NetBIOS or NWNBLink (Microsoft Extensions to Novell NetBIOS.) Here are a few of these parameters.

> **Hive:** HKEY_LOCAL_MACHINE
> **Key:** System\CurrentControlSet\Services\NWNBLink\Parameters
> **Value Name:** BroadcastTimeout
> **Data Type:** REG_DWORD
> **Value:** 1

This value is the interval, in 500-millisecond increments, that Windows NT waits between sending find-name requests. Depending on the speed and congestion of your network, you may want to increase the value to decrease overall network broadcasts.

I-382

> **Hive:** HKEY_LOCAL_MACHINE
> **Key:** System\CurrentControlSet\Services\NWNBLink\Parameters
> **Value Name:** BroadcastCount
> **Data Type:** REG_DWORD
> **Value:** 3

Use this value to determine the number of times a particular broadcast is sent. Increasing this value could result in congested networks; however, certain slower links may require it.

I-383

> **Hive:** HKEY_LOCAL_MACHINE
> **Key:** System\CurrentControlSet\Services\NWNBLink\Parameters
> **Value Name:** Internet
> **Data Type:** REG_DWORD
> **Value:** 1

This value alters the behavior of broadcast packets the NWNBLink protocol sends. If the value is 1, NWNBLink uses Novell-style WAN broadcasts. If you are using the BroadcastCount or BroadcastTimeout registry values, you must set this parameter to 0.

I-384   The next two values determine how Windows NT handles connection probes. The initiator of a session sends connection probes when a remote connection to a machine fails. Adjust these parameters according to your network speed and congestion.

Hive: HKEY_LOCAL_MACHINE
Key: System\CurrentControlSet\Services\NWNBLink\Parameters
Value Name: ConnectionCount
Data Type: REG_DWORD
Value: 5

This value sets the total number of times that Windows NT sends a connection probe. The default is 5; valid values range from 1 to 65,535.

I-385

Hive: HKEY_LOCAL_MACHINE
Key: System\CurrentControlSet\Services\NWNBLink\Parameters
Value Name: ConnectionTimeout
Data Type: REG_DWORD
Value: 5

This value dictates how long Windows NT waits between sending connection probes. The default is five 500-millisecond intervals, or 2.5 seconds. Changing this parameter can affect overall network congestion.

I-386

Hive: HKEY_LOCAL_MACHINE
Key: System\CurrentControlSet\Services\NWNBLink\Parameters
Value Name: InitialRetransmissionTime
Data Type: REG_DWORD
Value: 2

This value is used in conjunction with the RetransmitMax parameter, below. Changing this value can greatly reduce the amount of traffic on your network by delaying the interval that a sender waits before resending data. The default value (in 500-millisecond intervals) is 1; change it to 2 to reduce traffic.

I-387

Hive: HKEY_LOCAL_MACHINE
Key: System\CurrentControlSet\Services\NWNBLink\Parameters
Value Name: RetransmitMax
Data Type: REG_DWORD
Value: 8

This value governs how many times a computer retransmits data before it treats the network path as a bad path. As you can imagine, a slow link requires more time than a faster one. You can tune this value accordingly.

I-388 If you have applications that use keep-alive packets, these two registry entries can give you some measure of control over how often NWNBLink sends this type of traffic over your servers and workstations. Fine-tuning this parameter helps reduce network congestion. Using these two values in tandem really helps you control keep-alive traffic.

Hive: HKEY_LOCAL_MACHINE
Key: System\CurrentControlSet\Services\NWNBLink\Parameters
Value Name: KeepAliveCount
Data Type: REG_DWORD
Value: 8

This value determines how many times a session-alive frame is sent before the initiator gives up on the receiving computer.

I-389

Hive: HKEY_LOCAL_MACHINE
Key: System\CurrentControlSet\Services\NWNBLink\Parameters
Value Name: KeepAliveTimeout
Data Type: REG_DWORD
Value: 60

This registry value is very important. It determines how often session-alive frames are sent. The value is the number of 500-millisecond blocks it waits before sending a new session-alive frame.

NWLINK

I-390   These registry parameters let you tweak IPX/SPX. One way to think of it is that you can use these entries to manipulate the actual network adapters that NWLink is bound to. If you are troubleshooting the network adapter running NWLink, this is the place to be.

> **Hive:** HKEY_LOCAL_MACHINE
> **Key:** System\CurrentControlSet\Services\NWLink\NetConfig\Driver01
> **Value Name:** MaxPktSize
> **Data Type:** REG_DWORD
> **Value:** 0

This value controls the largest frame size that the network adapter allows. If the value is set to 0, NWLink obtains this value from the network it is running on. Otherwise, you may set a limit that the adapter doesn't support. This setup can be particularly useful if you are on a fast network and the station you are talking with is on a slower connection.

I-391

> **Hive:** HKEY_LOCAL_MACHINE
> **Key:** System\CurrentControlSet\Services\NWLink\NetConfig\Driver01
> **Value Name:** NetworkNumber
> **Data Type:** REG_DWORD
> **Value:** 0

If this value is set to 0, NWLink gets the value from the network it is currently running on. For those of you who were or are NetWare administrators, this value sets the internal IPX network number. The value is stored in hexadecimal and is 8 hex characters long; for example, AAAABEEF.

I-392   NWLink supports five different packet types. If you need to set the specific packet type for an adapter, this registry parameter lets you specify the packet types for each adapter.

> **Hive:** HKEY_LOCAL_MACHINE
> **Key:** System\CurrentControlSet\Services\NWLink\NetConfig\ Driver01
> **Value Name:** PktType
> **Data Type:** REG_DWORD
> **Value:** 3

Valid values are

0	Ethernet II
1	Ethernet 802.3
2	802.2
3	SNAP
4	Arcnet

I-393   The next two values control the routing information protocol (RIP) as it pertains to NWLink. NWLink uses RIP primarily to keep a list of remote machine names that it can use for name resolution. The list can affect the speed at which your computer can locate other computers on the network.

> **Hive:** HKEY_LOCAL_MACHINE
> **Key:** System\CurrentControlSet\Services\NWLink\NetConfig\ Driver01
> **Value Name:** RipAgeTime
> **Data Type:** REG_DWORD
> **Value:** 0

This value determines how many minutes NWLink waits before requesting a RIP update for a particular entry. The value is reset when a valid RIP announcement is received.

I-394

> **Hive:** HKEY_LOCAL_MACHINE
> **Key:** System\CurrentControlSet\Services\NWLink\NetConfig\ Driver01
> **Value Name:** RipUsageTime
> **Data Type:** REG_DWORD
> **Value:** 0

This value controls the length of time a current RIP cache entry is valid. Modifying this parameter with the RipAgeTime parameter lets you reduce your overall RIP-based traffic on a heavily congested network.

I-395   If you have many computers and routers on your LAN, you may want to consider source-routing with your NWLink protocol. NWLink has several registry
entries that give you some control over how it uses source-routing. The following four values control the bulk of source-routing features.

> **Hive:** HKEY_LOCAL_MACHINE
> **Key:** System\CurrentControlSet\Services\NWLink\NetConfig\
> Driver01
> **Value Name:** SourceRouteBcast
> **Data Type:** REG_DWORD
> **Value:** 0

If this value is 0, the broadcast is transmitted to the single-route broadcast. If
the value is set to 1, the all-routes broadcast is used. This setting can make a
huge difference in network overhead.

I-396

> **Hive:** HKEY_LOCAL_MACHINE
> **Key:** System\CurrentControlSet\Services\NWLink\NetConfig\
> Driver01
> **Value Name:** SourceRouteDef
> **Data Type:** REG_DWORD
> **Value:** 0

This value is very similar to the SourceRouteBcast value; it affects those broadcasts destined for machines that are not in the route table. If NWLink finds the
computer in the route table, it uses that route; otherwise, if the value is 0, it
uses the single-route broadcast. If the value is 1, NWLink uses the all-routes
broadcast.

I-397

> **Hive:** HKEY_LOCAL_MACHINE
> **Key:** System\CurrentControlSet\Services\NWLink\NetConfig\
> Driver01
> **Value Name:** SourceRouting
> **Data Type:** REG_DWORD
> **Value:** 0

This value specifies whether source-routing should be used on a Token-Ring
adapter. This value pertains only to Token-Ring adapters.

I-398

    Hive: HKEY_LOCAL_MACHINE
    Key: System\CurrentControlSet\Services\NWLink\NetConfig\
    Driver01
Value Name: SourceRouteMcast
  Data Type: REG_DWORD
     Value: 0

This value affects multicast addresses. If the value is 0, NWLink uses the single-route broadcast. If the value is 1, NWLink uses the all-routes broadcast.

I-399   These next seven values affect IPX/SPX globally. The values under the adapters section affect only a specific card; these values work for the whole NWLink transport.

    Hive: HKEY_LOCAL_MACHINE
    Key: System\CurrentControlSet\Services\NWLink\Parameters
Value Name: WindowSize
  Data Type: REG_DWORD
     Value: 4

This value sets the number of packets the receiving node can receive at a time. The SPX protocol uses the allocation field of the SPX packet to inform remote nodes of the available window size. This value sets the allocation field in the SPX packet.

I-400   These next two values pertain to RIP on an IPX/SPX network. Altering these settings affects all adapters running NWLink.

    Hive: HKEY_LOCAL_MACHINE
    Key: System\CurrentControlSet\Services\NWLink\Parameters
Value Name: RipCount
  Data Type: REG_DWORD
     Value: 5

This value determines how many times RIP tries to find a route on a network before it declares the route unusable. Depending on network traffic levels, adjusting this value can increase the likelihood that RIP finds routes.

I-401

Hive: HKEY_LOCAL_MACHINE
Key: System\CurrentControlSet\Services\NWLink\Parameters
Value Name: RipTimeout
Data Type: REG_DWORD
Value: 1

This value works in conjunction with RipCount to determine in 500-millisecond intervals how long RIP waits between sending request packets for a particular route.

I-402

Hive: HKEY_LOCAL_MACHINE
Key: System\CurrentControlSet\Services\NWLink\Parameters
Value Name: ConnectionCount
Data Type: REG_DWORD
Value: 10

This value determines how long NWLink tries to connect to a remote machine. If SPX does not get a response within the allotted number of tries, an error occurs. If you have a heavily congested network, tuning this parameter and the ConnectionTimeout parameter below may help you reduce connection timeouts.

I-403

Hive: HKEY_LOCAL_MACHINE
Key: System\CurrentControlSet\Services\NWLink\Parameters
Value Name: ConnectionTimeout
Data Type: REG_DWORD
Value: 2

This value is how many 500-millisecond intervals NWLink waits between sending connection probes. A value of 2 represents 1 second. By increasing this value and decreasing the ConnectionTimeout value, you can reduce congestion and still maintain your connections.

I-404

Hive: HKEY_LOCAL_MACHINE
Key: System\CurrentControlSet\Services\NWLnkSpx\Parameters
Value Name: KeepAliveTimeout
Data Type: REG_DWORD
Value: 12

This value is how many 500-millisecond intervals NWLink waits before sending a keep-alive packet to a remote station to verify that the SPX connection is still functioning.

I-405

     Hive: HKEY_LOCAL_MACHINE
      Key: System\CurrentControlSet\Services\NWLink\Parameters
  Value Name: KeepAliveCount
   Data Type: REG_DWORD
     Value: 12

This value is the number of keep-alive status requests that are sent. If you have long-term connections that are often idle for much of their connect life, you may want to tweak these parameters accordingly.

REMOTE ACCESS SERVER (RAS)

I-406 If you share phone lines with voice or fax and need to change the number of rings RAS waits before it answers the phone, change this registry parameter.

     Hive: HKEY_LOCAL_MACHINE
      Key: System\CurrentControlSet\Services\RasMan\Parameters
  Value Name: NumberOfRings
   Data Type: REG_DWORD
     Value: 1 - 20; default is 1

If you try to set the value to a number greater than 20, the default value (1) is used. Restart RAS for this value to take effect. This registry entry only affects UNIMODEM devices.

I-407 From time to time it is necessary to exclude certain dial addresses from the service. Basically, changing this value lets you hide certain RAS addresses without deleting them. If your RAS dialer is set up to choose alternates when it encounters a busy signal, you can appreciate the convenience of this feature. To exclude an address, add it under the following registry value.

     Hive: HKEY_CURRENT_USER
      Key: Software\Microsoft\RAS Autodial\Control
  Value Name: DisabledAddresses
   Data Type: REG_MULTI_SZ
     Value: <disabled addresses>

All addresses are case sensitive. This registry value is automatically created the first time you run AutoDial. After it is created, AutoDial does not modify it; you add the addresses you want to deactivate for the AutoDial service.

1-408 If you are experiencing a slight delay after you type your credentials in the "Connecting to" dialog box, you may have accumulated too many cached passwords. This registry entry lets you disable the caching feature.

> **Hive:** HKEY_LOCAL_MACHINE
> **Key:** System\CurrentControlSet\Services\RasMan\Parameters

Add this value under the Parameters key:

> **Value Name:** DisableSavePassword
> **Data Type:** REG_DWORD
> **Value:** 1

Changing this value to 1 effectively clears all cached passwords and prevents RAS from caching any further phonebook entries. The default value is 0, which enables the password-caching feature. Restart your machine for these values to take effect.

1-409 Logging off closes all RAS connections. If you have a remote machine connected to your corporate LAN and multiple people use it, you might want to keep RAS connections open even when a person logs out. This registry entry keeps RAS connections even if you log out.

> **Hive:** HKEY_LOCAL_MACHINE
> **Key:** Software\Microsoft\Windows NT\CurrentVersion\Winlogon

Add this value under the Winlogon key:

> **Value Name:** KeepRasConnections
> **Data Type:** REG_SZ
> **Value:** 1

Restart the RAS service for this change to take effect.

1-410 You can control the time your RAS server's modem waits before it calls back and authenticates a remote user. This registry entry lets you specify a value between 1 and 255 seconds.

> **Hive:** HKEY_LOCAL_MACHINE
> **Key:** System\CurrentControlSet\Services\RasMan\PPP
> **Value Name:** DefaultCallbackDelay
> **Data Type:** REG_DWORD
> **Value:** 12

The default is 12 seconds. Restart RAS for these values to take effect.

I-411 Are your non-Windows NT and non-Windows 95 clients having trouble connecting to your Windows NT RAS server? If you told the NT server to use clear-text authentication, but you're still having trouble, try setting these registry parameters to help solve your problem.

> **Hive:** HKEY_LOCAL_MACHINE
> **Key:** System\CurrentControlSet\Services\RasMan\PPP
> **Value Name:** ForceEncryptedData
> **Data Type:** REG_DWORD
> **Value:** 0

I-412

> **Hive:** HKEY_LOCAL_MACHINE
> **Key:** System\CurrentControlSet\Services\RasMan\PPP
> **Value Name:** ForceEncryptedPassword
> **Data Type:** REG_DWORD
> **Value:** 0

Restart Windows NT for these changes to take effect.

I-413 Do you want the "Logon Using Dialup Networking" checkbox in the logon screen to be checked by default? This registry entry tells Windows NT to use dialup networking for logon by default.

> **Hive:** HKEY_LOCAL_MACHINE
> **Key:** Software\Microsoft\Windows NT\CurrentVersion\Winlogon
> **Value Name:** RASForce
> **Data Type:** REG_SZ
> **Value:** 1

Restart Windows NT for these changes to take effect.

I-414 VanJacobsen (VJ) compression confuses some older dial-up clients. You can't disable VJ compression on the client, so use these entries to disable it on the server.

> **Hive:** HKEY_LOCAL_MACHINE
> **Key:** System\CurrentControlSet\Services\RasMan\IPCP\Parameters

Add the following value under the Parameters key:

> **Value Name:** RequestVJCompression
> **Data Type:** REG_DWORD
> **Value:** 0

I-415 You must also change this registry entry to disable VJ compression:

> **Hive:** HKEY_LOCAL_MACHINE
> **Key:** System\CurrentControlSet\Services\RasMan\IPCP\Parameters
> **Value Name:** AcceptVJCompression
> **Data Type:** REG_DWORD
> **Value:** 0

You must restart RAS for this change to take effect.

I-416 If you want to keep track of who is using your RAS server by having RAS write in the Event Log, change this entry.

> **Hive:** HKEY_LOCAL_MACHINE
> **Key:** System\CurrentControlSet\Services\RasMan\Parameters

Add the following value under the Parameters key:

> **Value Name:** Logging
> **Data Type:** REG_DWORD
> **Value:** 1

I-417 You recently established service with an ISP. The problem is, you can ping the LAN before you dial up your ISP, but not after. Modify these registry entries to fix this problem.

> **Hive:** HKEY_LOCAL_MACHINE
> **Key:** System\CurrentControlSet\Services\RasMan\PPP\IPCP

Add the following value under the IPCP key:

> **Value Name:** PriorityBasedOnSubnet
> **Data Type:** REG_DWORD
> **Value:** 1

I-418

> **Hive:** HKEY_LOCAL_MACHINE
> **Key:** System\CurrentControlSet\Services\RasMan\Parameters\PPP
> **Value Name:** Logging
> **Data Type:** REG_DWORD
> **Value:** 1

This value controls the logging action of PPP events that the RAS server handles. A value of 1 enables logging and 0, the default, disables logging.

I-419   If you recently added Internet access to your LAN via the RAS server and can get out just fine but everything coming back stops at the default gateway machine, then change this registry entry.

>   **Hive:** HKEY_LOCAL_MACHINE
>   **Key:** System\CurrentControlSet\Services\RasArp\Parameters

Add the following value under the Parameters key:

>   **Value Name:** DisableOtherSrcPackets
>   **Data Type:** REG_DWORD
>   **Value:** 0

Now all your Internet data will make it back to the right machine.

I-420   Are you having problems with your dial-up connections? Are you getting more retries than you should? You may need to enable the FIFO buffer on your serial card (if you have one, and you should). In addition, you may want to lower the receive buffer. These registry entries let you govern the size of the FIFO buffer for both receiving and transmitting.

>   **Hive:** HKEY_LOCAL_MACHINE
>   **Key:** System\CurrentControlSet\Services\Serial:
>   **Value Name:** ForceFifoEnable
>   **Data Type:** REG_DWORD
>   **Value:** 1

Enable the FIFO buffer by setting this value to 1. Restart the machine and see if this helps. If you still experience problems, try reducing the value of the receive FIFO buffer to 4; if you still have problems, drop it to 1.

I-421

>   **Value Name:** RxFIFO
>   **Data Type:** REG_DWORD
>   **Value:** 4

This value governs the receive buffer.

I-422

>   **Value Name:** TxFIFO
>   **Data Type:** REG_DWORD
>   **Value:** 8

This value governs the transmittal buffer.

I-423 Have you noticed that your laptop seems to receive files when you're connected to the corporate Ethernet but chokes when you're connected at a lesser speed (i.e., on a 28.8 modem connection)? Try modifying this parameter.

Hive: HKEY_LOCAL_MACHINE
Key: System\CurrentControlSet\Services\TCPIP\Parameters

Add the following value under the Parameters key:

Value Name: TcpWindowSize
Data Type: REG_DWORD
Value: 8192

Generally, slower connections benefit from a higher value; however some RAS connections work better with the value set to around 2768. For maximum efficiency, this value should be an even multiple of the TCP maximum segment size.

ROUTING INFORMATION PROTOCOL (RIP)

I-424 Does your Windows NT reject host routes or default routes that are broadcast by RIP-enabled routers? These registry entries will fix you right up.

Hive: HKEY_LOCAL_MACHINE
Key: System\CurrentControlSet\Services\IpRip\Parameters

Add the following value under the Parameters key:

Value Name: AcceptHostRoutes
Data Type: REG_DWORD
Value: 1

The default value is 0. Reboot your machine for these changes to take effect.

I-425

Hive: HKEY_LOCAL_MACHINE
Key: System\CurrentControlSet\Services\IpRip\Parameters

Add the following value under the Parameters key:

Value Name: AcceptDefaultRoutes
Data Type: REG_DWORD
Value: 1

The default value is 0. Reboot your machine for these changes to take effect.

I-426 Do you want to broadcast your default routes to other RIP-enabled routers in your network? Set this registry parameter to enable this function.

> **Hive:** HKEY_LOCAL_MACHINE
> **Key:** System\CurrentControlSet\Services\IpRip\Parameters

Add the following value under the Parameters key:

> **Value Name:** AnnounceDefaultRoutes
> **Data Type:** REG_DWORD
> **Value:** 1

The default value is 0. Reboot your machine for these changes to take effect.

I-427 Do you want to broadcast your host routes to other RIP-enabled routers in your network? Set this registry parameter to enable this feature.

> **Hive:** HKEY_LOCAL_MACHINE
> **Key:** System\CurrentControlSet\Services\IpRip\Parameters

Add the following value under the Parameters key:

> **Value Name:** AnnounceHostRoutes
> **Data Type:** REG_DWORD
> **Value:** 1

The default value is 0. Reboot your machine for these changes to take effect.

I-428 By default, any new route information or metric change automatically triggers a RIP update. Do you need to disable this feature? This registry entry shows you how.

> **Hive:** HKEY_LOCAL_MACHINE
> **Key:** System\CurrentControlSet\Services\IpRip\Parameters

Add the following value under the Parameters key:

> **Value Name:** EnableTriggeredUpdates
> **Data Type:** REG_DWORD
> **Value:** 0

The default value is 1. Reboot your machine for these changes to take effect.

I-429   This value is used in conjunction with the EnableTriggeredUpdates registry entry; it sets the number of seconds between triggered updates.

> **Hive:** HKEY_LOCAL_MACHINE
> **Key:** System\CurrentControlSet\Services\IpRip\Parameters

Add the following value under the Parameters key:

> **Value Name:** MaxTriggeredUpdateFrequency
> **Data Type:** REG_DWORD
> **Value:** 5

The default value is 5; valid values range from 1 to 86,400 seconds. Reboot your machine for these changes to take effect.

I-430   If you have a lot of dynamic routes created on your network, this registry entry may help you increase performance on your network. This value regulates when a route should be designated as a garbage route.

> **Hive:** HKEY_LOCAL_MACHINE
> **Key:** System\CurrentControlSet\Services\IpRip\Parameters

Add the following value under the Parameters key:

> **Value Name:** RouteTimeout
> **Data Type:** REG_DWORD
> **Value:** 180

The default value is 180; valid values can range from 1 to 259,200 seconds. Reboot your machine for these changes to take effect.

I-431   Are garbage routes on your network not removed as quickly as you would like? This registry entry lets you set how often garbage routes are discarded.

> **Hive:** HKEY_LOCAL_MACHINE
> **Key:** System\CurrentControlSet\Services\IpRip\Parameters

Add the following value under the Parameters key:

> **Value Name:** GarbageTimeout
> **Data Type:** REG_DWORD
> **Value:** 120

The default value is 120; valid values can range from 15 to 259,200 seconds (72 hours). Reboot your machine for these changes to take effect.

I-432 If you're trying to debug RIP problems, this registry entry lets you adjust the amount of information RIP records to the logging file.

> **Hive:** HKEY_LOCAL_MACHINE
> **Key:** System\CurrentControlSet\Services\IpRip\Parameters

Add the following value under the Parameters key:

> **Value Name:** LoggingLevel
> **Data Type:** REG_DWORD
> **Value:** 1

The default value is 1. Valid values are

0	No logging
1	Errors only
2	Errors and warnings
3	Errors, warnings, and informational messages

Restart your computer for these changes to take effect.

I-433 Are RIP announcements overloading your network? Do you want to silence periodic updates, yet still send triggered updates and receive all other RIP information? This registry entry suppresses periodic RIP announcements.

> **Hive:** HKEY_LOCAL_MACHINE
> **Key:** System\CurrentControlSet\Services\IpRip\Parameters

Add the following value under the Parameters key:

> **Value Name:** SilentRip
> **Data Type:** REG_DWORD
> **Value:** 1

The default value is 0. Setting the value to 1 suppresses periodic RIP announcements. Restart your machine for changes to take effect.

I-434 If you still want to send periodic updates (updates that contain the entire routing table for a given multiprotocol router), but not as often, you can regulate the frequency of the periodic updates with this registry entry.

Hive: HKEY_LOCAL_MACHINE
Key: System\CurrentControlSet\Services\IpRip\Parameters

Add the following value under the Parameters key:

Value Name: UpdateFrequency
Data Type: REG_DWORD
Value: 30

The default value is 30 seconds; valid values range from 15 to 86,400 seconds. Restart your machine for these changes to take effect.

Section II

HARDWARE

In this section, you find registry information pertaining to hardware peripherals, such as network adapters, disk controllers, and CD-ROMs. I try to provide as specific information as possible for different brands of peripherals.

MOUSE

II-1 If you get an error message stating that the ring buffer of your mouse over-
flowed, you may want to increase the size of the ring buffer. Change this registry entry.

>   **Hive:** HKEY_LOCAL_MACHINE
>   **Key:** System\CurrentControlSet\Services\Sermouse\Parameters
> **Value Name:** MouseDataQueSize
>   **Data Type:** REG_DWORD
>   **Value:** 0x64

The default is 0x64; increase this value to increase the size of the buffer.
Reboot for this change to take effect.

KEYBOARD

II-2 If you get an error message stating that the ring buffer of your keyboard over-
flowed, you might want to increase the size of the ring buffer. Change this
registry entry.

>   **Hive:** HKEY_LOCAL_MACHINE
>   **Key:** System\CurrentControlSet\Services\KbdClass\Parameters
> **Value Name:** KeyboardDataQueSize
>   **Data Type:** REG_DWORD
>   **Value:** 0x64

The default is 0x64; increase this value to increase the size of the buffer.
Reboot for this change to take effect.

MODEMS

II-3 NT 4.0 uses the unimodem protocol to recognize modems. If you have an
old modem that isn't unimodem-compliant and you want NT to use Modem.inf
to set the parameters, change this entry.

>   **Hive:** HKEY_LOCAL_MACHINE
>   **Key:** Software\Microsoft\RAS\Protocols

Add the following value under the Protocols key:

> **Value Name:** EnableUnimodem
>   **Data Type:** REG_DWORD
>   **Value:** 0

II-4   If you need to find the firmware revision on your hard drive without physi-
cally removing it, these registry entries show you how.

> **Hive:** HKEY_LOCAL_MACHINE
> **Key:** Hardware\DeviceMap\SCSI\ScsiPort0\TargetId0\
> LogicalUnitId0
> **Value Name:** Identifier
> **Data Type:** REG_SZ
> **Value:** Quantum Fireball_TM3 A6B

II-5

> **Value Name:** Type
> **Data Type:** REG_SZ
> **Value:** DiskPeripheral

These two entries control the first SCSI peripheral, or in this example, an IDE
Quantum Fireball drive. Even though the Fireball is an IDE device, you can
look at these keys to obtain the information. Note the Type value, which provides extra verification that you are indeed looking at the right peripheral.

II-6

> **Hive:** HKEY_LOCAL_MACHINE
> **Key:** Hardware\DeviceMap\SCSI\ScsiPort1\TargetId0\
> LogicalUnitId0
> **Value Name:** Identifier
> **Data Type:** REG_SZ
> **Value:** Toshiba CD-ROM XM-5702B 2826

II-7

> **Value Name:** Type
> **Data Type:** REG_SZ
> **Value:** CdRomPeripheral

These two entries control the second SCSI peripheral, or in this case, an IDE
Toshiba 12 X CD-ROM. Again, note the Type value, which provides extra verification that you are indeed looking at the correct peripheral.

HARDWARE

CPU

II-8   To see what kind of processor chip you are running on a remote computer, look in the registry. These entries give you information about the class of CPU the target machine is running. If you have more than one CPU, the Central-Processor key has numbered subkeys (1, 2, 3).

> **Hive:** HKEY_LOCAL_MACHINE
> **Key:** Hardware\Description\System\CentralProcessor\0
> **Value Name:** Identifier
> **Data Type:** REG_SZ
> **Value:** x86 Family 6 Model 1 Stepping 7

This value gives you information about the specific CPU revision.

II-9

> **Value Name:** VendorIdentifier
> **Data Type:** REG_SZ
> **Value:** GenuineIntel

This value gives you the manufacturer of the CPU.

II-10

> **Value Name:** ~MHz
> **Data Type:** REG_DWORD
> **Value:** 0xc7

This value is the actual speed of the CPU. This example says my CPU is faster than 199 Mhz, which it is. I tested this on a 200 Mhz Pentium Pro.

NETWORK CARDS

DIAMOND NET COMMANDER

II-11   If you have installed a Diamond Multimedia Net Commander ISDN adapter and are having problems, you may want to check these registry entries.

> **Hive:** HKEY_LOCAL_MACHINE
> **Key:** Software\Diamond Multimedia\NetCommander\ncVector
> **Value Name:** Status
> **Data Type:** REG_SZ
> **Value:** In Service

If the Net Commander is functioning properly, the value for Status is In Service. If the value is anything else, the card is not functioning properly.

II-12 Problem: after installing the software necessary to run the Net Commander, the configuration screen pop ups every time you reboot. Modify the following registry entry to keep the screen from popping up.

   Hive: HKEY_LOCAL_MACHINE
   Key: Software\Microsoft\Windows\CurrentVersion\Run
 Value Name: NetCmdrSetup
  Data Type: REG_SZ
   Value:

Delete anything in the Value field. Restart the machine for this change to take effect.

DIGIBOARD

II-13 If RAS can't see all the ports on your Digiboard multiport serial I/O board, make sure the following registry value is set correctly.

   Hive: HKEY_LOCAL_MACHINE
   Key: System\CurrentControlSet\Services\Asyncmac\Parameters
 Value Name: Ports
  Data Type: REG_DWORD
   Value: <number of ports>

If you have eight ports available, this value should be 8. Restart the machine for these changes to take effect.

IOMEGA ZIP DRIVE

II-14 You just bought an Iomega Zip Drive. From time to time you don't have it connected to your computer, which generates an error. To disable the message, change this entry; it stops the driver from reporting an error to the system log.

   Hive: HKEY_LOCAL_MACHINE
   Key: System\Current\Controlset\Services\PPA3NT\Parameters

Add the following value under the Parameters key:

 Value Name: ErrorControl
  Data Type: REG_DWORD
   Value: 0

HARDWARE

VIDEO CARDS

DIAMOND FIRE GL

II-15 When using your Diamond Multimedia Fire GL card, you get this error in the Event Viewer: "Glint Error: VideoPortGetAccessRanges failed." Try changing this registry entry to solve the problem.

> **Hive:** HKEY_LOCAL_MACHINE
> **Key:** System\CurrentControlSet\Servies\Glint\Device0

Add the following value:

> **Value Name:** UseBiosAddresses
> **Data Type:** REG_DWORD
> **Value:** 1

Restart Windows NT for these values to take effect.

STB VIRGE VELOCITY 3D

II-16 To set the advanced parameters of your STB ViRGE Velcoity 3D Video Card under NT, change the parameters under the following registry key. Several parameters control these advanced settings.

> **Hive:** HKEY_LOCAL_MACHINE
> **Key:** System\ControlSet\HardwareProfiles\0001\System\
> CurrentControlSet\Services\STBViRGE\Device0
> **Value Name:** DefaultSettings.BitsPerPel
> **Data Type:** REG_DWORD
> **Value:** 0x18

II-17
> **Value Name:** DefaultSettings.Flags
> **Data Type:** REG_DWORD
> **Value:** 0

II-18
> **Value Name:** DefaultSettings.VRefresh
> **Data Type:** REG_DWORD
> **Value:** 0x4b

II-19

    Value Name: DefaultSettings.XPanning
    Data Type: REG_DWORD
        Value: 0

II-20

    Value Name: DefaultSettings.XResolution
    Data Type: REG_DWORD
        Value: 0x400

II-21

    Value Name: DefaultSettings.YPanning
    Data Type: REG_DWORD
        Value: 0x0

II-22

    Value Name: DefaultSettings.YResolution
    Data Type: REG_DWORD
        Value: 0x300

II-23 If you need to find the system's refresh rate, check this registry entry.

            Hive: HKEY_LOCAL_MACHINE
            Key: System\ControlSet\Hardware Profiles\0001\System\
                        CurrentControlSet\Services\STBViRGE\Device0
    Value Name: Vrefresh
    Data Type: REG_DWORD
        Value: 0x4b

This example value is the refresh rate for an STB ViRGE video card. You must find the appropriate key for your video card, for example, an ATI or Matrox. The value is stored in hexadecimal.

HARDWARE

MATROX MILLENIUM AND MATROX MYSTIQUE

If you invested in a top-flight video card, you deserve to get the most out of it. These registry settings let you maximize the performance of your Matrox video cards, both the Millenium and the Mystique models.

II-24

Hive: HKEY_LOCAL_MACHINE
Key: System\CurrentControlSet\Services\mga64\Device0

Device0 refers to the first video card installed on your system.
Value Name: User.AlternateLines
Data Type: REG_BINARY
Value: 0

When set to 1, this value enables the faster AUTOLINE opcode of the drawing engine to draw lines defined by integer coordinates. The convention that determines which pixels contribute to a given line is slightly different in AUTOLINE and in Windows NT. Setting AlternateLines to 1 trades off compliance with the Windows NT conventions for performance. A value of 0 enforces compliance. Lines defined by non-integer endpoint coordinates are not affected by this setting.

II-25

Hive: HKEY_LOCAL_MACHINE
Key: System\CurrentControlSet\Services\mga64\Device0
Value Name: User.ComplexBlt
Data Type: REG_BINARY
Value: 1

Device0 in the key refers to the first video card installed on your system. When set to 1, this value lets your video card hardware accelerate some complex Raster OPerations (ROPs) by executing a sequence of simple ROPs (ORing, ANDing, etc.) on the display. Artifacts in the target display area may flash because an intermediate result, which will be replaced by the final image on the next cycle, is displayed in video RAM on a given refresh cycle. A value of 0 for the entry means that complex ROPs are performed in software.

II-26

     Hive: HKEY_LOCAL_MACHINE
     Key: System\CurrentControlSet\Services\mga64\Device0
Value Name: User.DeviceBitmaps
 Data Type: REG_BINARY
    Value: 1

Device0 in the key refers to the first video card installed on your system. Setting this value to 1 lets the hardware accelerate drawing bitmaps by using off-screen memory for caching them. A value of 0 disables bitmap caching and lets the CPU draw onto all bitmaps. Bitmap caching is internally disabled when a desktop requiring more than one card is in use, regardless of the registry setting.

II-27

     Hive: HKEY_LOCAL_MACHINE
     Key: System\CurrentControlSet\Services\mga64\Device0
Value Name: User.EnableUSWC
 Data Type: REG_BINARY
    Value: 1

Device0 refers to the first video card installed on your system. When set to 1, the value lets the frame buffer directly access the write-combining feature of the Pentium Pro processor. Setting this value to 0 may result in slightly slower performance.

II-28

     Hive: HKEY_LOCAL_MACHINE
     Key: System\CurrentControlSet\Services\mga64\Device0
Value Name: User.MgaInfoFile
 Data Type: REG_BINARY
    Value: 1

Device0 refers to the first video card installed on your system. When set to 1, this value lets the MGA PowerDesk software control refresh rates. A value of 0 allows all available refresh rates to be listed.

II-29

Hive: HKEY_LOCAL_MACHINE
Key: System\CurrentControlSet\Services\mga64\Device0
Value Name: User.SynchronizeDac
Data Type: REG_BINARY
Value: 0

Device0 refers to the first video card installed on your system. When set to 1, this value requests the driver to wait for a vertical sync before programming the ramdac with a new pointer shape or a new palette. If you notice stray pixels flashing around the pointer, setting this value to 1 might fix the problem. Setting it to 0 gives you slightly better performance.

II-30

Hive: HKEY_LOCAL_MACHINE
Key: System\CurrentControlSet\Services\mga64\Device0
Value Name: User.SynchronizeEngine
Data Type: REG_BINARY
Value: 0

Device0 refers to the first video card installed on your system. When set to 1, this value requires the driver to wait until the Millennium hardware is ready to accept new data before programming the next operation. Setting it to 0 results in better performance. On most x86-based systems, the PCI logic should ensure that such a check is redundant. If you're experiencing problems that might be related to timing (with communication programs, for instance), setting this value to 1 may help.

II-31

Hive: HKEY_LOCAL_MACHINE
Key: System\CurrentControlSet\Services\mga64\Device0
Value Name: User3D.DoubleBuffer
Data Type: REG_BINARY
Value: 1

Device0 refers to the first video card installed on your system. When set to 1, this value requires the Matrox Millennium or Mystique memory to allocate a back buffer. Set this value to 0 if you don't require a back buffer. Set this value to 1 to fully accelerate 3D animation.

II-32

Hive: HKEY_LOCAL_MACHINE
Key: System\CurrentControlSet\Services\mga64\Device0
Value Name: User3D.Zbuffer
Data Type: REG_BINARY
Value: 1

Device0 refers to the first video card installed on your system. When set to 1, this value requires the Matrox Millennium or Mystique memory to allocate a Z buffer. Set it to 0 if you don't require a Z buffer. To accelerate your 3D rendering, set this value to 1. Setting this value and the User3D.DoubleBuffer to 0 effectively disables any 3D hardware acceleration.

MGA POWERDESK

These registry entries let you tweak the features and performance of the PowerDesk software that ships with the Matrox Millenium and Mystique cards.

II-33

Hive: HKEY_LOCAL_MACHINE
Key: System\CurrentControlSet\Services\MGACtrl\PowerDesk
Value Name: PowerDeskPath
Data Type: REG_SZ
Value: C:\Program Files\MGA NT PowerDesk

This value sets the path to the configuration files for the Matrox PowerDesk configuration software. For example, to find out where the monitor configuration files are, look here for the path, then look in the MON subdirectory located under this path.

II-34

Hive: HKEY_LOCAL_MACHINE
Key: System\CurrentControlSet\Services\MGACtrl\PowerDesk\
CurrentSettings
Value Name: BitsperPixel
Data Type: REG_DWORD
Value: 08h

This value sets the number of colors that the card is currently configured to display in bits per pixel (bpp). Valid values are 08h (8 bpp, or 256 colors); 0Fh (15 bpp, or 32 K colors), 10h (16bpp, or 64 K colors), 18h (24 bpp, or 16,777,216 colors), and 20h (32bpp, or true color).

HARDWARE

II-35 The next two settings determine the resolution (in pixels) of your desktop
area, which includes your entire Windows workspace.

     Hive: HKEY_LOCAL_MACHINE
     Key: System\CurrentControlSet\Services\MGACtrl\PowerDesk\
      CurrentSettings
   Value Name: Mga.DesktopX
    Data Type: REG_DWORD
      Value: 0x400

II-36

     Hive: HKEY_LOCAL_MACHINE
     Key: System\CurrentControlSet\Services\MGACtrl\PowerDesk\
      CurrentSettings
   Value Name: Mga.DesktopY
    Data Type: REG_DWORD
      Value: 0x300

Your Windows workspace consists of everything you see on-screen and in the
off-screen area when you're using a "virtual desktop." (You use a virtual
desktop, or viewport, when your desktop area is larger than your display area.)

II-37 These two settings govern the resolution (in pixels) of your display area.

     Hive: HKEY_LOCAL_MACHINE
     Key: System\CurrentControlSet\Services\MGACtrl\PowerDesk\
      CurrentSettings
   Value Name: Mga.DesktopX
    Data Type: REG_DWORD
      Value: 0x400

II-38

     Hive: HKEY_LOCAL_MACHINE
     Key: System\CurrentControlSet\Services\MGACtrl\PowerDesk\
      CurrentSettings
   Value Name: Mga.DesktopY
    Data Type: REG_DWORD
      Value: 0x300

Your display area is your on-screen workspace, or the actual resolution that
the video card sets your monitor to. Generally, these settings are set to the
same values as your Desktop settings, though these values can be set smaller
than the desktop values to create a viewport into your desktop.

CD-ROM

II-39 Sometimes when running NT 4.0, you get frequent Event Viewer messages specifying an ATAPI source error, Event #9: "The device \device\scsiport0 did not respond within the timeout period." You can tell Windows NT to stop polling the CD-ROM for disk changes by changing the following registry entry.

        Hive: HKEY_LOCAL_MACHINE
         Key: System\CurrentControlSet\Services\CdRom
Value Name: Autorun
  Data Type: REG_DWORD
      Value: 0

SCSI CONTROLLERS

II-40 You recently decided to add a SCSI CD-ROM to your system, and you add a 1522 just for the CD-ROM. You boot NT and it hangs after trying to boot from the 1522. How can you dictate the boot process? This registry entry does the trick.

        Hive: HKEY_LOCAL_MACHINE
         Key: System\CurrentControlSet\Services\
             SCSI_CONTROLLER_NAME
Value Name: Tag
  Data Type: REG_DWORD
      Value:

You'll need the value from the new SCSI controller and from the original controller. If you swap these values, your system should boot from the original controller.

HARDWARE

11-41   If you use the Sparrow.sys driver for your SCSI adapter, you may have noticed that by default it is assigned IRQ 11 and this assignment seems to be hardcoded. Do not despair. This registry entry lets you override the hardcoded IRQ 11 and change it to anything you want.

> **Hive:** HKEY_LOCAL_MACHINE
> **Key:** System\CurrentControlSet\Services\Sparrow

Add the following key under the Sparrow key.

> **Key:** Parameters

Now that you have the Parameters key, you need to add another subkey: Device(n). The n is the device number you are changing the IRQ for. If you only have one adapter, it is Device0.

> **Key:** Device0

Next, you need to add the actual value that lets you change the IRQ settings:

> **Hive:** HKEY_LOCAL_MACHINE
> **Key:** System\CurrentControlSet\Services\Sparrow\Parameters\Device0
> **Value Name:** DriverParameter
> **Data Type:** REG_SZ
> **Value:** IRQ=12 (or any other valid IRQ setting)

You must reboot the machine for this change to take effect.

11-42   To increase the throughput of your SCSI adapter, try changing this registry entry.

> **Hive:** HKEY_LOCAL_MACHINE
> **Key:** CurrentControlSet\Services\aic78xx

Add the following key under the aic78xx key:

> **Key:** Parameters

Now add an additional subkey:

> **Key:** Device

Now we are ready to change the value that improves throughput.

> **Hive:** HKEY_LOCAL_MACHINE
> **Key:** CurrentControlSet\Services\aic78xx\Parameters\Device
> **Value Name:** MaximumSGList
> **Data Type:** REG_DWORD
> **Value:** 0xFF

This change works with Adaptec cards and may work with other SCSI adapters, too. As always, make sure you've backed up your registry before proceeding.

SOUND

II-43 You just applied the Windows NT 4.0 upgrade and now your audio doesn't work. Try this registry modification to fix it.

> **Hive:** HKEY_CURRENT_USER
> **Key:** Control Panel\Sound

Make sure the following value exists.

> **Value Name:** Beep
> **Data Type:** REG_SZ
> **Value:** yes

Reboot the system for these changes to take effect

II-44 Your sound card locks up any time you play a .wav file. The only solution is to restart the computer. Try this registry parameter to help solve the problem.

> **Hive:** HKEY_LOCAL_MACHINE
> **Key:** System\CurrentControlSet\Control\GraphicsDrivers

Add the following key under the GraphicsDrivers Key:

> **Key:** DisableUSWC

You don't need to specify anything else. By adding this key, you tell Windows NT not to use Uncache Speculative Write Combining on the video cards. Reboot the machine for this change to take effect.

HP DESKSCAN II 2.3

II-45   You upgraded to HP DeskScan II 2.3 from version 2.1 or older, and the program doesn't run. Changing the following registry entries should solve your problem.
>   **Hive:** HKEY_LOCAL_MACHINE
>   **Key:** System\CurrentControlSet\Services

Add the following Key and the next two values:
>   **Key:** Aspi32
>   **Value Name:** ErrorControl
>   **Data Type:** REG_DWORD
>   **Value:** 1

>   **Value Name:** Start
>   **Data Type** REG_DWORD
>   **Value:** 2

>   **Value Name:** Type
>   **Data Type:** REG_DWORD
>   **Value:** 1

II-46   This entry is the second part of installing the new DeskScan II 2.3 software.
>   **Hive:** HKEY_CURRENT_USER
>   **Key:** Control Panel\Mmcpl

Add the following value under the Mmcpl key:
>   **Value Name:** HP_Scanjet
>   **Data Type:** REG_SZ
>   **Value:** %systemroot%\system\hpscnmgr.dll

Reboot your system for these changes to take effect. Windows NT now runs the correct driver.

Section III

APPLICATIONS

This section contains registry entries for all types of software, from Microsoft SQL Server to Netscape to Windows NT system information. Office 97 applications have their own section.

SMS 1.2

III-1 When SMS creates a package for distribution, it first compresses all the files in the package and then sends the package to the site server. The site server expands the compressed package into a Temp directory. By default, SMS creates the Temp directory on the biggest drive with at least 100 megabytes of available space. Changing this registry value lets you specify which drive SMS uses as the preferred drive. If the minimum conditions aren't met (100 MB and NTFS), SMS searches for a more suitable drive.

       Hive: HKEY_LOCAL_MACHINE
       Key: Software\Microsoft\SMS\Components\SMS_DESPOOLER
Value Name: PreferredDriveForTempDirectory
  Data Type: REG_SZ
      Value: < valid drive letter >

Restart the machine for these values to take effect.

III-2 SMS needs a directory to copy the decompressed package to. By default, it looks at the drive that contains the SMS_SHR and determines whether that drive has at least 100 MB of free space. If it does, SMS creates the SMS_PKGx directory there. SMS by default uses the NTFS volume with the most free space. To change the minimum drive space required for this process, change the following registry entry.

       Hive: HKEY_LOCAL_MACHINE
       Key: Software\Microsoft\SMS\Components\SMS_DESPOOLER
Value Name: SMSDriveMinimumFreeSpaceinMBytes
  Data Type: REG_DWORD
      Value: 0x64

The value is in hexadecimal. Restart the machine for these values to take effect.

III-3 Your most effective tools for troubleshooting SMS performance problems are the different service logs. These registry entries let you maximize the amount of logging SMS performs. By analyzing these logs, you can get a pretty good picture of where the SMS bottlenecks are on your system.

> **Hive:** HKEY_LOCAL_MACHINE
> **Key:** Software\Microsoft\SMS\Tracing
> **Value Name:** SQLEnabled
> **Data Type:** REG_DWORD
> **Value:** 1

This value enables SMS to log its interactions with SQL Server. Restart the SMS Executive for this change to take effect.

III-4

> **Hive:** HKEY_LOCAL_MACHINE
> **Key:** Software\Microsoft\SMS\Tracing
> **Value Name:** Enabled
> **Data Type:** REG_DWORD
> **Value:** 1

This value enables SMS logging. When this value is set to 1, SMS logs the results for all SMS services. Setting this value to 0 disables logging. Restart the SMS Executive for this change to take effect.

III-5 SMS stores individual packages in compressed form before it ships them for distribution. This entry gives you the location of important information about these packages. This information is incredibly useful when debugging site distribution problems.

> **Hive:** HKEY_LOCAL_MACHINE
> **Key:** Software\Microsoft\SMS\Components\SMS_DESPOOLER\
> MasterPackages
> **Key:** < Package Name >

SMS creates a key for each package. This key stays in the registry of the site server until the package is removed from the site server. See III-19 for more about SMS packages.

APPLICATIONS

III-6

           Hive: HKEY_LOCAL_MACHINE
           Key: Software\Microsoft\SMS\Components\SMS_DESPOOLER\
           MasterPackages
Value Name: FileName
  Data Type: REG_DWORD
      Value: < fully qualified path to the compressed package file >

This value is the location where the compressed file for each job is stored; along with the directory, the value includes the filename in the format of JobID.wks. An example value is \\Machine_Name\SMS_SHRD\site.srv\ despoolr.box\store\< JobID >.wks.

III-7 To change the number of inventory attempts SMS tries before rolling the client into another domain, change this registry value.

           Hive: HKEY_LOCAL_MACHINE
           Key: Software\Microsoft\SMS\Components\
           SMS_MAINTENANCE_MANAGER
Value Name: Inventory False Logon Limit
  Data Type: REG_DWORD
      Value: 3

A common use for this value is when you upgrade SMS versions. If you inadvertently change the site code or site name, you can see problems. Reducing this value lets the clients roll over into the new domain faster. In effect, you are moving them from the old site to a new site.

III-8

           Hive: HKEY_LOCAL_MACHINE
           Key: Software\Microsoft\SMS\Components\SMS_DESPOOLER\
           CancelHistory
           Key: < PackageName >

When SMS cancels a job, it creates a key for each job under the CancelHistory key. The only value stored under these keys is the time stamp for when the job was canceled.

III-9

Hive: HKEY_LOCAL_MACHINE
Key: Software\Microsoft\SMS\Components\SMS_DESPOOLER\
TransferPackages
Key: < Package Name >

If you choose a server other than the site server to distribute a package, a key is created for each job under the Transfer Packages key. Under this key, you find a key for each server that has been designated to distribute the package.

III-10

Hive: HKEY_LOCAL_MACHINE
Key: Software\Microsoft\SMS\Components\SMS_DESPOOLER\
TransferPackages
Value Name: < Machine Name >

This key stores information about the package.

III-11

Hive: HKEY_LOCAL_MACHINE
Key: Software\Microsoft\SMS\Components\SMS_DESPOOLER\
TransferPackages\< Machine Name >
Value Name: ShareName
Data Type: REG_SZ
Value: < any valid share name >

This value determines where on the distribution server the site server copies the decompressed package files. The share is in the format SMS_PKGx, where x is a letter; for example, SMS_PKGD.

III-12 This registry entry stores the name of the default servers that distribute SMS packages. This information is useful if certain servers are used as package servers when you do not want them performing this function.

Hive: HKEY_LOCAL_MACHINE
Key: Software\Microsoft\SMS\Components\SMS_DESPOOLER
Value Name: DefaultPackageServers
Data Type: REG_MULTI_SZ
Value: < Machine Name >

You must restart the SMS services for these changes to take effect.

III-13   Each of these values sets different aspects of SMS connections.
   Hive: HKEY_LOCAL_MACHINE
   Key: Software\Microsoft\SMS\Components\SMS_DESPOOLER
   Value Name: ForcedDisconnectionDelayInMinutes
   Data Type: REG_DWORD
   Value: 0x5

III-14
   Hive: HKEY_LOCAL_MACHINE
   Key: Software\Microsoft\SMS\Components\SMS_DESPOOLER
   Value Name: NumberofRetriesBeforeForcedDisconnection
   Data Type: REG_DWORD
   Value: 0xc

III-15
   Hive: HKEY_LOCAL_MACHINE
   Key: Software\Microsoft\SMS\Components\SMS_DESPOOLER
   Value Name: UseForcedDisconnect
   Data Type: REG_DWORD
   Value: 0

III-16
   Hive: HKEY_LOCAL_MACHINE
   Key: Software\Microsoft\SMS\Components\SMS_DESPOOLER
   Value Name: PollingInterval
   Data Type: REG_DWORD
   Value: 0x1

III-17
   Hive: HKEY_LOCAL_MACHINE
   Key: Software\Microsoft\SMS\Components\SMS_DESPOOLER
   Value Name: InventoryChange
   Data Type: REG_DWORD
   Value: 0

III-18 This registry entry stores a key for each SMS job that was canceled. If you can't track the status of a particular job, be sure that it doesn't have a corresponding key under the CancelHistory key.

> **Hive:** HKEY_LOCAL_MACHINE
> **Key:** Software\Microsoft\SMS\Components\SMS_DESPOOLER\ CancelHistory\NTL001

In this example, NTL001 is a valid name for an SMS job. You need to know the name of the specific SMS job you want to track.

> **Value Name:** TimeStamp
> **Data Type:** REG_DWORD
> **Value:** < the time at which the job was canceled; for example, 0x33166b0a >

SMS creates a key for each job that is canceled. You can decipher the time stamp if you want, but the presence of a key means a job was canceled.

III-19 This registry entry stores a key for each SMS Master package. This information lets you see different packages that have been created over time.

> **Hive:** HKEY_LOCAL_MACHINE
> **Key:** Software\Microsoft\SMS\Components\SMS_DESPOOLER\ MasterPackages\W_NTL00001

In this example, W_NTL00001 is a valid name for an SMS package. You need to know the name of the specific SMS package you want to track.

> **Value Name:** TimeStamp
> **Data Type:** REG_DWORD
> **Value:** < the time at which the job was canceled; for example, 0x33166b0a >

SMS creates a key for each job that is canceled. You can decipher the time stamp if you want, but the presence of a key means a job was canceled.

APPLICATIONS

PCANYWHERE32

III-20 Are you having either of these problems getting Windows NT to work with your PCAnywhere 7.0 client?
- After you install the software, the Novell logon dialog box does not appear before users log on.
- You get the message "Novell NetWare Client for Windows NT has detected another 3rd party GINA authenticator installed. Do you want to replace it with Novell NetWare Client for Windows NT GINA authenticator?"

These registry entries fix the problem. You add two keys and a value — and be sure to add them in the correct order.

> **Hive:** HKEY_LOCAL_MACHINE
> **Key:** Software\Symantec\pcANYWHERE

Add a 7.0 key after the pcANYWHERE key.

> **Hive:** HKEY_LOCAL_MACHINE
> **Key:** Software\Symantec\pcANYWHERE\7.0

Add the System key after the 7.0 key.

III-21

> **Hive:** HKEY_LOCAL_MACHINE
> **Key:** Software\Symantec\pcANYWHERE\7.0\System
> **Value Name:** GinaDLL
> **Data Type:** REG_SZ
> **Value:** Nwgina.dll

SCHEDULE PLUS 7.0A

III-22 To run your current Schedule Plus configuration in workgroup mode, change this registry entry.

> **Hive:** HKEY_CURRENT_USER
> **Key:** Software\Microsoft\Schedule+\Application
> **Value Name:** MailDisabled
> **Data Type:** REG_DWORD
> **Value:** 0

Setting this value to 0 pops up a dialog box asking if you want to run Schedule Plus in workgroup mode. Exit Schedule Plus before changing this value.

III-23 To find out where your critical Schedule Plus files are stored, check these two registry entries, which point you to their locations.

        Hive: HKEY_CURRENT_USER
        Key: Software\Microsoft\Schedule+\Application
Value Name: LocalPath
    Data Type: REG_SZ
       Value: < drive:pathname\username.scd >

This value is the fully qualified path to your current Schedule Plus data file. Changing this value causes Schedule Plus to use data in the file contained in this value.

III-24

        Hive: HKEY_CURRENT_USER
        Key: Software\Microsoft\Schedule+\Application
Value Name: ArchiveFile
    Data Type: REG_SZ
       Value: < drive:pathname\ARCHIVEmmyy.scd >

This value sets the fully qualified path to the current archive file. It is in the format ARCHIVEmmyy.SCD, where mm is the numeric representation of the month the data was archived and yy is the year.

EXCHANGE INFORMATION STORE

III-25 Do you need to tighten security on your Exchange Server? It is possible to force Exchange to assign specific TCP/IP ports to RPCs that access the directory or information store. By default, Exchange assigns ports randomly. To use a packet filter and force Exchange to use a specific port, change this registry entry.

        Hive: HKEY_LOCAL_MACHINE
        Key: System\CurrentControlSet\ServicesMSExchangeDS\Parameters

Add the following values under the parameters key:

Value Name: TCP/IP Port
    Data Type: REG_DWORD
       Value: < your port number >

This change forces Exchange to use whatever port number you assign for access to the Directory Store.

APPLICATIONS

III-26

      Hive: HKEY_LOCAL_MACHINE
      Key: System\CurrentControlSet\ServicesMSExchangeIS\Parameters

Add the following values under the parameters key:
    Value Name: TCP/IP Port
    Data Type: REG_DWORD
      Value: < your port number >

This change forces Exchange to use whatever port number you assign for access to the Information Store. Restart Exchange for either of these changes to take effect.

III-27 **D**o you need to disable the circular logging Exchange Server 4.0 performs? If you have lots of disk and want to keep your logs for a longer time, use this registry entry to disable circular logging. You can disable circular logging for both the Directory Store and the Information Store.
      Hive: HKEY_LOCAL_MACHINE
      Key: System\CurrentControlSet\ServicesMSExchangeDS\Parameters

Add the following values under the parameters key:
    Value Name: Circular Logging
    Data Type: REG_DWORD
      Value: 0

This change disables circular logging for the Directory Store.

III-28

      Hive: HKEY_LOCAL_MACHINE
      Key: System\CurrentControlSet\ServicesMSExchangeIS\Parameters

Add the following values under the parameters key:
    Value Name: Circular Logging
    Data Type: REG_DWORD
      Value: 0

This change disables circular logging for the Information Store. Restart the Exchange server for either of these changes to take effect.

III-29 If you need to find out where Exchange stores its files (information that's very useful for moving files remotely or archiving files), the following registry values point you to the pertinent locations.

> **Hive:** HKEY_LOCAL_MACHINE
> **Key:** System\CurrentControlSet\Services\MSExchangeDS\ Parameters
> **Value Name:** Database Log Files Path
> **Data Type:** REG_SZ
> **Value:** < fully qualified path >

This value is where Exchange stores the log files for the Data Store.

III-30

> **Hive:** HKEY_LOCAL_MACHINE
> **Key:** System\CurrentControlSet\Services\MSExchangeDS\ Parameters
> **Value Name:** DSA Database File
> **Data Type:** REG_SZ
> **Value:** < fully qualified path\dir.edb >

This value is where Exchange stores the database file for the DSA (Directory Service Agent).

III-31

> **Hive:** HKEY_LOCAL_MACHINE
> **Key:** System\CurrentControlSet\Services\MSExchangeDS\ Parameters
> **Value Name:** DSA Hierarchy Table File
> **Data Type:** REG_SZ
> **Value:** < fully qualified path\hierarch.dat >

This value is where Exchange stores the hierarchy table file for the DSA.

III-32

> **Hive:** HKEY_LOCAL_MACHINE
> **Key:** System\CurrentControlSet\Services\MSExchangeDS\ Parameters
> **Value Name:** DSA Temporary File
> **Data Type:** REG_SZ
> **Value:** < fully qualified path\temp.edb >

This value is name of the temporary work file where Exchange stores the DSA.

APPLICATIONS

III-33

Hive: HKEY_LOCAL_MACHINE
Key: System\CurrentControlSet\Services\MSExchangeDS\
Parameters
Value Name: DSA Working Directory
Data Type: REG_SZ
Value: < fully qualified path >

This value is the directory where Exchange stores the temporary work file or files for the DSA.

III-34

Hive: HKEY_LOCAL_MACHINE
Key: System\CurrentControlSet\Services\MSExchangeDS\
ParametersPublic
Value Name: DB Path
Data Type: REG_SZ
Value: < fully qualified path\PUB.EDB >

This value is where Exchange stores the Information Store (IS) database file.

III-35

Hive: HKEY_LOCAL_MACHINE
Key: System\CurrentControlSet\Services\MSExchangeIS\
ParametersSystem
Value Name: DB Log Path
Data Type: REG_SZ
Value: < fully qualified path >

This value is the directory where Exchange stores the system log files.

III-36

Hive: HKEY_LOCAL_MACHINE
Key: System\CurrentControlSet\Services\MSExchangeIS\
ParametersSystem
Value Name: POP3 Protocol Log Path
Data Type: REG_SZ
Value: < fully qualified path >

This value is where Exchange stores the log files that are created during a POP3 transaction.

III-37

> **Hive:** HKEY_LOCAL_MACHINE
> **Key:** System\CurrentControlSet\Services\MSExchangeIS\
> ParametersSystem
> **Value Name:** Working Directory
> **Data Type:** REG_SZ
> **Value:** < fully qualified path >

This value is the working system directory for Exchange.

III-38

> **Hive:** HKEY_LOCAL_MACHINE
> **Key:** System\CurrentControlSet\Services\MSExchangeIS\
> ParametersPrivate
> **Value Name:** DB Path
> **Data Type:** REG_SZ
> **Value:** < fully qualified path\priv.edb >

This value is the location of the database for the Exchange private store.

NOVELL NETWARE

You can enable your Windows NT client to log on to your Novell server unattended. If you do, your server is no longer secure; however, you can do it. Change these entries to give the Novell client a default server, user name, and password to use for unattended logon.

III-39

> **Hive:** HKEY_LOCAL_MACHINE
> **Key:** Software\Novell\NWGINA\Login Screen

Add the following value under the Parameters key:
> **Value Name:** DefaultNetwareUserName
> **Data Type:** REG_SZ
> **Value:** < username >

III-40

> **Hive:** HKEY_LOCAL_MACHINE
> **Key:** Software\Novell\NWGINA\Login Screen

Add the following value under the Parameters key:
> **Value Name:** DefaultNetwarePassword
> **Data Type:** REG_SZ
> **Value:** < user password >

APPLICATIONS

III-41

      Hive: HKEY_LOCAL_MACHINE
      Key: Software\Novell\NWGINA\Login Screen

Add the following value under the Parameters key:
    Value Name: DefaultNDSContext
    Data Type: REG_SZ
    Value: < NDS context >

III-42

      Hive: HKEY_LOCAL_MACHINE
      Key: Software\Novell\NWGINA\Login Screen

Add the following value under the Parameters key:
    Value Name: DefaultNDSServer
    Data Type: REG_SZ
    Value: < server name >

III-43

      Hive: HKEY_LOCAL_MACHINE
      Key: Software\Novell\NWGINA\Login Screen

Add the following value under the Parameters key:
    Value Name: DefaultNDSTree
    Data Type: REG_SZ
    Value: < tree name >

III-44

      Hive: HKEY_LOCAL_MACHINE
      Key: Software\Novell\NWGINA\Login Screen

Add the following value under the Parameters key:
    Value Name: NetwareAutoAdminLogon
    Data Type: REG_SZ
    Value: 1

NETSCAPE 3.0

III-45 If you want to fiddle with the Netscape Navigator bookmark file or address book, these registry entries show you where the values are stored.

> **Hive:** HKEY_CURRENT_USER
> **Key:** Software\Netscape\Netscape Navigator\Bookmark List
> **Value Name:** File Location
> **Data Type:** REG_SZ
> **Value:** < fully qualified path and file name >

III-46

> **Value Name:** Add URLs Under
> **Data Type:** REG_SZ
> **Value:** Top Level Listing

III-47

> **Value Name:** Start Menu With
> **Data Type:** REG_SZ
> **Value:** Entire Listing

III-48

> **Hive:** HKEY_CURRENT_USER
> **Key:** Software\Netscape\Netscape Navigator\Address Book
> **Value Name:** File Location
> **Data Type:** REG_SZ
> **Value:** < fully qualified path and file name >

You can change the names of these files or verify that a particular registry entry points to the correct files. This information is very useful in debugging missing bookmarks and address books or creating a common set of bookmarks and address books to distribute.

III-49 If Netscape Navigator's caching feature doesn't work properly, be sure these registry entries refer to the correct directory for caching and match the settings displayed on the navigator administration screens.

> **Hive:** HKEY_CURRENT_USER
> **Key:** Software\Netscape\Netscape Navigator\Cache
> **Value Name:** Cache Dir
> **Data Type:** REG_SZ
> **Value:** < fully qualified path and file name >

This value is the directory where Navigator stores cached images and files.

APPLICATIONS

III-50

> **Value Name:** Disk Cache Size
> **Data Type:** REG_SZ
> **Value:** 0x00001388 (5000)

This value shows how much disk space Navigator can use to store cached information.

III-51

> **Value Name:** Disk Cache SSL
> **Data Type:** REG_SZ
> **Value:** No

This value determines whether Navigator caches Secure Socket Layer (SSL) pages.

III-52

> **Value Name:** Disk Cache Size
> **Data Type:** REG_SZ
> **Value:** 0x00000400 (1024)

This value determines how much memory Navigator uses to keep objects cached.

CITRIX WINFRAME

III-53 If your Winframe server runs certain applications slowly, don't fret. WinFrame is actually trying to do you a favor — it spots bad software and tries to reduce the resources it allocates to these bad applications. To modify this feature, change these registry entries.

> **Hive:** HKEY_LOCAL_MACHINE
> **Key:** Software\CITRIX\Compatibility\Applications

Add a key under the Applications key with the name of your applications.

> **Key:** < myapp >

Add the following values under the key you just created (whatever you called your myapp key).

> **Value Name:** FirstCountMsgQPeeksSleepBadApp
> **Data Type:** REG_DWORD
> **Value:** 0xf

III-54

> **Value Name:** Flags
> **Data Type:** REG_DWORD
> **Value:** 0xc

III-55

> **Value Name:** MsgQBadAppSleepTimeInMillisec
> **Data Type:** REG_DWORD
> **Value:** 3

III-56

> **Value Name:** NthCountMsgQPeeksSleepBadApp
> **Data Type:** REG_DWORD
> **Value:** 0x5

Restart the machine for these changes to take effect.

RIGHTFAX

III-57 If your client gets an RPC error message when using RightFax, you need to make sure that both the client and the server machines are using the same maximum IPX packet size. This registry entry lets you set the size.

> **Hive:** HKEY_LOCAL_MACHINE
> **Key:** System\CurrentControlSet\Services\NWLinkIPX\
> NetConfig\< adapter name >
> **Value Name:** MaxPktSize
> **Data Type:** REG_DWORD
> **Value:** 0

If the value is not present or the data is set to 0, it is up to the network adapter to set the MaxPktSize. You need to consult your user manual for your specific network card.

III-58 To test RightFax without installing a fax card, try this registry entry.

> **Hive:** HKEY_LOCAL_MACHINE
> **Key:** Software\RightFAX\BoardServer
> **Value Name:** Fakeboards
> **Data Type:** REG_DWORD
> **Value:** 1

Now you can simulate fax operations without having any hardware installed.

III-59 To change the separator value for an e-mail or fax address, use the following registry entry.

> **Hive:** HKEY_LOCAL_MACHINE
> **Key:** Software\RightFAX\Gateway
> **Value Name:** Separator
> **Data Type:** REG_SZ
> **Value:** < any character >

Restart the gateway for this value to take effect.

HOTSYNC 1.1

Are you having problems updating from HotSync 1.0 to 1.1? You may need to delete these registry keys for the new version to install properly.

III-60

> **Hive:** HKEY_CURRENT_USER
> **Key:** Software\Palm Computing\Pilot Desktop\Component0

III-61

> **Hive:** HKEY_CURRENT_USER
> **Key:** Software\Palm Computing\Pilot Desktop\Component1

III-62

> **Hive:** HKEY_CURRENT_USER
> **Key:** Software\Palm Computing\Pilot Desktop\Component2

III-63

> **Hive:** HKEY_CURRENT_USER
> **Key:** Software\Palm Computing\Pilot Desktop\Component3

III-64

> **Hive:** HKEY_CURRENT_USER
> **Key:** Software\Palm Computing\Pilot Desktop\HotSync

After deleting these keys, install the new version of HotSync.

MICROSOFT INDEX SERVER

III-65

Hive: HKEY_LOCAL_MACHINE
Key: System\CurrentControlSet\Control\ContentIndex
Value Name: FilterContents
Data Type: REG_SZ
Value: 0x1

This value determines whether Microsoft Index Server filters both the contents and properties of a file or only the properties of the file. A value of 0 specifies that the contents are not filtered. Otherwise, the contents and properties are both filtered.

III-66

Value Name: DaemonResponseTimeout
Data Type: REG_SZ
Value: 0x5

This value specifies, in minutes, a period during which the CiDaemon process should provide an appropriate response. The CiDaemon might time out by trying to index a corrupt file.

III-67

Value Name: FilterDirectories
Data Type: REG_DWORD
Value: 0x0

This value identifies whether Index Server filters directories for system properties and displays them in query results. When this value is not 0, directories are filtered.

III-68

Value Name: FilterFilesWithUnknownExtensions
Data Type: REG_DWORD
Value: 0x1

This value identifies whether Index Server filters files with extensions that have not been registered. When this value is set to 0, only registered file types are filtered.

III-69

Value Name: FilterRetries
Data Type: REG_DWORD
Value: 0x4

This value identifies the maximum number of times Index Server tries to filter a file if the initial attempt to filter the file fails.

III-70

    Value Name: ForcedNetPathScanInterval
       Data Type: REG_DWORD
          Value: 0x78

This value identifies the time, in minutes, between forced scans on directories with no notifications.

III-71

    Value Name: GenerateCharacterization
       Data Type: REG_DWORD
          Value: 0x1

This value controls the automatic generation of file characterizations (abstracts).

III-72

    Value Name: GrovelIISRegistry
       Data Type: REG_DWORD
          Value: 0x1

This value controls whether Index Server automatically indexes all virtual roots within Internet Information Server.

III-73

    Value Name: IsapiDefaultCatalogDirectory
       Data Type: REG_SZ
          Value: c:\bo

This value identifies the default directory that contains the content index catalog.

III-74

    Value Name: IsapiMaxEntriesInQueryCache
       Data Type: REG_DWORD
          Value: 0xa

This value identifies the maximum number of cached queries.

III-75

    Value Name: IsapiMaxRecordsInResultSet
       Data Type: REG_DWORD
          Value: 0x1388

This value identifies the maximum number of rows to fetch for a single query.

III-76
  Value Name: IsapiMaxRecordsPerGetRows
  Data Type: REG_DWORD
  Value: 0xa

This value identifies the maximum number of rows that are returned in a single fetch (get) operation. You can combine multiple fetches to make up a result set.

III-77
  Value Name: IsapiQueryCachePurgeInterval
  Data Type: REG_DWORD
  Value: 0x5

This value identifies the time interval during which a query cache item remains active.

III-78
  Value Name: IsapiRequestQueueSize
  Data Type: REG_DWORD
  Value: 0x18

This value identifies the maximum number of Web query requests to queue during periods of high server activity.

III-79
  Value Name: IsapiRequestThresholdFactor
  Data Type: REG_DWORD
  Value: 0x5

This value specifies a number of threads per processor; when processors reach this threshold, remaining query requests are queued.

III-80
  Hive: HKEY_LOCAL_MACHINE
  Key: System\CurrentControlSet\Control\
    ContentIndexIsapiVirtualServerCatalogs
 Value Name: < No Name >
  Data Type: REG_SZ
  Value: c:\bo

Each key in this section associates a virtual server with a specific catalog. The key name is the IP address of the virtual server (NULL is used for the default server), and the value is the location of the catalog as you would enter it in the CiCatalog parameter of an .idq file.

APPLICATIONS

III-81

Value Name: MasterMergeCheckpointInterval
Data Type: REG_DWORD
Value: 0x100

This value identifies the interval at which Index Server conducts checkpoints during master merges. This parameter determines how often data is written to the new master index and is critical when a master merge is paused and restarted.

III-82

Value Name: MasterMergeTime
Data Type: REG_DWORD
Value: 0x0

This value specifies when a master merge occurs. This value is the number of minutes after midnight.

III-83

Value Name: MaxActiveQueryThreads
Data Type: REG_DWORD
Value: 0x3

This value identifies the maximum number of asynchronous query threads that are processed concurrently.

III-84

Value Name: MaxCharacterization
Data Type: REG_DWORD
Value: 0x140

This value identifies the maximum number of characters in the automatically generated characterization (abstract).

III-85

Value Name: MaxFilesizeFiltered
Data Type: REG_DWORD
Value: 0x100

This value identifies the maximum size of a single file filtered with the default filter. If a file exceeds this size, only file properties are filtered. This limit does not apply to registered file types; that is, to those file types that do not use the default filter.

III-86

Value Name: MaxFilesizeMultiplier
Data Type: REG_DWORD
Value: 0x8

This value identifies the maximum amount of data that can be generated from a single file, based on its size. This value is a multiplier used in conjunction with the current file size to determine the maximum file size after content indexing. For example, a value of 2 means that a file can generate up to 2 times its size in content index data.

III-87

Value Name: MaxFreshCount
Data Type: REG_DWORD
Value: 0x4e20

This value identifies the maximum number of newly indexed files that cause a master merge to start.

III-88

Value Name: MaxIdealIndexes
Data Type: REG_DWORD
Value: 0x5

This value identifies the maximum number of indexes considered acceptable in an ideal system. If the number of indexes exceeds this value and the system is idle, an annealing merge brings the total count of indexes to this number.

III-89

Value Name: MaxIdealIndexes
Data Type: REG_DWORD
Value: 0x32

This value identifies the maximum number of persistent indexes in the catalog. If this number is exceeded, a shadow merge brings the total below this number.

III-90

Value Name: MaxMergeInterval
Data Type: REG_DWORD
Value: 0xa

This value identifies the sleep time between merges. Index Server often activates this to determine whether an annealing (most common), shadow, or master merge is necessary.

APPLICATIONS

III-91

Value Name: MaxPendingDocuments
Data Type: REG_DWORD
Value: 0x20

This value identifies the maximum number of pending documents that are filtered before the content index is considered out-of-date for property queries.

III-92

Value Name: MaxQueryExecutionTime
Data Type: REG_DWORD
Value: 0x2710

This value identifies the maximum execution time of a query. If a query takes more than this amount of CPU time, its processing is stopped and an error is returned.

III-93

Value Name: MaxQueryTimeslice
Data Type: REG_DWORD
Value: 0x32

This value identifies the maximum time allowed for Index Server to execute a query in a single CPU time slice. If more asynchronous queries are active than allowed query threads, Index Server puts a query back in the pending queue after this time interval. CPU time slicing is performed only after a matching row is found, so the time spent in a time slice may overrun this and a considerable number of rows may be examined in the time slice.

III-94

Value Name: MaxQueueChunks
Data Type: REG_DWORD
Value: 0x14

This value identifies the maximum number of in-memory buffers (queue chunks) allotted to keep track of pending documents. The higher the number, the less frequently the memory buffers are written to disk.

III-95

Value Name: MaxRestrictionNodes
Data Type: REG_DWORD
Value: 0xfa

This value identifies the minimum number of restriction nodes created by query normalization. If this value is exceeded, the query fails with the status of QUERY_E_TOOCOMPLEX. This status message means the query was too complex to be completed because the limit imposed in this registry key was reached. This key keeps a user from overloading the server's capacity with an overly large query.

III-96

Value Name: MaxShadowFreeForceMerge
Data Type: REG_SZ
Value: 0x1f4

When disk space occupied by the shadow indexes exceeds this value and the free space on the catalog disk drive falls below the MinDiskFreeForceMerge value, Index Server executes a master merge.

III-97

Value Name: MaxShadowIndexSize
Data Type: REG_DWORD
Value: 0xf

When the disk space occupied by the shadow indexes exceeds this percentage of the catalog drive, Index Server executes a master merge.

III-98

Value Name: MaxWordLists
Data Type: REG_DWORD
Value: 0x5

This value determines the maximum number of concurrent word lists that can exist.

III-99

Value Name: MaxWordlistSize
Data Type: REG_DWORD
Value: 0x5

This value, in 128K chunks, identifies the maximum amount of memory consumed by an individual word list. When this limit is reached, Index Server finishes the document it's currently filtering and adds that document only. Any other documents are re-filed and placed in another word list later.

III-100
Value Name: MinIdleQueryThreads
Data Type: REG_DWORD
Value: 0x2

This value sets the minimum number of idle threads kept alive to process incoming queries.

III-101
Value Name: MinMergeIdleTime
Data Type: REG_DWORD
Value: 0x5a

This value identifies when Index Server should perform an annealing merge because the system was idle more than average during the previous merge check period.

III-102
Value Name: MinSizeMergeWordlists
Data Type: REG_SZ
Value: 0x400

This value identifies the minimum combined size of word lists that forces a shadow merge.

III-103
Value Name: MinWordlistMemory
Data Type: REG_DWORD
Value: 0x5

This value identifies the minimum free memory used to create word lists.

III-104
Value Name: PropertyStoreMappedCache
Data Type: REG_DWORD
Value: 0x60

This value identifies the maximum size of memory buffers used for Property Cache.

III-105
Value Name: ThreadPriorityMerge
Data Type: REG_DWORD
Value: 0xfffffffe

This value identifies the priority of the merge thread.

III-106

Value Name: MinDiskFreeForceMerge
Data Type REG_DWORD
Value: 15

This value is the minimum free disk space needed before the content indexer forces a merge. Acceptable values range from 5 percent to 25 percent.

III-107

Hive: HKEY_LOCAL_MACHINE
Key: System\CurrentControlSet\Control\ContentIndex\Language
Value Name: InstalledLangs
Data Type: REG_MULTI_SZ
Value: English_US English_UK French_French German_German Italian_Italian Japanese_Default Neutral Spanish_Modern Swedish_Default

The InstalledLangs value lists the set of languages installed. Each string in the InstalledLangs value names a subkey below the Language key.

III-108

Hive: HKEY_LOCAL_MACHINE
Key: System\CurrentControlSet\Control\ContentIndex\ Language\English_US
Value Name: ISAPIDefaultErrorFile
Data Type: REG_SZ
Value: /Scripts/Samples/Search/DefError.htx

This value gives the full virtual path to the generic error template file that's displayed to the user. This .htx template is processed when none of the specific error pages applies. The CiRestriction, CiErrorMessage, and CiErrorNumber variables can all be referenced in the .htx file.

III-109

Value Name: ISAPIHTXErrorFile
Data Type: REG_SZ
Value: /Scripts/Samples/Search/HTXError.htx

This value identifies the full virtual path to the error page returned in response to errors in the .htx file. The CiRestriction, CiErrorMessage, and CiErrorNumber variables can all be referenced in the .htx file.

APPLICATIONS

III-110

Value Name: ISAPIIDQErrorFile
Data Type: REG_SZ
Value: /Scripts/Samples/Search/IDQError.htx

This value identifies the full virtual path to the error page returned in response to errors in the .idq file. The CiRestriction, CiErrorMessage, and CiErrorNumber variables can all be referenced in the .htx file.

III-111

Value Name: ISAPIRestrictionErrorFile
Data Type: REG_SZ
Value: /Scripts/Samples/Search/ResError.htx

This value identifies the full virtual path to the error page returned in response to errors in the query restriction (CiRestriction). This is the error page that users see most often. The CiRestriction, CiErrorMessage, and CiErrorNumber variables can all be referenced in the .htx file.

III-112

Value Name: Locale
Data Type: REG_DWORD
Value: 0x409

This value associates the registry section with a specific locale.

III-113

Value Name: NoiseFile
Data Type: REG_SZ
Value: noise.enu

This value identifies the file name of the noise-word list for this locale. The file must be located in the %SystemRoot%\System32 directory.

III-114

Value Name: StemmerClass
Data Type: REG_SZ
Value: {eeed4c20-7f1b-11ce-be57-00aa0051fe20}

This value identifies the ActiveX class ID of the class used for locale-specific stemming.

III-115
Value Name: WbreakerClass
Data Type: REG_SZ
Value: {59E09780-8099-101B-8DF3-00000B65C3B5}

This value identifies the ActiveX class ID of the class used to split phrases for this locale.

III-116 **I**f Microsoft Index Server is currently indexing all your files, you can make it quit by limiting Index Server to indexing just those files you register.
Hive: HKEY_LOCAL_MACHINE
Key: System\CurrentControlSet\Control\ContentIndex
Value Name: FilterFilesWithUnknownExtensions
Data Type: REG_DWORD
Value: 0

A value of 0 tells the Content indexer to Index only those file types that have been registered and ignore the rest. This feature is handy when you don't want to index .exe files and .com files, for example.

SQL SERVER

III-117 **Y**ou can specify the protocol you want SQL Executive to use in its Advanced tab, but if you need to specify a particular protocol for SQL Executive to use when connecting to servers, you need to add the following registry entry.
Hive: HKEY_LOCAL_MACHINE
Key: Software\Microsoft\MSSQLServer\SQLExecutive\
Value Name: ServerHost
Data Type: REG_SZ
Value: < server >

You must still create a specific server connection in the Advanced tab of the SQL Client Configuration Utility. Then set the ServerHost value in the SQL Executive section of the registry to the appropriate server name. SQL should then use the defined protocol on all its connection attempts to subscribing servers.

APPLICATIONS

III-118 To increase the concurrent number of SQLExec tasks that use a DB-Library connection, change the following registry value.

Hive: HKEY_LOCAL_MACHINE
Key: Software\Microsoft\MSSQLServer\SQLExecutive
Value Name: MaxDBProcesses
Data Type: REG_DWORD
Value: 61

The number of available concurrent tasks is the number of MaxDBProcesses — three for SQL overhead. Restart your SQL server for these changes to take effect.

III-119 If the SQLMonitor Service on Windows NT won't start and you recently changed the SQL Server SA accounts password, you should change it back. If you can't remember the password, here's how to fix the problem.

Hive: HKEY_LOCAL_MACHINE
Key: Software\Microsoft\SQLServer\SQLMONITOR\Parameters
Value Name: Password
Data Type: REG_SZ

Type the new SA account password for the value.

Value: password

Restart the machine for these changes to take effect.

III-120 You've installed SQL Server 6.5, but SQL Executive does not come up. When you try to start it from the Control Panel, you get an Error 109. To fix the problem, change this registry value.

Hive: HKEY_LOCAL_MACHINE
Key: Software\Microsoft\SQLServer\CurrentVersion
Value Name: CurrentVersion
Data Type: REG_SZ
Value: 6.50.201

Restart the machine for these changes to take effect.

EXCHANGE SERVER 4.0

III-121   If you have tried to change your Exchange password, chances are you have encountered this error: "The NT Domain password could not be changed. A required action was not successful due to an unspecified error." You need to add the following registry parameters to fix this problem.

> **Hive:** HKEY_LOCAL_MACHINE
> **Key:** CurrentControlSet\Control\LSA

Add the following value under the LSA key:

> **Value Name:** NetWareClientSupport
> **Data Type:** REG_DWORD
> **Value:** 1

Use this entry if you are running NWLINK.

III-122

> **Hive:** HKEY_LOCAL_MACHINE
> **Key:** CurrentControlSet\Control\LSA

Add the following value under the LSA key:

> **Value Name:** TcpipClientSupport
> **Data Type:** REG_DWORD
> **Value:** 1

Use this entry if you are running TCP/IP. Restart the machine for these changes to take effect.

III-123   If you cannot communicate with your Exchange Server using your Exchange client and have recently installed a firewall, you may need to change the following registry entries.

> **Hive:** HKEY_LOCAL_MACHINE
> **Key:** System\CurrentControlSet\Services\MSExchangeIS\
> ParametersSystem
> **Value Name:** TCP/IP Port
> **Data Type:** REG_DWORD
> **Value:** < valid TCP/IP Port number >

III-124

Hive: HKEY_LOCAL_MACHINE
Key: System\CurrentControlSet\Services\MSExchangeIS\
Parameters
Value Name: TCP/IP Port
Data Type: REG_DWORD
Value: < valid TCP/IP Port number >

Some Internet firewall software doesn't accept the TCP/IP ports Exchange uses to communicate via RPC. You need to modify these ports on the Exchange server to something that your firewall software can use. Restart Exchange for these changes to take effect.

III-125 The Exchange client installs multiple protocols so that it can connect to the server using any one. As a result, sometimes it seems that Exchange takes forever to load. You can speed things up by eliminating the protocols you don't use. For example, if you use only TCP/IP, you can change the following registry entry.

Hive: HKEY_LOCAL_MACHINE
Key: System\CurrentControlSet\ServicesMSExchangeMTA\
Parameters\MT
Value Name: gateway clients
Data Type: REG_DWORD
Value: 0x20

The default setting is 0x8 and is fine under normal conditions. If your installation has several gateways or connections configured, try increasing this parameter.

INTERNET NEWS AND MAIL

III-126 If you need to move the address book file, you need to modify these two registry values. This change is especially useful if you have just upgraded your hard drive and want to move some of the larger files to a disk with more room.

Hive: HKEY_CURRENT_USER
Key: Software\Microsoft\Internet Mail and News
Value Name: Store Root
Data Type: REG_SZ
Value: < fully qualified path and directory >

This value sets where Internet Explorer stores the address book files. Be sure to include the drive and fully qualified path.

III-127

> **Hive:** HKEY_CURRENT_USER
> **Key:** Software\Microsoft\WAB\
> **Value Name:** Wab File Name
> **Data Type:** REG_SZ
> **Value:** < fully qualified path and directory >

This value is the actual location of the .wab files, in the format username.wab. If your login is tim, your wab file is tim.wab.

PEER WEB SERVICES

III-128 Have you ever tried to change the port numbers for the personal Web server or FTP server that comes with Front Page? Well, now you can. Each of the values below represents its corresponding services TCP/IP port number in hexadecimal. You can change them to any valid port number. Restart your machine for any changes to take effect.

> **Hive:** HKEY_LOCAL_MACHINE
> **Key:** System\CurrentControlSet\Control\ServiceProvider\ ServiceTypes
> **Value Name:** MSFTPSVC
> **Data Type:** REG_DWORD
> **Value:** port number in hex

This value is the TCP/IP port number for the FTP Service.

III-129

> **Hive:** HKEY_LOCAL_MACHINE
> **Key:** System\CurrentControlSet\Control\ServiceProvider\ ServiceTypes
> **Value Name:** W3SVC
> **Data Type:** REG_DWORD
> **Value:** port number in hex

This value is the TCP/IP port number for the Web Service.

APPLICATIONS

III-130

     Hive: HKEY_LOCAL_MACHINE
    Key: System\CurrentControlSet\Control\ServiceProvider\
       ServiceTypes
 Value Name: GOPHERSVC
  Data Type: REG_DWORD
    Value: port number in hex

This value is the TCP/IP port number for the Gopher Service.

III-131

     Hive: HKEY_LOCAL_MACHINE
    Key: System\CurrentControlSet\Control\ServiceProvider\
       ServiceTypes
 Value Name: MicrosoftInternetInformationServer
  Data Type: REG_DWORD
    Value: port number in hex

This value is the TCP/IP port number that the administration program for Peer Web services listens on.

NETSCAPE NAVIGATOR 3.0

III-132 You recently joined a domain, and some of your settings were wiped out for Netscape Navigator. You invested a lot of time in setting up Netscape Navigator, and now you can access the correct version only if you boot locally. This registry location shows where Netscape stores its information.

    Hive: HKEY_CURRENT_USER
    Key: Software\Netscape

Save the key and then log on to NT as the domain user. Restore the saved key and you're back in business.

III-133 Do you need to browse Japanese, Chinese, or Korean HTML files with your Netscape browser? Follow these steps.

1. First, download the following free fonts from Microsoft.
   * Traditional Chinese — http://ms.www.conxion.com/msdownload/ ieinstall/ie3lpktw.exe
   * Japanese — http://ms.www.conxion.com/msdownload/ieinstall/ ie3lpkja.exe
   * Korean — http://ms.www.conxion.com/msdownload/ieinstall/ ie3lpkko.exe
   * Simplified Chinese — http://ms.www.conxion.com/msdownload/ ieinstall/ie3lpkcn.exe
   * Pan European — http://ms.www.conxion.com/msdownload/ieinstall/ ie3lpkpe.exe

2. Change the following registry key:

   > **Hive:** HKEY_CURRENT_USER
   > **Key:** Software\Netscape\Netscape\Navigator\INTL

   Add the following value under the INTL key:
   Value Name: UseUnicodeFont
   Data Type: REG_DWORD
   Value: 1

3. Now run Navigator and select the font from General Preference menu. Choose the language and select the font you downloaded. Follow the same procedure for fixed fonts.

GOPHER

III-134 To change the Administrator name for your Gopher service, change this registry entry.

> **Hive:** HKEY_LOCAL_MACHINE
> **Key:** System\CurrentControlSet\Services\GOPHERSVC\Parameters

Add the following value under the Parameters key:
Value Name: AdminName
Data Type: REG_SZ
Value: Administrator

The default value is Administrator. Change this value to the name that's appropriate for your site. Restart the service for these changes to take effect.

APPLICATIONS

III-135 To change the Administrator e-mail address for your Gopher service, change this registry entry.

> **Hive:** HKEY_LOCAL_MACHINE
> **Key:** System\CurrentControlSet\Services\GOPHERSVC\Parameters

Add the following value under the Parameters key:

> **Value Name:** AdminEmail
> **Data Type:** REG_SZ
> **Value:** Admin@corp.com

The default value is admin@corp.com. Change this address to the appropriate name for your site. Restart the service for these changes to take effect.

III-136 To control the duration of a log file generated by the Gopher service, change this registry entry.

> **Hive:** HKEY_LOCAL_MACHINE
> **Key:** System\CurrentControlSet\Services\GOPHERSVC\Parameters

Add the following value under the Parameters key:

> **Value Name:** LogFilePeriod
> **Data Type:** REG_DWORD
> **Value:** 1

The values for LogFilePeriod are as follows:

0   never open a new log file. Instead, log file size is governed by LogFileTruncateSize

1   open a new log file every day

2   open a new log file every week

3   open a new log file every month

The default is 0. Restart the service for this value to take effect.

III-137 This registry entry determines the maximum size, in bytes, a Gopher log file can be before the Gopher Server logging service opens a new file.

> **Hive:** HKEY_LOCAL_MACHINE
> **Key:** System\CurrentControlSet\Services\GOPHERSVC\Parameters

Add the following value under the Parameters key:

> **Value name:** LogFileTruncateSize
> **Data Type:** REG_DWORD
> **Value:** 1388000

The default value is 1,388,000. If this value is set to 0, the log file grows to fill the available disk space. A value other than 0 specifies the maximum size of the log file before a new log file is opened.

III-138 To limit the maximum number of user connections your Gopher service allows, change this registry entry. It controls how many people can access your gopher server at a given time.

> **Hive:** HKEY_LOCAL_MACHINE
> **Key:** System\CurrentControlSet\Services\GOPHERSVC\Parameters

Add the following value under the Parameters key:

> **Value Name:** MaxConnections
> **Data Type:** REG_DWORD
> **Value:** 0x186a0

Restart the service for this value to take effect.

WORKS 4.0

III-139 If you recently installed MS Works 4.0 and cannot perform a spellcheck in Exchange, check the following registry values.

> **Hive:** HKEY_LOCAL_MACHINE
> **Key:** SharedTools\ProofingTools\CustomDictionaries
> **Value Name:** 1
> **Data Type:** REG_SZ
> **Value:** < fully qualified path and directory >

Sometimes MS Works incorrectly sets this value to an invalid path. You need to find the correct path and change the value 1 to the correct path name.

FTP

III-140 To annotate the directories that are displayed with the FTP service, check this registry entry. It lets you customize the directory display.

> **Hive:** HKEY_LOCAL_MACHINE
> **Key:** System\CurrentControlSet\Services\MSFTPSVC\Parameters

Add the following value under the Parameters key:

> **Value Name:** AnnotateDirectories
> **Data Type:** REG_DWORD
> **Value:** 0

The FTP service lets you customize your directories by displaying special text stored in a file called ~ftpsvc~ckm in the directory you wish to customize. The default value for this entry is 0, which disables the feature. Change the value to 1 to enable this feature. Restart the service for this value to take effect.

III-141 To provide a custom greeting and exit message for your FTP users, change this registry entry.

> **Hive:** HKEY_LOCAL_MACHINE
> **Key:** System\CurrentControlSet\Services\MSFTPSVC\Parameters

Add the following value under the Parameters key:

> **Value Name:** GreetingMessage
> **Data Type:** REG_SZ
> **Value:** < string >

III-142 For an exit message, add the following value under the Parameters key:

> **Value Name:** ExitMessage
> **Data Type:** REG_SZ
> **Value:** < string >

III-143   Do you ever need to change the default TCP/IP port IIS, Gopher, Microsoft Internet Service Manager, or FTP uses? You can try to change it using the Microsoft Internet Service Manager. If that doesn't work, and a lot of times it doesn't, try this registry entry.

> **Hive:** HKEY_LOCAL_MACHINE
> **Key:** System\CurrentControlSet\Control\ServiceProvider\
> ServiceType\MSFTPSVC
> **Value Name:** TcpPort
> **Data Type:** REG_DWORD
> **Value:** < desired port number >

This value regulates the FTP service.

III-144

> **Hive:** HKEY_LOCAL_MACHINE
> **Key:** System\CurrentControlSet\Control\ServiceProvider\
> ServiceType\GOPHERSVC
> **Value Name:** TcpPort
> **Data Type:** REG_DWORD
> **Value:** < desired port number >

This value regulates the Gopher service.

III-145

> **Hive:** HKEY_LOCAL_MACHINE
> **Key:** System\CurrentControlSet\Control\ServiceProvider\
> ServiceType\Microsoft Internet Information Server
> **Value Name:** TcpPort
> **Data Type:** REG_DWORD
> **Value:** < desired port number >

This value regulates the Internet Information Server.

III-146

> **Hive:** HKEY_LOCAL_MACHINE
> **Key:** System\CurrentControlSet\Control\ServiceProvider\
> ServiceType\W3SVC
> **Value Name:** TcpPort
> **Data Type:** REG_DWORD
> **Value:** < desired port number >

This value sets the default port that the WWW service listens on.

APPLICATIONS

III-147 Problem: You have configured FTP on two servers. One server is a PDC and the other is a stand-alone server. You can FTP to the PDC just fine, but you have trouble using your domain accounts with the standalone server. This registry entry solves the problem.

> **Hive:** HKEY_LOCAL_MACHINE
> **Key:** System\CurrentControlSet\Services\FTPSVC
> **Value Name:** DefaultLogonDomain
> **Data Type:** REG_SZ
> **Value:** < domain name >

Restart the machine for these changes to take effect. You should make this change only on the stand-alone server, not the PDC (or any subsequent BDC).

III-148 Several hundred users with valid network accounts frequently access your FTP server. You also have many anonymous accesses. You can create a setup that logs only the anonymous users by modifying this registry entry.

> **Hive:** HKEY_LOCAL_MACHINE
> **Key:** System\CurrentControlSet\Services\MSFTPSVC\Parameters

Add the following value under the Parameters key.

> **Value Name:** LogNonAnonymous
> **Data Type:** REG_DWORD
> **Value:** 1

The default value is 1. Set this to 0 to disable logging users who have actual user accounts.

III-149 Are your users having problems downloading files from your FTP server even though they type the exact file names? This registry entry should solve the problem.

> **Hive:** HKEY_LOCAL_MACHINE
> **Key:** System\CurrentControlSet\Services\MSFTPSVC\Parameters

Add the following value under the Parameters key.

> **Value Name:** LowercaseFiles
> **Data Type:** REG_DWORD
> **Value:** 1

The default value is 0, or disabled. Set this value to 1 to enable lowercase file comparisons.

III-150 Do you want to change the Administrator name for your FTP service? Here is the registry entry that stores that value.

> **Hive:** HKEY_LOCAL_MACHINE
>   **Key:** System\CurrentControlSet\Services\MSFTPSVC\Parameters

Add the following value under the Parameters key:

> **Value Name:** AdminName
>   **Data Type:** REG_SZ
>   **Value:** Administrator

The default value is Administrator. Change it to the appropriate name for your site. Restart the service for these changes to take effect.

III-151 If you want to change the Administrator e-mail address for your FTP service, change this entry.

> **Hive:** HKEY_LOCAL_MACHINE
>   **Key:** System\CurrentControlSet\Services\MSFTPSVC\Parameters

Add the following value under the Parameters key:

> **Value Name:** AdminEmail
>   **Data Type:** REG_SZ
>   **Value:** Admin@corp.com

The default value is admin@corp.com. Change value to the appropriate name for your site. Restart the service for these changes to take effect.

III-152 Do you want to limit the maximum number of user connections your FTP service allows? These entries give you that control. This registry entry lets you control how many people can access your FTP server at a given time. You can set it to send a message to the clients refused access (MaxClientsMessage).

> **Hive:** HKEY_LOCAL_MACHINE
>   **Key:** System\CurrentControlSet\Services\MSFTPSVC\Parameters

Add the following value under the Parameters key:

> **Value Name:** MaxConnections
>   **Data Type:** REG_DWORD
>   **Value:** 100,000

This value is the number of clients that can connect to the FTP server at any given time. Restart the service for this value to take effect.

APPLICATIONS

III-153   This entry sends a message you specify when a user connection to your FTP server is refused.

> **Value Name:** MaxClientsMessage
> **Data Type:** REG_SZ
> **Value:** < string value >

The message in the string is sent when the value set in MaxConnections is exceeded. Restart the service for this value to take effect.

III-154   You have many FTP users who have user accounts from one particular domain and who continually forget to add the < domainname > parameter in front of their user names when they try to log on. To change the default logon domain so that they'll log on even when they forget to specify the domain name, change this registry entry.

> **Hive:** HKEY_LOCAL_MACHINE
> **Key:** System\CurrentControlSet\Services\MSFTPSVC\Parameters

Add the following value under the Parameters key:

> **Value Name:** DefaultLogonDomain
> **Data Type:** REG_SZ
> **Value:** < domain name >

Restart the service for this value to take effect.

III-155   To gain a little more control over the log files generated by the FTP service, change this registry entry — it lets you control the duration of a log file.

> **Hive:** HKEY_LOCAL_MACHINE
> **Key:** System\CurrentControlSet\Services\MSFTPSVC\Parameters

Add the following value under the Parameters key:

> **Value Name:** LogFilePeriod
> **Data Type:** REG_DWORD
> **Value:** 1

The valid values for LogFilePeriod are as follows:

0   Never open a new log file. The log file is governed by LogFileTruncateSize.
1   Open a new log file every day.
2   Open a new log file every week.
3   Open a new log file every month.

The default is 0. Restart the service for this value to take effect.

III-156 This entry sets the maximum size in bytes your FTP log file can be before a new file is opened by the FTP logging module.

> **Hive:** HKEY_LOCAL_MACHINE
> **Key:** System\CurrentControlSet\Services\MSFTPSVC\Parameters

Add the following value under the Parameters key:

> **Value Name:** LogFileTruncateSize
> **Data Type:** REG_DWORD
> **Value:** 1388000

The default value is 1,388,000. A value of 0 means "do not truncate."

III-157 If you need to change the default FTP port in IIS 3.0, try using the Microsoft Internet Service Manager. If that doesn't work, and a lot of times it doesn't, try this registry entry.

> **Hive:** HKEY_LOCAL_MACHINE
> **Key:** System\CurrentControlSet\Control\ServiceProvider\
> ServiceType\MSFTPSVC
> **Value Name:** TcpPort
> **Data Type:** REG_DWORD
> **Value:** < desired port number >

DR. WATSON

III-158

> **Hive:** HKEY_LOCAL_MACHINE
> **Key:** Software\Microsoft\DrWatson
> **Value Name:** LogFilePath
> **Data Type:** REG_SZ
> **Value:** %windir%

This value sets the directory that stores the log file Dr. Watson creates.

APPLICATIONS

III-159

Hive: HKEY_LOCAL_MACHINE
Key: Software\Microsoft\DrWatson
Value Name: AppendToLogFile
Data Type: REG_DWORD
Value: 0x00000001

This value controls how Dr. Watson records to the log file. If the value is 1, Dr. Watson appends to the log file; a value of 0 creates a new log file for each application error.

III-160

Hive: HKEY_LOCAL_MACHINE
Key: Software\Microsoft\DrWatson
Value Name: CreateCrashDump
Data Type: REG_DWORD
Value: 0x00000001

This value controls what Dr. Watson does after a crash. A value of 1 creates a crash dump file. A value of 0 suppresses the creation of a crash dump file.

III-161

Hive: HKEY_LOCAL_MACHINE
Key: Software\Microsoft\DrWatson
Value Name: CrashDumpFile
Data Type: REG_DWORD
Value: %windir%\user.dmp

This value controls where Dr. Watson writes the file after a Blue Screen of Death (BSOD).

III-162

Hive: HKEY_LOCAL_MACHINE
Key: Software\Microsoft\DrWatson
Value Name: SoundNotification
Data Type: REG_DWORD
Value: 0x00000001

This value controls whether Dr. Watson notifies you with a sound (wave file). A value of 1 turns on the feature; a value of 0 turns it off.

III-163

> **Hive:** HKEY_LOCAL_MACHINE
> **Key:** Software\Microsoft\DrWatson
> **Value Name:** WaveFile
> **Data Type:** REG_SZ
> **Value:** < fully qualified path and filename >

This value is the path to the wave file Dr. Watson plays to notify you.

III-164

> **Hive:** HKEY_LOCAL_MACHINE
> **Key:** Software\Microsoft\DrWatson
> **Value Name:** VisualNotification
> **Data Type:** REG_DWORD
> **Value:** 0x00000001

This value determines whether Dr. Watson displays the message box when it encounters an error. A value of 1 turns on the feature; a value of 0 turns it off.

INTERNET INFORMATION SERVER 3.0

III-165 To change the Administrator name for your Web service, change this entry.

> **Hive:** HKEY_LOCAL_MACHINE
> **Key:** System\CurrentControlSet\Services\W3SVC\Parameters

Add the following value under the Parameters key:

> **Value Name:** AdminName
> **Data Type:** REG_SZ
> **Value:** Administrator

The default value is Administrator. Change this to whatever name is appropriate for your site. Restart the service for these changes to take effect.

APPLICATIONS

III-166 To change the Administrator e-mail address for your Web service, change this entry.

> **Hive:** HKEY_LOCAL_MACHINE
> **Key:** System\CurrentControlSet\Services\W3SVC\Parameters

Add the following value under the Parameters key:

> **Value Name:** AdminEmail
> **Data Type:** REG_SZ
> **Value:** Admin@corp.com

The default value is admin@corp.com. Change this value to the appropriate name for your site. Restart the service for these changes to take effect

---

III-167 To control the duration of a log file generated by the Web service, change this registry entry.

> **Hive:** HKEY_LOCAL_MACHINE
> **Key:** System\CurrentControlSet\Services\W3SVC\Parameters

Add the following value under the Parameters key:

> **Value Name:** LogFilePeriod
> **Data Type:** REG_DWORD
> **Value:** 1

The values for LogFilePeriod are as follows:

0 Never open a new log file. The log file size is governed by the LogFileTruncateSize value.
1 Open a new log file every day.
2 Open a new log file every week.
3 Open a new log file every month.

The default is 0. Restart the service for this value to take effect.

III-168 This entry determines the maximum size, in bytes, your Web log file can be before the Web logging module opens a new file.

> **Hive:** HKEY_LOCAL_MACHINE
> **Key:** System\CurrentControlSet\Services\W3SVC\Parameters

Add the following value under the Parameters key:

> **Value Name:** LogFileTruncateSize
> **Data Type:** REG_DWORD
> **Value:** 1,388,000

The default value is 1388000. A value of 0 means "do not truncate."

III-169 Is your IIS not properly recognizing MIDI files? That's because you need to add this registry key.

Hive: HKEY_LOCAL_MACHINE
Key: System\CurrentControlSet\Services\InetInfo\Parameters\ MimeMap

Add the following Key under the MimeMap key:
Key: audio/midi,mid,,

Now when you want to play MIDI files, add this string:

```
<EMBED SRC="music1.mid" VOLUME=30 WIDTH=144 HEIGHT=60
AUTOSTART=true hidden=true loop=true>
<bgsound src="music2.mid" loop=-1>
```

It will work.

III-170 Do you want to limit the maximum number of user connections your Web service allows? This registry entry lets you control how many people can access your Web server at a given time. You can set it up to send a message to the client that was refused access. You can specify the content of this message in the AccessDeniedMessage value.

Hive: HKEY_LOCAL_MACHINE
Key: System\CurrentControlSet\Services\W3SVC\Parameters

Add the following value under the Parameters key:
Value Name: MaxConnections
Data Type: REG_DWORD
Value: 0x186a0

Restart the service for this value to take effect.

III-171 This entry sets the message displayed when a user is denied a connection to your Web server.

Hive: HKEY_LOCAL_MACHINE
Key: System\CurrentControlSet\Services\W3SVC\Parameters

Add the following value under the Parameters key:
Value Name: AccessDeniedMessage
Data Type: REG_SZ
Value: < string value >

Restart the service for this change to take effect.

III-172   Have you ever needed to change the location of the virtual root directories that IIS installs for its various services? These registry entries let you change the virtual roots for the main Web directory, the admin directory, the scripts directory, and others.

      Hive: HKEY_LOCAL_MACHINE
       Key: System\CurrentControlSet\Services\W3SVC\Parameters\VirtualRoots
Value Name: /:
  Data Type: REG_SZ
     Value: C:\InetPub\wwwroot,1

III-173

      Hive: HKEY_LOCAL_MACHINE
       Key: System\CurrentControlSet\Services\W3SVC\Parameters\VirtualRoots
Value Name: /iisadmin
  Data Type: REG_SZ
     Value: C:\NTS40\System32\inetsrv\iisadmin,,1

III-174

      Hive: HKEY_LOCAL_MACHINE
       Key: System\CurrentControlSet\Services\W3SVC\Parameters\VirtualRoots
Value Name: /Scripts
  Data Type: REG_SZ
     Value: C:\InetPub\scripts,,1

III-175

      Hive: HKEY_LOCAL_MACHINE
       Key: System\CurrentControlSet\Services\W3SVC\Parameters\VirtualRoots
Value Name: /srchadm
  Data Type: REG_SZ
     Value: C:\InetPub\wwwroot\srchadm,,1

The value after the path corresponds to the permission level. A value of 1 gives read-only permission; a value of 4 gives execute permission. A value of 5 gives both read and execute permission.

III-176 If you have an IIS-based Website and want to turn on server caching, change this entry.

> **Hive:** HKEY_LOCAL_MACHINE
> **Key:** System\CurrentControlSet\Services\InetInfo\Parameters

Add the following value under the Parameters key:

> **Value Name:** DisableMemoryCache
> **Data Type:** REG_DWORD
> **Value:** 0

The default value is 0, which disables server caching. Changing it to 1 enables server caching. Restart the IIS service for these changes to take effect.

III-177 If your site has heavy traffic and you are trying to squeeze every ounce of performance out of your machines, try this registry entry to speed things up a bit.

> **Hive:** HKEY_LOCAL_MACHINE
> **Key:** System\CurrentControlSet\Services\InetInfo\Parameters

Add the following value under the Parameters key:

> **Value Name:** ListenBackLog
> **Data Type:** REG_DWORD
> **Value:** 50

This value can range from 1 to infinity. A value of 50 works well for sites with heavy traffic.

III-178 You have many Web users with user accounts from one particular domain who continually forget to add the < domainname > parameter in front of their user names when they try to log on. To change the default logon domain so that they'll log in even when they forget to specify the domain name, change this registry entry.

> **Hive:** HKEY_LOCAL_MACHINE
> **Key:** System\CurrentControlSet\Services\W3SVC\Parameters

Add the following value under the Parameters key:

> **Value Name:** DefaultLogonDomain
> **Data Type:** REG_SZ
> **Value:** Domain Name

Restart the service for this value to take effect.

APPLICATIONS

III-179   When you install IIS, it creates an anonymous user, generally in the form of IUSR_machinename. To change that user ID, change these entries.

> **Hive:** HKEY_LOCAL_MACHINE
> **Key:** System\CurrentControlSet\Services\W3SVC\Parameters

Add the following value under the Parameters key:

> **Value Name:** AnonymousUserName
> **Data Type:** REG_SZ
> **Value:** valid user name

III-180   Change this value as well.

> **Hive:** HKEY_LOCAL_MACHINE
> **Key:** Software\Microsoft\InetStp
> **Value Name:** AnonymousUser
> **Data Type:** REG_SZ
> **Value:** user_name

Stop and start the IIS service for these changes to take effect.

III-181   You can customize the default help that comes with IIS to include instructions that are specific to your Web site. This registry entry shows you the location for the Help file for InetManager; it's an HTML document, so you can modify it with standard tools.

> **Hive:** HKEY_LOCAL_MACHINE
> **Key:** Software\Microsoft\InetMgr\Parameters
> **Value Name:** HelpLocation
> **Data Type:** REG_SZ
> **Value:** iisadmin\htmldocs\inetdocs.htm

III-182 Are your users complaining of interrupted file transfers? Increasing the value of this registry parameter can help alleviate these symptoms. This value determines how long your server tries to transfer a file to a user before killing the file. The default value is 1000.

> **Hive:** HKEY_LOCAL_MACHINE
> **Key:** System\CurrentControlSet\Services\InetInfo\Parameters

Add the following value under the Parameters key:

> **Value Name:** MinFileKbSec
> **Data Type:** REG_DWORD
> **Value:** 1000

Here is how this value works. The server establishes a timeout value based on the following formula: The timeout equals the timeout value specified in the Internet Service Manager plus the size of the file being transferred divided by MinFileKbSec registry key.

III-183 If you run a tight ship and have several other applications running on your Web machine, you may want to investigate this parameter. It lets you specify how many threads the server keeps ready to handle input/output requests even when there is no activity. The default is 86,400 seconds, or 24 hours, which keeps threads active all the time. You can adjust this parameter according to your needs.

> **Hive:** HKEY_LOCAL_MACHINE
> **Key:** System\CurrentControlSet\Services\InetInfo\Parameters

Add the following value under the Parameters key:

> **Value Name:** ThreadTimeout
> **Data Type:** REG_DWORD
> **Value:** 86400 (24 hours)

III-184 Problem: You just switched to IIS 3.0 and you're busy creating Active Server pages left and right. Within minutes of deploying your Active Server pages, you're flooded with e-mail. Apparently, Active Server is setting cookies and your users don't like it. The following registry modification fixes this problem.

> **Hive:** HKEY_LOCAL_MACHINE
> **Key:** System\CurrentControlSet\Services\W3SVC\ASP\Parameters
> **Value Name:** AllowSessionState
> **Data Type:** REG_DWORD
> **Value:** 0

Restart your Web machine — and presto, no more cookies.

APPLICATIONS

III-185 If your log files are particularly large, you might try adjusting this parameter in the registry. It gives you control over how much log data the system caches before it writes to the log file. Decreasing this parameter causes it to write more frequently; increasing it causes it to write less frequently.

> **Hive:** HKEY_LOCAL_MACHINE
> **Key:** System\CurrentControlSet\Services\InetInfo\Parameters

Add the following value under the Parameters key:

> **Value Name:** LogFileBatchSize
> **Data Type:** REG_DWORD
> **Value:** 64

The default value is 64 K. Restart the service for any change to take effect.

III-186 If you have a lot of users on your Web site who log on with a user account (not just via anonymous), this registry parameter can help speed access to your system. It determines whether IIS caches security information about a particular file object when it retrieves it and therefore doesn't need to check the file for subsequent users. The default value is 0, which disables security descriptor caching. A value of 1 enables security descriptor caching.

> **Hive:** HKEY_LOCAL_MACHINE
> **Key:** System\CurrentControlSet\Services\InetInfo\Parameters

Add the following value under the Parameters key:

> **Value Name:** CacheSecurityDescriptor
> **Data Type:** REG_DWORD
> **Value:** 1

III-187 To improve the performance of IIS by allocating more memory to cache, change this registry entry.

> **Hive:** HKEY_LOCAL_MACHINE
> **Key:** System\CurrentControlSet\Services\InetInfo\Parameters

Add the following value under the Parameters key:

> **Value Name:** MemoryCacheSize
> **Data Type:** REG_DWORD
> **Value:** 3072000

The default value is 3072000, or 3 MB. Valid values for this entry range from 0 to 4294967295 bytes. You must have sufficient RAM on your computer to accommodate your setting. Restart the service for this change to take effect.

III-188   Do you create a lot of pages dynamically on your Web site (who doesn't anymore)? You may want to adjust this parameter so that objects don't stay in cache too long.

> **Hive:** HKEY_LOCAL_MACHINE
>
> **Key:** System\CurrentControlSet\Services\InetInfo\Parameters

Add the following value under the Parameters key:

> **Value Name:** ObjectCacheTTL
>
> **Data Type:** REG_DWORD
>
> **Value:** 30

The value specifies the number of seconds any object stays in the cache; 30 seconds is the default value. If an object is not accessed during this time, it is removed from the cache memory. If your system is constrained by limited memory, reducing the value causes the system to use less memory.

III-189   If you have a lot of users with individual accounts accessing your system, changing this value should improve your performance, too.

> **Hive:** HKEY_LOCAL_MACHINE
>
> **Key:** System\CurrentControlSet\Services\InetInfo\Parameters

Add the following value under the Parameters key:

> **Value Name:** UserTokenTTL
>
> **Data Type:** REG_DWORD
>
> **Value:** 900

The security information for each user helps create a user token on the server that is used to access files or other resources. The token is cached so that verification takes place only the first time the account is accessed (or until the token falls out of the cache). This value determines in seconds how long the token remains in cache. The default is 900 seconds (15 minutes).

APPLICATIONS

INTERNET EXPLORER 3.0

III-190 To change the default download path for Internet Explorer 3.0 on any machine (even a remote machine), use this registry value.

> **Hive:** HKEY_CURRENT_USER
> **Key:** Software\Microsoft\InternetExplorer

Change the Value for DownloadDirectory under the InternetExplorer key.

> **Value Name:** DownloadDirectory
> **Data Type:** REG_SZ
> **Value:** < fully qualified path and directory >

Restart Internet Explorer for the changes to take effect.

III-191 Are you tired of looking at the same old boring Times New Roman font in Internet Explorer? This example changes the default font from Times New Roman to Wide Latin. Changing this entry changes all references to the default font in your style sheets and thus in Explorer.

> **Hive:** HKEY_CURRENT_USER
> **Key:** Software\Microsoft\Internet Explorer\Styles
> **Value Name:** IEPropFontName
> **Data Type:** REG_SZ
> **Value:** Wide Latin

III-192 Problem: You have the same problem with boring fonts, but you don't want to just change fonts. Instead, you want certain headers to be bold and others to be italic. You need to modify the style sheets Internet Explorer uses and then change the default style sheet. First, let's modify the style sheets.

Hive: HKEY_LOCAL_MACHINE

Key: Software\Microsoft\Internet Explorer\Styles

Each Style sheet has the following thirteen parts:
- Style_Sheet_Name_Address_font
- Style_Sheet_Name_BlockQuote_font
- Style_Sheet_Name_H1_font
- Style_Sheet_Name_H2_font
- Style_Sheet_Name_H3_font
- Style_Sheet_Name_H4_font
- Style_Sheet_Name_H5_font
- Style_Sheet_Name_H6_font
- Style_Sheet_Name_Listing_font
- Style_Sheet_Name_Normal_font
- Style_Sheet_Name_Plain Text_font
- Style_Sheet_Name_Pre_font
- Style_Sheet_Name_XMP_font

Each font has a value in the following format:

Style_Sheet_Name_html_type:REG_SZ:Fontname,Bold Toggle,Font Size,Italic Toggle,Underline Toggle.

In our example, for the Style Sheet SerifSmallest, we change Header 3 to Wide Latin and Header 4 to Wide Latin not bold with a size of 12 points.

Value Name: SerifSmallest_H3_font

Data Type: REG_SZ

Value: Wide Latin,Bold,10,NoItalic,NoUnderline

Value Name: SerifSmallest_H4_font

Data Type: REG_SZ

Value: Wide Latin,NoBold,12,NoItalic,NoUnderline

III-193 Now we change Internet Explorer's default style sheet.

> **Hive:** HKEY_CURRENT_USER
> **Key:** Software\Microsoft\Internet Explorer\Styles
> **Value Name:** Default_Style_Sheet
> **Data Type:** REG_SZ
> **Value:** SerifSmallest

If you have Internet Explorer running, exit it and reload. Your new style sheet is in place.

III-194 If you're having trouble finding Web sites, you can use the autosearch function in Internet Explorer 3.0 to help you. Type **go** in the address bar, followed by some keywords that describe what you are looking for; Internet Explorer starts searching using its default search engine, Yahoo! To change the search engine, modify the following registry key.

> **Hive:** HKEY_CURRENT_USER
> **Key:** Software\Microsoft\Internet Explorer\SearchUrl
> **Value Name:** Default
> **Data Type:** REG_SZ
> **Value:** home.microsoft.com/access/autosearch.asp?p=%s

Here are the values for some popular search engines:

Excite	www.excite.com/search.gw?search=%s
AltaVista	www.altavista.digital.com/cgi-bin/query?pg=q&q=%s
Magellan	searcher.mckinley.com/searcher.cgi?query=%s
InfoSeek	guide-p.infoseek.com/Titles?qt=%si
Lycos	www.lycos.com/cgi-bin/pursuit?query=%s
Yahoo! (plain search)	search.yahoo.com/bin/search?p=%s
Yahoo! (IE autosearch)	msie.yahoo.com/autosearch?p=%si

III-195 To change the background of Internet Explorer's toolbar, change this registry entry.

> **Hive:** HKEY_CURRENT_USER
> **Key:** Software\Microsoft\Internet Explorer\Toolbar

Add the following value:

> **Value Name:** BackBitmap
> **Data Type:** REG_SZ
> **Value:** < fully qualified path and filename of any bitmap file >

Restart Internet Explorer for these values to take effect.

III-196 Do you sometimes get that annoying blank page when you bring up Internet Explorer? To change it to something meaningful other than the ever-popular blank.htm, change this entry.

        Hive: HKEY_CURRENT_USER
        Key: Software\Microsoft\Internet Explorer\Main
  Value Name: Local Page
   Data Type: REG_SZ
       Value: D:\<system root>\System32\blank.htm

The default value is listed above. Change it to any fully qualified path and file name. Restart Internet Explorer for this value to take effect.

III-197 Internet Explorer displays the most recent addresses in the Address box below the toolbar. This registry entry shows you where these values are stored.

        Hive: HKEY_CURRENT_USER
        Key: Software\Microsoft\Internet Explorer\TypedURLs
  Value Name: Url(n) where n is a number. Example Url1, Url2 etc.
   Data Type: REG_SZ
       Value: any valid internet address. Example http://www.
                 winntmag.com

You can delete values from this registry key as well as add them. Restart Internet Explorer for any changes to take effect.

APPLICATIONS

MACAFEE NETSHIELD

III-198 You've installed MacAfee Netshield 2.5 for Windows NT and your users are having problems logging on. Both Windows 95 and Windows NT users receive the same error message at logon: "Not enough server storage is available to process this command." Windows for Workgroup users get a different error message: "Path not found." In either case, error #2011 is logged in the event log. This registry value should fix this problem for all these users.

> **Hive:** HKEY_LOCAL_MACHINE
> **Key:** CurrentControlSet\Services\LanmanServer

Add the value IRPStacksize

> **Value Name:** IRPStackSize
> **DataType:** REG_DWORD
> **Value:** 5

The value is the amount of memory, in 36-byte segments, set aside for the Input/Output Request Stack. The default value is 4; change it to 5. The range of valid values is 1 to 12.

SQL ANYWHERE 32

III-199 If you use SQL Server Anywhere and are connecting your 16-bit client application to either SQL Anywhere's 32-bit client or a 32-bit standalone server, you need to make sure that the following registry entries exist. If you are having problems connecting, checking these entries is a good place to start.

> **Hive:** HKEY_CURRENT_USER
> **Key:** Software\ODBC\ODBC.INI\< datasource name >
> **Value Name:** AutoStop
> **Data Type:** REG_SZ
> **Value:** yes

III-200
> **Value Name:** DatabaseName
> **Data Type:** REG_SZ
> **Value:** database name

III-201
> **Value Name:** Driver
> **Data Type:** REG_SZ
> **Value:** c:\sqlany50\win32\wod50t.dll

III-202

> **Value Name:** PWD
> **Data Type:** REG_SZ
> **Value:** SQL

III-203

> **Value Name:** Start
> **Data Type:** REG_SZ
> **Value:** c:\sqlany50\win32\dbeng50

III-204

> **Value Name:** UID
> **Data Type:** REG_SZ
> **Value:** DBA

The 16-bit ODBC Driver Manager (Odbc.dll), provided with SQL Anywhere, lets 16-bit applications access a 32-bit ODBC driver without any changes. However, you must define a datasource with the 32-bit administrator tool. When you create a datasource with the 32-bit ODBC admin tool, entries are created in the registry and in Odbc.ini. Make sure the registry and Odbc.ini are in sync.

Section IV

MICROSOFT OFFICE

MICROSOFT ASSISTANT FOR OFFICE 97

By now you've seen the paper clip that helps you through the trials and tribulations of using Office 97. You can add extra features to this little critter and bend his will to your own with these registry entries.

IV-1

        Hive: HKEY_LOCAL_MACHINE
        Key: Software\Microsoft\Office\8.0\Common\Assistant
Value Name: AsstPath
  Data Type: REG_SZ
      Value: C:\Program Files\Microsoft Office\Office\Actors

This value contains the path where the actor files are stored. It is almost certain that Microsoft and third-party vendors will make new actors available. This path lets you add new actor files as they become available. These files are the Office Assistant actor (. act) and preview (.acp) files that are located on your system.

IV-2

        Hive: HKEY_LOCAL_MACHINE
        Key: Software\Microsoft\Office\8.0\Common\Assistant
Value Name: AsstSourcePath
  Data Type: REG_SZ
      Value: E:\Office\Actors

This value stores the source path for the support files Office 97 needs for the actor files.

IV-3

Hive: HKEY_LOCAL_MACHINE
Key: Software\Microsoft\Office\8.0\Common\Assistant
Value Name: AsstFile
Data Type: REG_SZ
Value: Clippit.act

This key is handy if you don't want to dig out your Office 97 CD every time you change the assistant. This value is the name of the file that Office 97 uses for the assistant. Note that this value is just the filename, not the full path to the file. Valid values include

Clippit.act	Clippit Paper Clip
Dot.act	The Dot (Bouncing Ball)
Genius.act	The Genius (Einstein)
Hoverbot.act	Hover Bot
Logo.act	Office Logo
Mnature.act	Mother Nature
Powerpup.act	Power Pup (The Power Dog)
Scribble.act	Scribble (The Paper Cat)
Will.act	Will (William Shakespeare)

IV-4   These next two registry entries control the location of the Office Assistant on the screen.

Hive: HKEY_LOCAL_MACHINE
Key: Software\Microsoft\Office\8.0\Common\Assistant
Value Name: AsstTop
Data Type: REG_DWORD
Value:

IV-5

Hive: HKEY_LOCAL_MACHINE
Key: Software\Microsoft\Office\8.0\Common\Assistant
Value Name: AsstLeft
Data Type: REG_DWORD
Value:

For each of these keys, the value is the location where the Assistant appears on the screen, given in pixels. Set these values to determine the location of the top left corner of the Assistant.

MICROSOFT OFFICE

IV-6   Would you like to stop the Assistant from moving around on you while you're working on something?

> **Hive:** HKEY_LOCAL_MACHINE
> **Key:** Software\Microsoft\Office\8.0\Common\Assistant
> **Value Name:** AsstMoveWhenInTheWay
> **Data Type:** REG_DWORD
> **Value:** 1

Set this value to 0 to keep the Assistant from moving.

IV-7   The noises the Office Assistant makes are fun, but after hearing them about a thousand times, you want it to just shut up. This registry entry lets you do just that.

> **Hive:** HKEY_LOCAL_MACHINE
> **Key:** Software\Microsoft\Office\8.0\Common\Assistant
> **Value Name:** AsstSounds
> **Data Type:** REG_DWORD
> **Value:** 1

Setting this value to 0 disables sound for the Assistant.

IV-8

> **Hive:** HKEY_CURRENT_USER
> **Key:** Software\Microsoft\Office\8.0\Common\Assistant
> **Value Name:** AsstState
> **Data Type:** REG_DWORD
> **Value:** 0x5 (5)

This value lets you control the size of the Assistant window. Valid values are

0x5	Large and Visible
0x9	Small and Visible
0x6	Large but Hidden
0xa	Small but Hidden

IV-9   Microsoft includes tip wizards with all the Office 97 products. These next seven registry entries let you enable or disable the wizards.

> **Hive:** HKEY_LOCAL_MACHINE
> **Key:** Software\Microsoft\Office\8.0\Common\Assistant
> **Value Name:** AsstShowTipOfDay
> **Data Type:** REG_DWORD
> **Value:** 1

Tired of seeing all the tips of the day? Setting this value to 0 disables these tips.

`IV-10`

Hive: HKEY_LOCAL_MACHINE
Key: Software\Microsoft\Office\8.0\Common\Assistant
Value Name: AsstFeatureTips
Data Type: REG_DWORD
Value: 1

Setting this value to 1 shows tips for features you may not know about and suggests better ways to use the features you do know about.

`IV-11`

Hive: HKEY_LOCAL_MACHINE
Key: Software\Microsoft\Office\8.0\Common\Assistant
Value Name: AsstKeyboardShortcutTips
Data Type: REG_DWORD
Value: 1

Setting this value to 1 makes the Office Assistant show you keyboard shortcuts for functions that take complicated mouse and menu commands to accomplish.

`IV-12`

Hive: HKEY_LOCAL_MACHINE
Key: Software\Microsoft\Office\8.0\Common\Assistant
Value Name: AsstMouseTips
Data Type: REG_DWORD
Value: 1

Setting this value to 1 makes the Office Assistant watch your mouse commands and show you tips for using your mouse more effectively.

`IV-13`

Hive: HKEY_LOCAL_MACHINE
Key: Software\Microsoft\Office\8.0\Common\Assistant
Value Name: AsstAssistWithHelp
Data Type: REG_DWORD
Value: 1

Setting this value to 1 shows the Office Assistant when you press the F1 key in any Microsoft Office application. Setting this value to 0 makes the Help function appear instead of the Office Assistant. Note: In some areas, Help appears when you press the F1 key regardless of this setting.

MICROSOFT OFFICE

IV-14

       Hive: HKEY_LOCAL_MACHINE
       Key: Software\Microsoft\Office\8.0\Common\Assistant
Value Name: AsstAssistWithAlerts
  Data Type: REG_DWORD
      Value: 1

Setting this value to 1 enables the Office Assistant to show you help messages.

IV-15

       Hive: HKEY_LOCAL_MACHINE
       Key: Software\Microsoft\Office\8.0\Common\Assistant
Value Name: AsstGuessHelp
  Data Type: REG_DWORD
      Value: 1

Setting this value to 1 enables context-sensitive help. Set this value to 0 if you do not want help topics to appear unless you specifically ask for help.

IV-16

       Hive: HKEY_LOCAL_MACHINE
       Key: Software\Microsoft\Office\8.0\Common\Assistant
Value Name: AsstOnlyHighPriorityTips
  Data Type: REG_DWORD
      Value: 1

Setting this value to 1 shows you only the tips that are important, such as those that alert you to timesaving features. This feature is great for moving from a beginner to an advanced user.

IV-17

       Hive: HKEY_LOCAL_MACHINE
       Key: Software\Microsoft\Office\8.0\Common\Assistant
Value Name: AsstOfficeWizards
  Data Type: REG_DWORD
      Value: 1

Setting this value to 1 enables the Office Assistant to provide help with most of the wizards in Microsoft Office applications.

MICROSOFT EXCEL 8.0/97

The following registry keys control the various options that are available within Microsoft Excel 97. Note that to change any of these options, you must exit Excel, change the registry key, then restart Excel.

IV-18

Hive: HKEY_CURRENT_USER
Key: Software\Microsoft\Office\8.0\Excel\Microsoft Excel
Value Name: DefaultPath
Data Type: REG_SZ
Value: D:\My Documents

This value sets the default storage location and search path for documents that you create or use in Microsoft Excel 97. This value overrides the path set in the HKEY_CURRENT_USER\Software\Microsoft\Windows\CurrentVersion\Explorer \User Shell Folders\Personal registry key.

IV-19

Hive: HKEY_CURRENT_USER
Key: Software\Microsoft\Shared Tools\Outlook\Journaling\ Microsoft Excel
Value Name: Enabled
Data Type: REG_DWORD
Value: 0x1

This value controls the Journaling feature in Microsoft Outlook and tracks when and how long you work with any Microsoft Excel Documents.

IV-20

Hive: HKEY_CURRENT_USER
Key: Software\Microsoft\Office\8.0\Excel\Microsoft Excel
Value Name: Maximized
Data Type: REG_DWORD
Value: 0x3

This value controls how Excel displays its window and workbook window when starting up. Note that Excel overwrites this value with its current settings when it exits. You have the following options for this value:

3   Excel and Workbook window maximized
2   Workbook window maximized
1   Excel maximized, Workbook window not maximized
0   Nothing maximized

IV-21

          Hive: HKEY_CURRENT_USER
           Key: Software\Microsoft\Office\8.0\Excel\Microsoft Excel
Value Name: Pos
  Data Type: REG_SZ
       Value: left, top, right, bottom

This value tells Excel how big to make its window and the position of the Top, Left, Right and Bottom corners of its window. An example of a valid value is 66,66,600,411

IV-22

          Hive: HKEY_CURRENT_USER
           Key: Software\Microsoft\Office\8.0\Excel\Microsoft Excel
Value Name: Default Chart
  Data Type: REG_SZ
       Value: <type:charttype, subtype>

This value sets Excel's default chart, which is a two-dimensional column chart. The type can be Standard, Built-in, or User-defined; for the charttype variable, select one of the charts listed in the Chart Type menu on the Chart/Chart Type dialog box. Similarly, for the subtype variable, choose one of the Chart subtypes found in the same dialog box. The default value is Standard:1,1. Note that user-defined chart formats are stored in a file called Xlusrgal.xls, which is located in the Program Files\Microsoft Office\Office folder.

IV-23

          Hive: HKEY_CURRENT_USER
           Key: Software\Microsoft\Office\8.0\Excel\Microsoft Excel
Value Name: DefSheets
  Data Type: REG_DWORD
       Value: 0x3

This value tells Excel how many worksheets to create in a new workbook. If you set this to 1, a new workbook contains only one worksheet.

IV-24

Hive: HKEY_CURRENT_USER
Key: Software\Microsoft\Office\8.0\Excel\Microsoft Excel
Value Name: MoveEnterDir
Data Type: REG_DWORD
Value: 0x1

If the "Move selection after Enter" function is enabled, this value controls the direction the selection cursor moves after you press Enter in the current cell. Valid values are

0   Down
1   Right
2   Up
3   Left

IV-25

Hive: HKEY_CURRENT_USER
Key: Software\Microsoft\Office\8.0\Excel\Microsoft Excel
Value Name: DefFileMRU
Data Type: REG_DWORD
Value: 0x4

This value controls the number of most recently used files to display under the File Menu.

IV-26

Hive: HKEY_CURRENT_USER
Key: Software\Microsoft\Office\8.0\Excel\Microsoft Excel
Value Name: Font
Data Type: REG_SZ
Value: Arial,10

This value specifics the default font and size to use for new worksheets. It also controls the default font used for the Normal style and for the row and column headings.

IV-27

Hive: HKEY_CURRENT_USER
Key: Software\Microsoft\Office\8.0\Excel\Microsoft Excel
Value Name: MenuKey
Data Type: REG_DWORD
Value: 47

This value specifies the key to use to activate Excel menus or Help functions; normally this value is a forward slash (/), which is the menu key used for Lotus 1-2-3. This is the value of the key in ASCII.

IV-28
Hive: HKEY_CURRENT_USER
Key: Software\Microsoft\Office\8.0\Excel\Microsoft Excel
Value Name: Randomize
Data Type: REG_DWORD
Value: 1

This value causes Microsoft Excel to generate a unique random number each time you use the RAND function.

IV-29 The next two registry keys control where Excel's dialog boxes appear on the screen. Excel updates these values when it closes.
Hive: HKEY_CURRENT_USER
Key: Software\Microsoft\Office\8.0\Excel\Microsoft Excel
Value Name: StickyPtX
Data Type: REG_DWORD
Value: 479

IV-30
Hive: HKEY_CURRENT_USER
Key: Software\Microsoft\Office\8.0\Excel\Microsoft Excel
Value Name: StickyPtY
Data Type: REG_DWORD
Value: 241

IV-31
Hive: HKEY_CURRENT_USER
Key: Software\Microsoft\Office\8.0\Excel\Microsoft Excel
Value Name: SortCaseSensitive
Data Type: REG_DWORD
Value: 0x0

This value controls the default Case Sensitive setting for the sorting algorithm that Microsoft Excel uses.

IV-32
Hive: HKEY_CURRENT_USER
Key: Software\Microsoft\Office\8.0\Excel\Microsoft Excel
Value Name: CustomSortOrder
Data Type: REG_DWORD
Value: 0x0

This value controls the default setting of the First key sort order, which appears under the Sort/Options dialog box.

IV-33

Hive: HKEY_CURRENT_USER
Key: Software\Microsoft\Office\8.0\Excel\Microsoft Excel
Value Name: AutoFormat
Data Type: REG_DWORD
Value: 0x2

This value is the default AutoFormat choice that appears under the AutoFormat dialog box. The value specifies an index number that points to a Table Format.

IV-34

Hive: HKEY_CURRENT_USER
Key: Software\Microsoft\Office\8.0\Excel\Microsoft Excel
Value Name: AutoFormat Options
Data Type: REG_DWORD
Value: 0x3f (63)

This value controls the format options specified in the AutoFormat registry key; the options correspond to the attributes in the AutoFormat dialog box. The available options are

  1 Number
  2 Font
  4 Alignment
  8 Border
 16 Patterns
 32 Width/Height

Simply add the values of the options you want. The final value is their sum. For example, if you wanted just the Border and Font options, add 8 and 2 for a value of 10.

IV-35

Hive: HKEY_CURRENT_USER
Key: Software\Microsoft\Office\8.0\Excel\Recent File List
Value Name: File1 or File2 or File3, etc.
Data Type: REG_SZ
Value: <last used file>

These values show the most recently used files that appear on the bottom of the File menu.

IV-36

> **Hive:** HKEY_CURRENT_USER
> **Key:** Software\Microsoft\Office\8.0\Excel\Microsoft Excel
> **Value Name:** Basics
> **Data Type:** REG_DWORD
> **Value:** 1

If this value is set to 0, Microsoft Excel starts up with the Office Assistant, which displays a menu that lets you see key information. After you click "Start using Microsoft Excel," Excel sets this value to 1, thereby disabling this function. If you want to go back and learn about the new features, set this value to 0.

IV-37

> **Hive:** HKEY_CURRENT_USER
> **Key:** Software\Microsoft\Office\8.0\Excel\Microsoft Excel
> **Value Name:** AddIn Path
> **Data Type:** REG_SZ
> **Value:** <paths of add-on programs>

In this value, you tell Excel the directories to search in for add-on programs and tools. Separate multiple paths with semicolons (;).

IV-38

> **Hive:** HKEY_CURRENT_USER
> **Key:** Software\Microsoft\Office\8.0\Excel\Microsoft Excel
> **Value Name:** AltStartup
> **Data Type:** REG_SZ
> **Value:** <path of alternate startup folder>

This value specifies the location of the alternate startup folder. Microsoft Excel automatically loads files from this directory after loading files from the Xlstart folder.

IV-39

> **Hive:** HKEY_CURRENT_USER
> **Key:** Software\Microsoft\Office\8.0\Excel\Microsoft Excel
> **Value Name:** 3dDialogs
> **Data Type:** REG_DWORD
> **Value:** 0x1

This value tells Microsoft Excel to use 3-D dialog boxes. If you prefer the look of regular dialog boxes, set this value to 0.

IV-40

Hive: HKEY_CURRENT_USER
Key: Software\Microsoft\Office\8.0\Excel\Microsoft Excel
Value Name: AutoCalculate
Data Type: REG_DWORD
Value: <index value>

This value sets the AutoCalculation function. Your options are

0	Count Nums
4	Sum
5	Average
6	Min
7	Max
169	Count

IV-41

Hive: HKEY_CURRENT_USER
Key: Software\Microsoft\Office\8.0\Excel\Microsoft Excel
Value Name: User
Data Type: REG_SZ
Value: <user name>

This value is the user name that Microsoft Excel attaches to Workbooks.

IV-42

Hive: HKEY_CURRENT_USER
Key: Software\Microsoft\Office\8.0\Excel\Microsoft Excel
Value Name: CfDDELink
Data Type: REG_SZ
Value: 1

If this value is set to 1, Microsoft Excel remembers the last clipboard format used for a successful DDE operation. Setting this option helps reduce the time required for future DDE operations.

MICROSOFT OFFICE

IV-43 Have you ever run across this message: "Microsoft Excel was unable to save this file because you do not have rename or delete privileges on the file server where you tried to save it. A temporary file was created on the server. You can re-open this temporary file, and save it to another drive." Great! Now what? Try this registry entry to solve your problem.

> **Hive:** HKEY_LOCAL_MACHINE
> **Key:** SYSTEM\CurrentControlSet\LANMAN\Server\Parameters

Add the following value under the Parameters key:

> **Value Name:** CachedOpenLimit
> **Data Type:** REG_DWORD
> **Value:** 0

Reboot your machine for these changes to take effect.

MICROSOFT WORD 8.0/97

The following registry keys control the various options that are available in Microsoft Word 97. To change any of these options, you must exit Word, change the registry key, then restart Microsoft Word.

IV-44 If your Word is crashing or you're getting lots of Dr. Watson dialog boxes while you are using Word, try exiting Word and deleting the next two keys. Microsoft Word rebuilds them based on the information stored under the HKEY_LOCAL_MACHINE\Software\Microsoft\Office\8.0\New User Settings\Word registry key.

> **Hive:** HKEY_CURRENT_USER
> **Key:** Software\Microsoft\Office\8.0\Word\Data
> **Value Name:** Toolbars
> **Data Type:** REG_BINARY
> **Value:** <lots of data, varies by user>

This values stores your personal toolbar settings for Microsoft Word.

IV-45

> **Hive:** HKEY_CURRENT_USER
> **Key:** Software\Microsoft\Office\8.0\Word\Data
> **Value Name:** Settings
> **Data Type:** REG_BINARY
> **Value:** <lots of data, varies by user>

This is where your personal settings for Microsoft Word are stored.

IV-46   When using Word 97 to edit an HTML file, you are unceremoniously dumped with an error in Gdi.exe. To fix this problem, you need to have the Office 97 CD handy as well as Regedt32.exe.

> **Hive:** HKEY_CURRENT_USER
> **Key:** Software\Microsoft\Office\8.0\Word\Data

Delete the Settings value under the data key.

> **Value Name:** Settings
> **Data Type:** REG_BINARY
> **Value:** <binary value>

Exit Regedt32.exe. Run setup from your Office 97 CD and choose Reinstall/Update. After Office 97 finishes updating the file, reboot the machine and the problem should go away.

IV-47

> **Hive:** HKEY_CURRENT_USER
> **Key:** Software\Microsoft\Office\8.0\Word\Default Save
> **Value Name:** Default Format
> **Data Type:** REG_SZ
> **Value:**

Would you like Microsoft Word to save its documents in a format other than Word 97? Just modify this key to indicate the format that you want, and it automatically saves any new document to the chosen format. It also prompts you if you try saving your document in a different format than you specified via this key. Specify one of the following values for this key. Note that <blank> means you must leave the field blank.

<blank>	Word 8.0/97 (*.doc)
MSWord6Exp	Word 6.0/95 (*.doc)
WrdPrfctWin	Word Perfect 5.x for Windows (*.doc)
WrdPrfctDOS51	Word Perfect 5.1 for DOS (*.doc)
WrdPrfctDat	Word Perfect 5.1 or 5.2 Secondary File (*.doc)
WrdPrfctDOS50	Word Perfect 5.0 for DOS (*.doc)
WrdPrfctDat50	Word Perfect 5.0 Secondary File (*.doc)
HTML	HTML Document (*.html; *.htm; *.htx)
Text	Text Only (*.txt)
CRText	Text Only with Line Breaks (*.txt)
8Text	MS-DOS Text (*.txt)
8CRText	MS-DOS Text with Line Breaks (*.txt)
Unicode	Unicode Text (*.txt)
rtf	Rich Text Format (*.rtf)
Dot	Document Template (*.dot)

IV-48

> **Hive:** HKEY_LOCAL_MACHINE
> **Key:** Software\Microsoft\Office\8.0\Common\Default Save
> **Value Name:** Prompt Text
> **Data Type:** REG_SZ
> **Value:** "Other people may not have the latest version of Office, so if you plan to share this file, you should save it in the following format."

This value sets the text that the Assistant displays when you have Default Save set to something other than Word 97 and you use the "Save As" command under the File menu. If you want users to save their documents to a specific standard, you can type the string into this value.

IV-49

> **Hive:** HKEY_CURRENT_USER
> **Key:** Software\Microsoft\Office\8.0\Word\Options
> **Value Name:** EnableMacroVirusProtection
> **Data Type:** REG_SZ
> **Value:** 1 (default)

If this value is enabled, which is the default setting, it turns on a warning message that appears whenever you open a document that might contain macro viruses — documents with macros, customized toolbars, menus, or shortcuts. Set this value to 0 to disable this feature.

IV-50

> **Hive:** HKEY_CURRENT_USER
> **Key:** Software\Microsoft\Office\8.0\Word\Options
> **Value Name:** AutoSpell
> **Data Type:** REG_SZ
> **Value:** 1 (default)

This value controls the spelling checker in Word 97. Set this value to 0 to stop Word from checking your spelling while you are working on a document.

IV-51

> **Hive:** HKEY_CURRENT_USER
> **Key:** Software\Microsoft\Office\8.0\Word\Options
> **Value Name:** AutoGrammar
> **Data Type:** REG_SZ
> **Value:** 1

This value controls the grammar checker in Word 97. If you want to stop Word from checking your grammar while you are working on a document, set this value to 0.

IV-52

Hive: HKEY_CURRENT_USER
Key: Software\Microsoft\Office\8.0\Word\Options
Value Name: BackgroundSave
Data Type: REG_SZ
Value: 1

This value enables or disables background saving, which lets Word save your document in the background while you keep working. Setting this value to 0 disables background saving.

IV-53

Hive: HKEY_CURRENT_USER
Key: Software\Microsoft\Office\8.0\Word\Options
Value Name: BackgroundPrint
Data Type: REG_SZ
Value: 1 (default)

This value enables or disables background printing, which lets you print documents in the background and continue working. Setting this value to 0 disables background printing.

IV-54

Hive: HKEY_CURRENT_USER
Key: Software\Microsoft\Office\8.0\Word\Options
Value Name: NoEditTime
Data Type: REG_SZ
Value: 0

By default, Microsoft Word tracks the total editing time for a given document. This statistic appears on the File/Properties dialog box under the Statistics tab. When this value is 0, which is the default, Word tracks total editing time; setting it to 1 turns off this feature.

IV-55

Hive: HKEY_CURRENT_USER
Key: Software\Microsoft\Office\8.0\Word\Options
Value Name: StartWhatIsNew
Data Type: REG_SZ
Value: 0

If this value is set to 0, when Word starts up, Office Assistant gives you the options of learning what's new in Word 97, learning about the Office Assistant, or starting Word. After you choose to start Word, Word 97 sets this to 1, thereby disabling this function. If you bypassed your other options the first time and want to learn about the new features in Word 97, set this value to 0.

MICROSOFT OFFICE

IV-56

          Hive: HKEY_CURRENT_USER
          Key: Software\Microsoft\Office\8.0\Word\Options
Value Name: LiveScrolling
   Data Type: REG_SZ
       Value: 1

With this feature turned on, Word changes the display as you move one of the scrollboxes; with it turned off, Word waits until you let go of the mouse button to update the screen. Set the value to 1, the default value, to turn on the feature; set it to 0 to turn it off. Note that this value affects only the scrollboxes, not any of the other scrolling controls. Turning off this function can be very useful if you have a slow video card.

IV-57

          Hive: HKEY_CURRENT_USER
          Key: Software\Microsoft\Office\8.0\Word\Options
Value Name: PlainTextAutoFormat
   Data Type: REG_SZ
       Value: 1

This value turns on the AutoFormat feature for plain-text WordMail messages when you open them. This value affects only WordMail messages; it does not affect pasted text or other text files. Set the value to 1 to turn on AutoFormat; set it to 0 to turn off AutoFormat.

IV-58

          Hive: HKEY_CURRENT_USER
          Key: Software\Microsoft\Office\8.0\Word\Options
Value Name: UpdateDictionaryNumber
   Data Type: REG_SZ
       Value: 1

This value specifies the custom dictionary where the spelling checker adds words; the number corresponds to the number in the custom dictionary list. Find this list by going to the Spelling tab, clicking Options, and choosing Custom Dictionaries.

IV-59

          Hive: HKEY_CURRENT_USER
          Key: Software\Microsoft\Office\8.0\Word\Options
Value Name: WPHelp
   Data Type: REG_SZ
       Value: 0

This value tells Microsoft Word to use WordPerfect commands along with its own. Setting this value to 0 disables this feature; setting it to 1 turns on this feature.

IV-60

        Hive: HKEY_CURRENT_USER
         Key: Software\Microsoft\Office\8.0\Word\Options
Value Name: Doc-Extension
  Data Type: REG_SZ
      Value: <extension>

This value specifies the default extension added to document filenames; the default value is .doc. To use a different filename extension, change the value of this key to your preferred extension (you're not limited to three letters). Don't forget the leading period.

IV-61

        Hive: HKEY_CURRENT_USER
         Key: Software\Microsoft\Office\8.0\Word\Options
Value Name: Dot-Extension
  Data Type: REG_SZ
      Value: <extension>

This value sets the default extension added to Word template filenames; the default value is .dot. To use a different filename extension, change the value of this key to your preferred extension (you're not limited to three letters). Don't forget the leading period.

IV-62

        Hive: HKEY_CURRENT_USER
         Key: Software\Microsoft\Office\8.0\Word\Options
Value Name: Bak-Extension
  Data Type: REG_SZ
      Value: <extension>

If you choose, Word saves a previous version of a document as a backup copy every time you save a document; the default filename extension Word assigns is .bak. To change the extension, change the value of this key to your preferred extension (you're not limited to three letters). Don't forget the leading period.

IV-63

        Hive: HKEY_CURRENT_USER
         Key: Software\Microsoft\Office\8.0\Word\Options
Value Name: ProgramDir
  Data Type: REG_SZ
      Value: D:\Program Files\Microsoft Office\Office

This value sets the path to the Microsoft Word executable (Winword.exe) program. Other programs use this path to locate the Word executable and install ancillary programs Word uses.

MICROSOFT OFFICE

IV-64

> **Hive:** HKEY_CURRENT_USER
> **Key:** Software\Microsoft\Office\8.0\Word\Options
> **Value Name:** Doc-Path
> **Data Type:** REG_SZ
> **Value:** D:\My Documents

This value sets the default storage location and search path for documents that you create or use in Microsoft Word 97. This value overrides the value set in the registry key HKEY_CURRENT_USER\Software\Microsoft\Windows\CurrentVersion\Explorer\User Shell Folders\Personal.

IV-65

> **Hive:** HKEY_CURRENT_USER
> **Key:** Software\Microsoft\Office\8.0\Word\Options
> **Value Name:** Autosave-Path
> **Data Type:** REG_SZ
> **Value:** D:\My Documents\Autorecover

This value determines where Word stores documents, templates, and other items that you create in Word; it's also where Word looks for its AutoRecover files. Setting this value can be very useful if your system crashes while you are working on a document. If you don't set this value, which is the default setting, Word stores these files in your Temp folder.

   If your system has become unusable but you can still access the files, save them in this directory, then set up a new system and restore your files into to the directory you specify in this value. When you start Word, it AutoRecovers your documents.

IV-66

> **Hive:** HKEY_CURRENT_USER
> **Key:** Software\Microsoft\Office\8.0\Word\Options
> **Value Name:** Picture-Path
> **Data Type:** REG_SZ
> **Value:** D:\Program Files\Microsoft Office\Clipart

This value sets where Microsoft Word looks for pictures, such as clipart, when you select Insert/Pictures/From File. You may want to change this value to point to a common folder for your image files.

IV-67

> **Hive:** HKEY_CURRENT_USER
> **Key:** Software\Microsoft\Office\8.0\Word\Options
> **Value Name:** PicEditClas
> **Data Type:** REG_SZ
> **Value:** Word.Picture.8

This value specifies the object class name for the picture editor Word uses.

IV-68

> **Hive:** HKEY_CURRENT_USER
> **Key:** Software\Microsoft\Office\8.0\Word\Options
> **Value Name:** Tools-Path
> **Data Type:** REG_SZ
> **Value:** D:\Program Files\Microsoft Office\Office

This value specifies where Microsoft Word looks for tools (such as dictionaries).

IV-69

> **Hive:** HKEY_CURRENT_USER
> **Key:** Software\Microsoft\Office\8.0\Word\Options
> **Value Name:** Startup-Path
> **Data Type:** REG_SZ
> **Value:** D:\Program Files\Microsoft Office\Office\Startup

This value sets the Startup folder Word and any Word add-on products use.

IV-70

> **Hive:** HKEY_CURRENT_USER
> **Key:** Software\Microsoft\Office\8.0\Word\Options
> **Value Name:** WordMail-Path
> **Data Type:** REG_SZ
> **Value:** D:\Program Files\Microsoft Office\Office\
> WordMail\Favorites

This value sets the location for the document template files you need to use Word as an e-mail editor.

MICROSOFT OFFICE

IV-71   If Microsoft Word doesn't show up as one of your journaling options in Microsoft Outlook, you need to add the following key and values.

> **Hive:** HKEY_CURRENT_USER
>
> **Key:** Software\Microsoft\Shared Tools\Outlook\Journaling

Add the following key:

> **Key:** Microsoft Word

Next, add these five values:

> **Value Name:** Autojournaled
> **Data Type:** REG_DWORD
> **Value:** 0x1

> **Value Name:** Description
> **Data Type:** REG_SZ
> **Value:** Microsoft Word

> **Value Name:** Enabled
> **Data Type:** REG_DWORD
> **Value:** 0x1

> **Value Name:** Large Icon
> **Data Type:** REG_SZ
> **Value:** [16]

> **Value Name:** Small Icon
> **Data Type:** REG_SZ
> **Value:** [16]

You must change the values in both Autojournaled and Enabled for this change to take effect. A value of 1 turns on this feature; a value of 0 turns it off.

IV-72 You can do the same thing for Microsoft Access. Repeat the procedure but substitute Microsoft Access for the initial Key value and the Description value, as below:

> **Hive:** HKEY_CURRENT_USER
> **Key:** Software\Microsoft\Shared Tools\Outlook\Journaling

Add the following key:

> **Key:** Microsoft Access

> **Value Name:** Description
> **Data Type:** REG_SZ
> **Value:** Microsoft Access

Don't forget to add the three other values listed under Microsoft Word, above; their values don't change. As with Word, you must change the values in both Autojournaled and Enabled for this change to take effect. A value of 1 turns on this feature; a value of 0 turns it off.

IV-73

> **Hive:** HKEY_CURRENT_USER
> **Key:** Software\Microsoft\Office\8.0\Common\AutoCorrect
> **Value Name:** Path
> **Data Type:** REG_SZ
> **Value:** D:\WINNT\username.acl

This value sets Word's AutoCorrect (ACL) file. When you start up Word for the first time, it copies this value from the Mso97.acl file. To set up your own AutoCorrect file and have everyone use it, run Microsoft Word and add entries to the AutoCorrect list with the AutoCorrect command located under the Tools menu. Then exit Word and copy your AutoCorrect file over Mso97.acl or over the specific users' <username>.ACL file. You could also create a common file and point the users' AutoCorrect registry key to your common file.

IV-74

> **Hive:** HKEY_CURRENT_USER
> **Key:** Software\Microsoft\Office\8.0\Word\Options
> **Value Name:** BitmapMemory
> **Data Type:** REG_SZ
> **Value:** 1024

This value sets the maximum size, in K, of bitmap caching used for graphics. Increase this value for better graphics performance. The default cache size is 1,024K.

IV-75

> **Hive:** HKEY_CURRENT_USER
> **Key:** Software\Microsoft\Office\8.0\Word\Options
> **Value Name:** CacheSize
> **Data Type:** REG_SZ
> **Value:** 64

This value sets the maximum size, in K, of caching used for Word documents. Increase this value for better performance. The minimum and default cache size is 64K.

IV-76

> **Hive:** HKEY_CURRENT_USER
> **Key:** Software\Microsoft\Office\8.0\Word\Options
> **Value Name:** SlowShading
> **Data Type:** REG_SZ
> **Value:** Yes

Adding this line forces Word to use the Windows graphics device interface (GDI) to add shading instead of calling a printer escape code. When you select "Print TrueType As Graphics" in the printer driver dialog box, TrueType fonts print white-on-black shading. However, this method affects the way the shading looks and may slow down printing for documents that contain a lot of shading.

IV-77

> **Hive:** HKEY_CURRENT_USER
> **Key:** Software\Microsoft\Office\8.0\Word\Options
> **Value Name:** DraftFont
> **Data Type:** REG_SZ
> **Value:** 1

This value controls how Word displays documents. Using a draft font displays most character formatting as underlined and bold and displays graphics as empty boxes. To speed up screen display in documents with extensive formatting, enable draft font by setting this value to 1.

IV-78

> **Hive:** HKEY_CURRENT_USER
> **Key:** Software\Microsoft\Office\8.0\Word\Options
> **Value Name:** AskForPrinterPicture
> **Data Type:** REG_SZ
> **Value:** 0

This value controls how Microsoft Excel DDE results display in Word. A value of 0 sets the display to color; set the value to 1 to have it display in black and white.

IV-79

Hive: HKEY_CURRENT_USER
Key: Software\Microsoft\Office\8.0\Word\Options
Value Name: NetworkButtons
Data Type: REG_SZ
Value: <yes/no>

This value specifies whether to hide or show the Network button in dialog boxes such as Open, Save As, and Open Data Source. The default value is yes.

IV-80

Hive: HKEY_CURRENT_USER
Key: Software\Microsoft\Office\8.0\Word\Options
Value Name: MessageBeeps
Data Type: REG_SZ
Value: <yes/no>

This value determines whether the system beeps when Word displays a message box. The default value is yes.

IV-81

Hive: HKEY_CURRENT_USER
Key: Software\Microsoft\Office\8.0\Word\Options
Value Name: NoFontMRUList
Data Type: REG_SZ
Value: <yes/no>

This value specifies whether to hide the most recently used fonts on the Formatting toolbar Font list. The default setting is no.

IV-82

Hive: HKEY_LOCAL_MACHINE
Key: Software\Microsoft\Office\8.0\Common\Security
Value Name: DisablePwdCaching
Data Type: REG_ DWORD
Value: 0

This value controls whether passwords for password-protected documents in Office 97 applications are cached. A value of 0 disables password caching; a value of 1 enables password caching.

MICROSOFT OFFICE

IV-83

     Hive: HKEY_CURRENT_USER
     Key: Software\Microsoft\Windows\CurrentVersion\Explorer\
     User Shell Folders
Value Name: Personal
Data Type: REG_EXPAND_SZ
    Value: %USERPROFILE%\Personal

This value sets default storage location and search path for documents that you create or use in any of the Office 97 applications. The default is your Personal folder. Note that you can reset this value for each Office 97 application.

SOUNDS

If you want to add or change the sounds of events in the various Office 97 applications, you need to modify these entries. Three registry keys are associated with each sound: the Office 97 sound or event ID, the default sound file to play for that ID, and the currently configured sound file. Type everything in the Value field, including spaces.

IV-84

     Hive: HKEY_CURRENT_USER
     Key: AppEvents\EventLabels\Office97-NewItem
Value Name: <No Name>
Data Type: REG_SZ
    Value: New Item

     Key: AppEvents\Schemes\Apps\Office97\Office97-NewItem
Value Name: .Default
Data Type: REG_SZ
    Value: C:\WINNT\Media\Office97\NewItem.wav

Value Name: .Current
Data Type: REG_SZ
    Value: C:\WINNT\Media\Office97\NewItem.wav

You must provide a fully qualified path and file name to the wave file.

IV-85

Hive: HKEY_CURRENT_USER
Key: AppEvents\EventLabels\Office97-AddItemtoView
Value Name: <No Name>
Data Type: REG_SZ
Value: Add Item to View

Key: AppEvents\Schemes\Apps\Office97\Office97-AddItemtoView
Value Name: .Default
Data Type: REG_SZ
Value: C:\WINNT\Media\Office97\NewItem.wav

Value Name: .Current
Data Type: REG_SZ
Value: C:\WINNT\Media\Office97\NewItem.wav

You must provide a fully qualified path and file name to the wave file.

IV-86

Hive: HKEY_CURRENT_USER
Key: AppEvents\EventLabels\Office97-Alert
Value Name: <No Name>
Data Type: REG_SZ
Value: Alert

Key: AppEvents\Schemes\Apps\Office97\Office97-Alert
Value Name: .Default
Data Type: REG_SZ
Value: C:\WINNT\Media\Office97\Alert.wav

Value Name: .Current
Data Type: REG_SZ
Value: C:\WINNT\Media\Office97\Alert.wav

This value sets the sound that Office 97 applications use when alerting you to important events. You will also hear this when closing the Find window from within Word. You must provide a fully qualified path and file name to the wave file.

MICROSOFT OFFICE

IV-87

Hive: HKEY_CURRENT_USER
Key: AppEvents\EventLabels\Office97-Send
Value Name: \<No Name\>
Data Type: REG_SZ
Value: Send

Key: AppEvents\Schemes\Apps\Office97\Office97-Send
Value Name: .Default
Data Type: REG_SZ
Value: C:\WINNT\Media\Office97\Send.wav

Value Name: .Current
Data Type: REG_SZ
Value: C:\WINNT\Media\Office97\Send.wav

This value sets the sound you hear when you send something, such an e-mail message. You must provide a fully qualified path and file name to the wave file.

IV-88

Hive: HKEY_CURRENT_USER
Key: AppEvents\EventLabels\Office97-Sort
Value Name: \<No Name\>
Data Type: REG_SZ
Value: Sort

Key: AppEvents\Schemes\Apps\Office97\Office97-Sort
Value Name: .Default
Data Type: REG_SZ
Value: C:\WINNT\Media\Office97\Sort.wav

Value Name: .Current
Data Type: REG_SZ
Value: C:\WINNT\Media\Office97\Sort.wav

This value sets the sound played when one of the Office 97 applications is sorting or resorting anything, such as a spreadsheet. You must provide a fully qualified path and file name to the wave file.

IV-89

Hive: HKEY_CURRENT_USER
Key: AppEvents\EventLabels\Office97-AutoCorrect
Value Name: <No Name>
Data Type: REG_SZ
Value: AutoCorrect

Key: AppEvents\Schemes\Apps\Office97\Office97-AutoCorrect
Value Name: .Default
Data Type: REG_SZ
Value: C:\WINNT\Media\Office97\AutoCorr.wav

Value Name: .Current
Data Type: REG_SZ
Value: C:\WINNT\Media\Office97\AutoCorr.wav

This value sets the sound that Office Applications (primarily Word) use when the AutoCorrect feature becomes active and AutoCorrects something. You must provide a fully qualified path and file name to the wave file.

IV-90

Hive: HKEY_CURRENT_USER
Key: AppEvents\EventLabels\Office97-BestFit
Value Name: <No Name>
Data Type: REG_SZ
Value: Best Fit

Key: AppEvents\Schemes\Apps\Office97\Office97-BestFit
Value Name: .Default
Data Type: REG_SZ
Value: C:\WINNT\Media\Office97\BestFit.wav

Value Name: .Current
Data Type: REG_SZ
Value: C:\WINNT\Media\Office97\BestFit.wav

This value sets the sound Office 97 applications play when you select the "Best Fit" feature. For example, you might select a column header and select the "Best Fit" option to make the column fit the data it's displaying. You must provide a fully qualified path and file name to the wave file.

MICROSOFT OFFICE

IV-91

Hive: HKEY_CURRENT_USER
Key: AppEvents\EventLabels\Office97-ProcessComplete
Value Name: <No Name>
Data Type: REG_SZ
Value: Process Complete

Key: AppEvents\Schemes\Apps\Office97\Office97-ProcessComplete
Value Name: .Default
Data Type: REG_SZ
Value: C:\WINNT\Media\Office97\ProcessComplete.wav

Value Name: .Current
Data Type: REG_SZ
Value: C:\WINNT\Media\Office97\ProcessComplete.wav

This value sets the sound Office 97 applications play when they are done performing some action, such as saving a document. You must provide a fully qualified path and file name to the wave file.

IV-92

Hive: HKEY_CURRENT_USER
Key: AppEvents\EventLabels\Office97-Undo
Value Name: <No Name>
Data Type: REG_SZ
Value: Undo

Key: AppEvents\Schemes\Apps\Office97\Office97-Undo
Value Name: .Default
Data Type: REG_SZ
Value: C:\WINNT\Media\Office97\Undo.wav

Value Name: .Current
Data Type: REG_SZ
Value: C:\WINNT\Media\Office97\Undo.wav

This value sets the sound played when you undo something in one of the Office 97 applications. You must provide a fully qualified path and file name to the wave file.

IV-93

Hive: HKEY_CURRENT_USER
Key: AppEvents\EventLabels\Office97-Redo
Value Name: <No Name>
Data Type: REG_SZ
Value: Redo

Key: AppEvents\Schemes\Apps\Office97\Office97-Redo
Value Name: .Default
Data Type: REG_SZ
Value: C:\WINNT\Media\Office97\Redo.wav

Value Name: .Current
Data Type: REG_SZ
Value: C:\WINNT\Media\Office97\Redo.wav

This value sets the sound played when you redo an action that you have undone. You must provide a fully qualified path and file name to the wave file.

IV-94

Hive: HKEY_CURRENT_USER
Key: AppEvents\EventLabels\Office97-Reminder
Value Name: <No Name>
Data Type: REG_SZ
Value: Reminder

Key: AppEvents\Schemes\Apps\Office97\Office97-Reminder
Value Name: .Default
Data Type: REG_SZ
Value: C:\WINNT\Media\Office97\Reminder.wav

Value Name: .Current
Data Type: REG_SZ
Value: C:\WINNT\Media\Office97\Reminder.wav

This value sets the sound played when an Office 97 application announces an appointment. You must provide a fully qualified path and file name to the wave file.

MICROSOFT OFFICE

IV-95

      Hive: HKEY_CURRENT_USER
      Key: AppEvents\EventLabels\Office97-Clear
Value Name: <No Name>
  Data Type: REG_SZ
     Value: Clear

      Key: AppEvents\Schemes\Apps\Office97\Office97-Clear
Value Name: .Default
  Data Type: REG_SZ
     Value: C:\WINNT\Media\Office97\Clear.wav

Value Name: .Current
  Data Type: REG_SZ
     Value: C:\WINNT\Media\Office97\Clear.wav

This value sets the sound played when you delete selected text in Microsoft
Word or clear out a cell or a range of cells in a Microsoft Excel spreadsheet.
You must provide a fully qualified path and file name to the wave file.

IV-96

      Hive: HKEY_CURRENT_USER
      Key: AppEvents\EventLabels\Office97-Cut&Clear
Value Name: <No Name>
  Data Type: REG_SZ
     Value: Cut & Clear

      Key: AppEvents\Schemes\Apps\Office97\Office97-Cut&Clear
Value Name: .Default
  Data Type: REG_SZ
     Value: C:\WINNT\Media\Office97\Cut.wav

Value Name: .Current
  Data Type: REG_SZ
     Value: C:\WINNT\Media\Office97\Cut.wav

You must provide a fully qualified path and file name to the Wave file.

IV-97

Hive: HKEY_CURRENT_USER
Key: AppEvents\EventLabels\Office97-Delete
Value Name: <No Name>
Data Type: REG_SZ
Value: Delete

Key: AppEvents\Schemes\Apps\Office97\Office97-Delete
Value Name: .Default
Data Type: REG_SZ
Value: C:\WINNT\Media\Office97\Delete.wav

Value Name: .Current
Data Type: REG_SZ
Value: C:\WINNT\Media\Office97\Delete.wav

This value sets the sound Microsoft Office 97 uses when you delete something. You must provide a fully qualified path and file name to the wave file.

IV-98

Hive: HKEY_CURRENT_USER
Key: AppEvents\EventLabels\Office97-DeleteRow
Value Name: <No Name>
Data Type: REG_SZ
Value: Delete Row

Key: AppEvents\Schemes\Apps\Office97\Office97-DeleteRow
Value Name: .Default
Data Type: REG_SZ
Value: C:\WINNT\Media\Office97\Delete.wav

Value Name: .Current
Data Type: REG_SZ
Value: C:\WINNT\Media\Office97\Delete.wav

This value sets the sound played when you delete a row from something; this sound is used most often within Excel. You must provide a fully qualified path and file name to the wave file.

MICROSOFT OFFICE

IV-99

> **Hive:** HKEY_CURRENT_USER
> **Key:** AppEvents\EventLabels\Office97-InsertRow
> **Value Name:** <No Name>
> **Data Type:** REG_SZ
> **Value:** Insert Row

> **Key:** AppEvents\Schemes\Apps\Office97\Office97-InsertRow
> **Value Name:** .Default
> **Data Type:** REG_SZ
> **Value:** C:\WINNT\Media\Office97\InsertRow.wav

> **Value Name:** .Current
> **Data Type:** REG_SZ
> **Value:** C:\WINNT\Media\Office97\InsertRow.wav

This value sets the sound played when you insert a row or column; it is used most often in Excel. You must provide a fully qualified path and file name to the wave file.

IV-100

> **Hive:** HKEY_CURRENT_USER
> **Key:** AppEvents\EventLabels\Office97-DialogCancel
> **Value Name:** <No Name>
> **Data Type:** REG_SZ
> **Value:** Dialog Cancel

> **Key:** AppEvents\Schemes\Apps\Office97\Office97-DialogCancel
> **Value Name:** .Default
> **Data Type:** REG_SZ
> **Value:** C:\WINNT\Media\Office97\Dialog.wav

> **Value Name:** .Current
> **Data Type:** REG_SZ
> **Value:** C:\WINNT\Media\Office97\Dialog.wav

This value sets the sound played when you click the cancel button on an Office 97 dialog box. You must provide a fully qualified path and file name to the wave file.

IV-101

Hive: HKEY_CURRENT_USER
Key: AppEvents\EventLabels\Office97-DialogOk
Value Name: <No Name>
Data Type: REG_SZ
Value: Dialog Ok

Key: AppEvents\Schemes\Apps\Office97\Office97-DialogOk
Value Name: .Default
Data Type: REG_SZ
Value: C:\WINNT\Media\Office97\Dialog.wav

Value Name: .Current
Data Type: REG_SZ
Value: C:\WINNT\Media\Office97\Dialog.wav

This value sets the sound played when you click the OK button in an Office 97 dialog box. You must provide a fully qualified path and file name to the wave file.

IV-102

Hive: HKEY_CURRENT_USER
Key: AppEvents\EventLabels\Office97-Drag
Value Name: <No Name>
Data Type: REG_SZ
Value: Drag

Key: AppEvents\Schemes\Apps\Office97\Office97-Drag
Value Name: .Default
Data Type: REG_SZ
Value: C:\WINNT\Media\Office97\Drag.wav

Value Name: .Current
Data Type: REG_SZ
Value: C:\WINNT\Media\Office97\Drag.wav

This value sets the sound played when you start to drag something in an Office 97 application. For example, when you select text in a Word document and drag it someplace, you'll hear this sound. You must provide a fully qualified path and file name to the wave file.

MICROSOFT OFFICE

IV-103

Hive: HKEY_CURRENT_USER
Key: AppEvents\EventLabels\Office97-Drop
Value Name: <No Name>
Data Type: REG_SZ
Value: Drop

Key: AppEvents\Schemes\Apps\Office97\Office97-Drop
Value Name: .Default
Data Type: REG_SZ
Value: C:\WINNT\Media\Office97\Drop.wav

Value Name: .Current
Data Type: REG_SZ
Value: C:\WINNT\Media\Office97\Drop.wav

This value sets the sound played when you drop something, such as text or a graphic, into an Office 97 application. You must provide a fully qualified path and file name to the wave file.

IV-104

Hive: HKEY_CURRENT_USER
Key: AppEvents\EventLabels\Office97-Expand/Collapse
Value Name: <No Name>
Data Type: REG_SZ
Value: Expand/Collapse

Key: AppEvents\Schemes\Apps\Office97\Office97-Expand/Collapse
Value Name: .Default
Data Type: REG_SZ
Value: C:\WINNT\Media\Office97\Sort.wav

Value Name: .Current
Data Type: REG_SZ
Value: C:\WINNT\Media\Office97\Sort.wav

This value sets the sound played when you expand or collapse a directory in Outlook. You must provide a fully qualified path and file name to the wave file.

IV-105

Hive: HKEY_CURRENT_USER
Key: AppEvents\EventLabels\Office97-FolderSwitch
Value Name: <No Name>
Data Type: REG_SZ
Value: Folder Switch

Key: AppEvents\Schemes\Apps\Office97\Office97-FolderSwitch
Value Name: .Default
Data Type: REG_SZ
Value: C:\WINNT\Media\Office97\Folder.wav

Value Name: .Current
Data Type: REG_SZ
Value: C:\WINNT\Media\Office97\Folder.wav

This value sets the sound played when you switch folders in Outlook. You must provide a fully qualified path and file name to the wave file.

IV-106

Hive: HKEY_CURRENT_USER
Key: AppEvents\EventLabels\Office97-GroupScopeSwitch
Value Name: <No Name>
Data Type: REG_SZ
Value: Group Scope Switch

Key: AppEvents\Schemes\Apps\Office97\
Office97-GroupScopeSwitch
Value Name: .Default
Data Type: REG_SZ
Value: C:\WINNT\Media\Office97\GroupScopeSwitch.wav

Value Name: .Current
Data Type: REG_SZ
Value: C:\WINNT\Media\Office97\GroupScopeSwitch.wav

This value sets is the sound played when you switch groups on the Outlook menu. You must provide a fully qualified path and file name to the wave file.

MICROSOFT OFFICE

`IV-107`

Hive: HKEY_CURRENT_USER
Key: AppEvents\EventLabels\Office97-GroupSwitch
Value Name: <No Name>
Data Type: REG_SZ
Value: Group Switch

Key: AppEvents\Schemes\Apps\Office97\Office97-GroupSwitch
Value Name: .Default
Data Type: REG_SZ
Value: C:\WINNT\Media\Office97\GroupSwitch.wav

Value Name: .Current
Data Type: REG_SZ
Value: C:\WINNT\Media\Office97\GroupSwitch.wav

You must provide a fully qualified path and file name to the wave file.

`IV-108`

Hive: HKEY_CURRENT_USER
Key: AppEvents\EventLabels\Office97-ModeSwitch
Value Name: <No Name>
Data Type: REG_SZ
Value: Mode Switch

Key: AppEvents\Schemes\Apps\Office97\Office97-ModeSwitch
Value Name: .Default
Data Type: REG_SZ
Value: C:\WINNT\Media\Office97\ModeSwitch.wav

Value Name: .Current
Data Type: REG_SZ
Value: C:\WINNT\Media\Office97\ModeSwitch.wav

This value sets the sound played when you preview a document you're printing and you change from Actual Size to Overview mode or when you change the icon size on the outlook bar. You must provide a fully qualified path and file name to the wave file.

IV-109

Hive: HKEY_CURRENT_USER
Key: AppEvents\EventLabels\Office97-ViewSwitch
Value Name: <No Name>
Data Type: REG_SZ
Value: View Switch

Key: AppEvents\Schemes\Apps\Office97\Office97-ViewSwitch
Value Name: .Default
Data Type: REG_SZ
Value: C:\WINNT\Media\Office97\ViewSwitch.wav

Value Name: .Current
Data Type: REG_SZ
Value: C:\WINNT\Media\Office97\ViewSwitch.wav

This value sets the sound played when you switch views of data. For example, if you change the message view in Outlook, you hear this sound. You must provide a fully qualified path and file name to the wave file.

IV-110

Hive: HKEY_CURRENT_USER
Key: AppEvents\EventLabels\Office97-ZoomIn
Value Name: <No Name>
Data Type: REG_SZ
Value: Zoom In

Key: AppEvents\Schemes\Apps\Office97\Office97-ZoomIn
Value Name: .Default
Data Type: REG_SZ
Value: C:\WINNT\Media\Office97\ZoomIn.wav

Value Name: .Current
Data Type: REG_SZ
Value: C:\WINNT\Media\Office97\ZoomIn.wav

This value sets the sound an Office 97 application plays when you zoom in on a spreadsheet or document (note that Word doesn't use this sound). You must provide a fully qualified path and file name to the wave file.

MICROSOFT OFFICE

IV-111

      Hive: HKEY_CURRENT_USER
       Key: AppEvents\EventLabels\Office97-ZoomOut
Value Name: <No Name>
  Data Type: REG_SZ
     Value: Zoom Out

       Key: AppEvents\Schemes\Apps\Office97\Office97-ZoomOut
Value Name: .Default
  Data Type: REG_SZ
     Value: C:\WINNT\Media\Office97\ZoomOut.wav

Value Name: .Current
  Data Type: REG_SZ
     Value: C:\WINNT\Media\Office97\ZoomOut.wav

This value sets the sound an Office 97 application plays when you zoom out on a spreadsheet or document (note that Word doesn't use this sound). You must provide a fully qualified path and file name to the wave file.

IV-112 The following registry keys control the sounds that Microsoft Office 97 makes when using the scrollbars. Note that some Office applications don't use these sounds.

      Hive: HKEY_CURRENT_USER
       Key: AppEvents\EventLabels\Office97-PlyScroll
Value Name: <No Name>
  Data Type: REG_SZ
     Value: Ply Scroll

       Key: AppEvents\Schemes\Apps\Office97\Office97-PlyScroll
Value Name: .Default
  Data Type: REG_SZ
     Value: C:\WINNT\Media\Office97\PlyScroll.wav

Value Name: .Current
  Data Type: REG_SZ
     Value: C:\WINNT\Media\Office97\PlyScroll.wav

You must provide a fully qualified path and file name to the wave file.

IV-113

          Hive: HKEY_CURRENT_USER
           Key: AppEvents\EventLabels\Office97-PlySelect
  Value Name: <No Name>
    Data Type: REG_SZ
       Value: Ply Select

           Key: AppEvents\Schemes\Apps\Office97\Office97-PlySelect
  Value Name: .Default
    Data Type: REG_SZ
       Value: C:\WINNT\Media\Office97\PlySelect.wav

  Value Name: .Current
    Data Type: REG_SZ
       Value: C:\WINNT\Media\Office97\PlySelect.wav

This value sets the sound played when you select a tab on the bottom of a workbook to choose a different spreadsheet. You must provide a fully qualified path and file name to the wave file.

IV-114

          Hive: HKEY_CURRENT_USER
           Key: AppEvents\EventLabels\Office97-ScrollArrow
  Value Name: <No Name>
    Data Type: REG_SZ
       Value: Scroll Arrow

           Key: AppEvents\Schemes\Apps\Office97\Office97-ScrollArrow
  Value Name: .Default
    Data Type: REG_SZ
       Value: C:\WINNT\Media\Office97\ScrollArrow.wav

  Value Name: .Current
    Data Type: REG_SZ
       Value: C:\WINNT\Media\Office97\ScrollArrow.wav

This value sets the sound played when you click one of the scroll bar arrows in most Office 97 applications except Word. You must provide a fully qualified path and file name to the wave file.

`IV-115`

Hive: HKEY_CURRENT_USER
Key: AppEvents\EventLabels\Office97-ScrollBar
Value Name: <No Name>
Data Type: REG_SZ
Value: Scroll Bar

Key: AppEvents\Schemes\Apps\Office97\Office97-ScrollBar
Value Name: .Default
Data Type: REG_SZ
Value: C:\WINNT\Media\Office97\ScrollBar.wav

Value Name: .Current
Data Type: REG_SZ
Value: C:\WINNT\Media\Office97\ScrollBar.wav

This value sets the sound played when you click a scrollbar in most Office 97 applications except Word. You must provide a fully qualified path and file name to the wave file.

`IV-116`

Hive: HKEY_CURRENT_USER
Key: AppEvents\EventLabels\Office97-ScrollThumb
Value Name: <No Name>
Data Type: REG_SZ
Value: Scroll Thumb

Key: AppEvents\Schemes\Apps\Office97\Office97-ScrollThumb
Value Name: .Default
Data Type: REG_SZ
Value: C:\WINNT\Media\Office97\ScrollThumb.wav

Value Name: .Current
Data Type: REG_SZ
Value: C:\WINNT\Media\Office97\ScrollThumb.wav

This value sets the sound played when you click the thumb control on a scroll bar in most Office 97 applications except Word. You must provide a fully qualified path and file name to the wave file.

IV-117 The following registry keys control the sounds of various toolbar actions.

> **Hive:** HKEY_CURRENT_USER
> **Key:** AppEvents\EventLabels\Office97-ToolbarClick
> **Value Name:** <No Name>
> **Data Type:** REG_SZ
> **Value:** Toolbar Click

> **Key:** AppEvents\Schemes\Apps\Office97\Office97-ToolbarClick
> **Value Name:** .Default
> **Data Type:** REG_SZ
> **Value:** C:\WINNT\Media\Office97\Click.wav

> **Value Name:** .Current
> **Data Type:** REG_SZ
> **Value:** C:\WINNT\Media\Office97\Click.wav

This value sets the sound played when you click one of the toolbar buttons. You must provide a fully qualified path and file name to the wave file.

IV-118

> **Hive:** HKEY_CURRENT_USER
> **Key:** AppEvents\EventLabels\Office97-ToolbarClose
> **Value Name:** <No Name>
> **Data Type:** REG_SZ
> **Value:** Toolbar Close

> **Key:** AppEvents\Schemes\Apps\Office97\Office97-ToolbarClose
> **Value Name:** .Default
> **Data Type:** REG_SZ
> **Value:** C:\WINNT\Media\Office97\Close.wav

> **Value Name:** .Current
> **Data Type:** REG_SZ
> **Value:** C:\WINNT\Media\Office97\Close.wav

This value sets the sound played when you close a toolbar menu. You must provide a fully qualified path and file name to the wave file.

MICROSOFT OFFICE

IV-119

         Hive: HKEY_CURRENT_USER
          Key: AppEvents\EventLabels\Office97-ToolbarDock
Value Name: <No Name>
 Data Type: REG_SZ
      Value: Toolbar Dock

          Key: AppEvents\Schemes\Apps\Office97\Office97-ToolbarDock
Value Name: .Default
 Data Type: REG_SZ
      Value: C:\WINNT\Media\Office97\Dock.wav

Value Name: .Current
 Data Type: REG_SZ
      Value: C:\WINNT\Media\Office97\Dock.wav

This value sets the sound you hear when you dock a toolbar onto one of the sides of an Office 97 application. You must provide a fully qualified path and file name to the wave file.

IV-120

         Hive: HKEY_CURRENT_USER
          Key: AppEvents\EventLabels\Office97-ToolbarUndock
Value Name: <No Name>
 Data Type: REG_SZ
      Value: Toolbar Undock

          Key: AppEvents\Schemes\Apps\Office97\
              Office97-ToolbarUndock
Value Name: .Default
 Data Type: REG_SZ
      Value: C:\WINNT\Media\Office97\Undock.wav

Value Name: .Current
 Data Type: REG_SZ
      Value: C:\WINNT\Media\Office97\Undock.wav

This value sets the sound played when you undock a toolbar from one of the sides of an Office 97 application. You must provide a fully qualified path and file name to the wave file.

IV-121

Hive: HKEY_CURRENT_USER
Key: AppEvents\EventLabels\Office97-ToolbarDrop
Value Name: <No Name>
Data Type: REG_SZ
Value: Toolbar Drop

Key: AppEvents\Schemes\Apps\Office97\Office97-ToolbarDrop
Value Name: .Default
Data Type: REG_SZ
Value: C:\WINNT\Media\Office97\Drop.wav

Value Name: .Current
Data Type: REG_SZ
Value: C:\WINNT\Media\Office97\Drop.wav

This value sets the sound played when you are dragging around a toolbar or toolbar window and you drop it (or let go of it). You must provide a fully qualified path and file name to the wave file.

IV-122

Hive: HKEY_CURRENT_USER
Key: AppEvents\EventLabels\Office97-ToolbarFocus
Value Name: <No Name>
Data Type: REG_SZ
Value: Toolbar Focus

Key: AppEvents\Schemes\Apps\Office97\Office97-ToolbarFocus
Value Name: .Default
Data Type: REG_SZ
Value: C:\WINNT\Media\Office97\Focus.wav

Value Name: .Current
Data Type: REG_SZ
Value: C:\WINNT\Media\Office97\Focus.wav

This value sets the sound played when you select one of the "windowed" toolbars. You must provide a fully qualified path and file name to the wave file.

MICROSOFT OFFICE

CURSORS

Did you know that Office 97 Applications can display different cursors when you do something such as highlight text in a document or delete a cell within a spreadsheet? With the following 22 registry keys, you can control which cursor Office 97 uses. Note: Some of these cursors show up only in place of the hourglass cursor when one of the Office 97 applications takes time to perform one of these tasks.

IV-123

Hive: HKEY_CURRENT_USER
Key: Software\Microsoft\Office\8.0\Common\Cursors
Value Name: AutoFormat
Data Type: REG_SZ
Value: C:\WINNT\Cursors\autofmt.ani

This value sets the cursor displayed while your text is AutoFormatted in one of the Office 97 applications such as Word or Excel. You must provide a fully qualified path and cursor file name.

IV-124

Hive: HKEY_CURRENT_USER
Key: Software\Microsoft\Office\8.0\Common\Cursors
Value Name: Charting
Data Type: REG_SZ
Value: C:\WINNT\Cursors\charting.ani

This value sets the cursor displayed when you create a chart or graph in one of the Office 97 applications such as Excel. You must provide a fully qualified path and cursor file name.

IV-125

Hive: HKEY_CURRENT_USER
Key: Software\Microsoft\Office\8.0\Common\Cursors
Value Name: Cut
Data Type: REG_SZ
Value: C:\WINNT\Cursors\cut.ani

If you want to change the cursor displayed when you cut something out of a document or delete an e-mail message, point this registry entry to the cursor file you wish to use. You must provide a fully qualified path and cursor file name.

IV-126

          Hive: HKEY_CURRENT_USER
          Key: Software\Microsoft\Office\8.0\Common\Cursors
Value Name: DataMap
    Data Type: REG_SZ
        Value: C:\WINNT\Cursors\msmap.ani

Microsoft Excel uses this registry key when performing a mapping function. You must provide a fully qualified path and cursor file name.

IV-127

          Hive: HKEY_CURRENT_USER
          Key: Software\Microsoft\Office\8.0\Common\Cursors
Value Name: HighlightTextHor
    Data Type: REG_SZ
        Value: C:\WINNT\Cursors\hilithor.ani

The cursor set in this value is displayed when you highlight text in one of the Office 97 applications. You must provide a fully qualified path and cursor file name.

IV-128

          Hive: HKEY_CURRENT_USER
          Key: Software\Microsoft\Office\8.0\Common\Cursors
Value Name: HighlightTextVert
    Data Type: REG_SZ
        Value: C:\WINNT\Cursors\hilitver.ani

This value sets the cursor displayed when you highlight something that is oriented vertically, such as part of a PowerPoint slide. You must provide a fully qualified path and cursor file name.

IV-129

          Hive: HKEY_CURRENT_USER
          Key: Software\Microsoft\Office\8.0\Common\Cursors
Value Name: Load
    Data Type: REG_SZ
        Value: C:\WINNT\Cursors\load.ani

This value sets the cursor shown when you load in a long file into one of the Office 97 applications. You must provide a fully qualified path and cursor file name.

MICROSOFT OFFICE

IV-130

Hive: HKEY_CURRENT_USER
Key: Software\Microsoft\Office\8.0\Common\Cursors
Value Name: MacroRecord
Data Type: REG_SZ
Value: C:\WINNT\Cursors\macrorec.ani

When you create a macro in one of the Office 97 applications, you might see a spinning cassette with a mouse cursor over it. To change the cursor, change the value in this entry. You must provide a fully qualified path and cursor file name.

IV-131

Hive: HKEY_CURRENT_USER
Key: Software\Microsoft\Office\8.0\Common\Cursors
Value Name: Object
Data Type: REG_SZ
Value: C:\WINNT\Cursors\object.ani

To change the cursor you see when you insert an object into a document, modify this registry entry. You must provide a fully qualified path and cursor file name.

IV-132

Hive: HKEY_CURRENT_USER
Key: Software\Microsoft\Office\8.0\Common\Cursors
Value Name: OpenShared
Data Type: REG_SZ
Value: C:\WINNT\Cursors\opshrfld.ani

The cursor specified in this value appears when you open a file that is already opened by someone else. You must provide a fully qualified path and cursor file name.

IV-133

Hive: HKEY_CURRENT_USER
Key: Software\Microsoft\Office\8.0\Common\Cursors
Value Name: PaintArrow
Data Type: REG_SZ
Value: C:\WINNT\Cursors\paintptr.ani

This value sets the cursor displayed when you use the Format Painter in any Office 97 application. You must provide a fully qualified path and cursor file name.

IV-134

Hive: HKEY_CURRENT_USER
Key: Software\Microsoft\Office\8.0\Common\Cursors
Value Name: PaintCell
Data Type: REG_SZ
Value: C:\WINNT\Cursors\paintcel.ani

The cursor set in this value appears when you use the Format Painter to apply formatting in an Excel spreadsheet. You must provide a fully qualified path and cursor file name.

IV-135

Hive: HKEY_CURRENT_USER
Key: Software\Microsoft\Office\8.0\Common\Cursors
Value Name: PaintTextHor
Data Type: REG_SZ
Value: C:\WINNT\Cursors\painthor.ani

The cursor set in this value appears when you use the Format Painter to paint text formatting horizontally — it's the same cursor you usually see when using the Format Painter to apply formatting. You must provide a fully qualified path and cursor file name.

IV-136

Hive: HKEY_CURRENT_USER
Key: Software\Microsoft\Office\8.0\Common\Cursors
Value Name: PaintTextVert
Data Type: REG_SZ
Value: C:\WINNT\Cursors\paintver.ani

This registry entry holds the path and file name of the cursor that appears when you apply the Format Painter to vertical text.

IV-137

Hive: HKEY_CURRENT_USER
Key: Software\Microsoft\Office\8.0\Common\Cursors
Value Name: Print
Data Type: REG_SZ
Value: C:\WINNT\Cursors\print.ani

To change the cursor that's displayed when you print, set the value of this registry key to a fully qualified path and cursor file name of the cursor that you wish to use.

MICROSOFT OFFICE

IV-138

     Hive: HKEY_CURRENT_USER
      Key: Software\Microsoft\Office\8.0\Common\Cursors
  Value Name: Recalc
   Data Type: REG_SZ
     Value: C:\WINNT\Cursors\recalc.ani

This value sets the cursor Excel uses when it recalculates a spreadsheet. You must provide a fully qualified path and cursor file name.

IV-139

     Hive: HKEY_CURRENT_USER
      Key: Software\Microsoft\Office\8.0\Common\Cursors
  Value Name: Repaginate
   Data Type: REG_SZ
     Value: C:\WINNT\Cursors\repag.ani

Change this entry to change the cursor Word uses when repaginating a document. You must provide a fully qualified path and cursor file name.

IV-140

     Hive: HKEY_CURRENT_USER
      Key: Software\Microsoft\Office\8.0\Common\Cursors
  Value Name: ReplaceAll
   Data Type: REG_SZ
     Value: C:\WINNT\Cursors\replace.ani

This value sets the cursor that appears when you tell an Office 97 application to search and replace in a document. You must provide a fully qualified path and cursor file name.

IV-141

     Hive: HKEY_CURRENT_USER
      Key: Software\Microsoft\Office\8.0\Common\Cursors
  Value Name: Save
   Data Type: REG_SZ
     Value: C:\WINNT\Cursors\save.ani

This value sets the cursor that appears when you save a document such as a spreadsheet within one of the Office 97 applications. You must provide a fully qualified path and cursor file name.

IV-142

> **Hive:** HKEY_CURRENT_USER
> **Key:** Software\Microsoft\Office\8.0\Common\Cursors
> **Value Name:** SendMail
> **Data Type:** REG_SZ
> **Value:** C:\WINNT\Cursors\sendmail.ani

This value sets the cursor Outlook displays when you send a message to someone. You must provide a fully qualified path and cursor file name.

IV-143

> **Hive:** HKEY_CURRENT_USER
> **Key:** Software\Microsoft\Office\8.0\Common\Cursors
> **Value Name:** Sorting
> **Data Type:** REG_SZ
> **Value:** C:\WINNT\Cursors\sort.ani

This value sets the cursor that appears when one of the Office 97 applications sorts or resorts anything, such as a spreadsheet. You must provide a fully qualified path and cursor file name.

IV-144

> **Hive:** HKEY_CURRENT_USER
> **Key:** Software\Microsoft\Office\8.0\Common\Cursors
> **Value Name:** WordCount
> **Data Type:** REG_SZ
> **Value:** C:\WINNT\Cursors\wrdcount.ani

This value sets the cursor that appears when Word counts the number of words in your document. You must provide a fully qualified path and cursor file name.

MICROSOFT POWERPOINT 8.0/97

The following registry keys control various options available in Microsoft PowerPoint 97. Note that to change any of these options, you must exit PowerPoint, change the registry key, then restart Microsoft PowerPoint.

IV-145

Hive: HKEY_CURRENT_USER
Key: Software\Microsoft\Office\8.0\PowerPoint\Options
Value Name: Always render high quality 24-bit images
Data Type: REG_DWORD
Value: 1

Setting this value to 1 enables PowerPoint's ability to render its images at the highest screen quality. Disabling this feature can speed up the display, but may produce a lower-quality display.

IV-146

Hive: HKEY_CURRENT_USER
Key: Software\Microsoft\Office\8.0\PowerPoint\Options
Value Name: AlwaysSuggest
Data Type: REG_DWORD
Value: 0

Setting this value to 0 makes PowerPoint automatically display a list of suggested spellings for misspelled words during a spelling check. Setting the value to 1 disables the feature.

IV-147

Hive: HKEY_CURRENT_USER
Key: Software\Microsoft\Office\8.0\PowerPoint\Options
Value Name: AppMaximized
Data Type: REG_DWORD
Value: 0

Setting this value to 1 causes PowerPoint to open at its maximum size.

IV-148

Hive: HKEY_CURRENT_USER
Key: Software\Microsoft\Office\8.0\PowerPoint\Options
Value Name: Background spell checking
Data Type: REG_DWORD
Value: 1

Setting this value to 1 causes PowerPoint to perform background spell-checking; setting it to 0 disables this feature.

IV-149

> **Hive:** HKEY_CURRENT_USER
> **Key:** Software\Microsoft\Office\8.0\PowerPoint\Options
> **Value Name:** BackgroundPrint
> **Data Type:** REG_DWORD
> **Value:** 1

Setting this value to 1 lets PowerPoint print presentations in the background so you can continue working in PowerPoint while you are printing. Setting this value to 1 disables this feature.

IV-150 The next four values set the screen position of the application window when it's not maximized. The values are in pixels, but you must type them in hexadecimal format. For clarity, the decimal value is in parentheses, but you should type only the hexadecimal.

> **Hive:** HKEY_CURRENT_USER
> **Key:** Software\Microsoft\Office\8.0\PowerPoint\Options
> **Value Name:** Left
> **Data Type:** REG_DWORD
> **Value:** 0x6e (110)

IV-151

> **Hive:** HKEY_CURRENT_USER
> **Key:** Software\Microsoft\Office\8.0\PowerPoint\Options
> **Value Name:** Bottom
> **Data Type:** REG_DWORD
> **Value:** 0x210 (528)

IV-152

> **Hive:** HKEY_CURRENT_USER
> **Key:** Software\Microsoft\Office\8.0\PowerPoint\Options
> **Value Name:** Right
> **Data Type:** REG_DWORD
> **Value:** 0x31c (796)

MICROSOFT OFFICE

IV-153

> **Hive:** HKEY_CURRENT_USER
> **Key:** Software\Microsoft\Office\8.0\PowerPoint\Options
> **Value Name:** Top
> **Data Type:** REG_DWORD
> **Value:** 0x69 (105)

The first of these entries sets the left coordinate, the second entry sets the position of the bottom of the window, the third sets the right coordinate, and the fourth sets the position of the top.

IV-154

> **Hive:** HKEY_CURRENT_USER
> **Key:** Software\Microsoft\Office\8.0\PowerPoint\Options
> **Value Name:** FrequencyToSaveAutoRecoveryInfo
> **Data Type:** REG_DWORD
> **Value:** 0xa (10)

This value sets how often PowerPoint creates an AutoRecovery file. The value is time in minutes, but you must type it in hexadecimal format. For clarity, the decimal value is in parentheses, but you should type only the hexadecimal.

IV-155

> **Hive:** HKEY_CURRENT_USER
> **Key:** Software\Microsoft\Office\8.0\PowerPoint\Options
> **Value Name:** Language Id
> **Data Type:** REG_DWORD
> **Value:** 0x409 (1033)

This value tells PowerPoint which language to use for its various options such as the spelling checker. Valid values are listed below, but you must type them in hexadecimal format. For clarity, the decimal value is in parentheses above and appears to the left below, but you should type only the hexadecimal.

1030	Danish
1031	German
1033	U.S. English
1034	Spanish
1036	French
1040	Italian
1043	Dutch
1044	Norwegian
1054	Swedish
2057	British English
2070	Portuguese
3081	Australian English

IV-156

Hive: HKEY_CURRENT_USER
Key: Software\Microsoft\Office\8.0\PowerPoint\Options
Value Name: LinkSoundSize
Data Type: REG_DWORD
Value: 0x64 (100)

This value determines how PowerPoint treats sound files. PowerPoint loads into your presentations those sounds files that are smaller than this value, and it links to sound files larger than this value. The value is in kilobytes, but you must type the value in hexadecimal format. For clarity, the decimal value is in parentheses, but you should type only the hexadecimal.

IV-157

Hive: HKEY_CURRENT_USER
Key: Software\Microsoft\Office\8.0\PowerPoint\Options
Value Name: Do not underline errors
Data Type: REG_DWORD
Value: 0

Setting this value to 1 hides the wavy red line under possible spelling errors in your presentation. Disabling this feature causes PowerPoint to mark possible spelling errors with a wavy red line that are visible on the screen but that do not print.

IV-158

Hive: HKEY_CURRENT_USER
Key: Software\Microsoft\Office\8.0\PowerPoint\Options
Value Name: DocMaximized
Data Type: REG_DWORD
Value: 1

Setting this value to 1 maximizes the document window when you open PowerPoint.

IV-159

Hive: HKEY_CURRENT_USER
Key: Software\Microsoft\Office\8.0\PowerPoint\Options
Value Name: DragAndDrop
Data Type: REG_DWORD
Value: 1

Setting this value to 1 allows drag-and-drop text editing; setting it to 0 causes PowerPoint to extend the selection when you drag the cursor over text.

MICROSOFT OFFICE

IV-160

> **Hive:** HKEY_CURRENT_USER
> **Key:** Software\Microsoft\Office\8.0\PowerPoint\Options
> **Value Name:** FastSaves
> **Data Type:** REG_DWORD
> **Value:** 1

Enabling this feature speeds up saving by recording only the changes in a presentation. Disabling this feature means that save commands take longer but save the entire presentation.

IV-161

> **Hive:** HKEY_CURRENT_USER
> **Key:** Software\Microsoft\Office\8.0\PowerPoint\Options
> **Value Name:** GuidesVisible
> **Data Type:** REG_DWORD
> **Value:** 0

If this value is set to 0, PowerPoint displays the vertical and horizontal alignment guides on your slides. The alignment guides are useful for aligning objects on your slides.

IV-162

> **Hive:** HKEY_CURRENT_USER
> **Key:** Software\Microsoft\Office\8.0\PowerPoint\Options
> **Value Name:** Ignore email and file names
> **Data Type:** REG_DWORD
> **Value:** 1

Setting this value to 1 tells PowerPoint's spelling checker to ignore e-mail and filenames.

IV-163

> **Hive:** HKEY_CURRENT_USER
> **Key:** Software\Microsoft\Office\8.0\PowerPoint\Options
> **Value Name:** Ignore UPPERCASE words
> **Data Type:** REG_DWORD
> **Value:** 1

Setting this value to 1 tells PowerPoint's spelling checker to ignore words in UPPERCASE letters.

IV-164

      Hive: HKEY_CURRENT_USER
      Key: Software\Microsoft\Office\8.0\PowerPoint\Options
Value Name: Ignore words with numbers
  Data Type: REG_DWORD
     Value: 1

Setting this value to 1 tells PowerPoint's spelling checker to ignore words that contain numbers.

IV-165

      Hive: HKEY_CURRENT_USER
      Key: Software\Microsoft\Office\8.0\PowerPoint\Options
Value Name: MacroVirusProtection
  Data Type: REG_DWORD
     Value: 1

Setting this value to 1 enables a warning dialog box that appears whenever you open a PowerPoint presentation that might contain macro viruses — any file that contains macros, customized toolbars, menus, or shortcuts.

IV-166

      Hive: HKEY_CURRENT_USER
      Key: Software\Microsoft\Office\8.0\PowerPoint\Options
Value Name: MRUListActive
  Data Type: REG_DWORD
     Value: 1

This value controls the most recently used file list. Setting this value to 1 displays the most recently used files under the File menu.

IV-167

      Hive: HKEY_CURRENT_USER
      Key: Software\Microsoft\Office\8.0\PowerPoint\Options
Value Name: NewSlideDialog
  Data Type: REG_DWORD
     Value: 1

Setting this value to 1 enables the Show Slide Layout dialog box when you insert new slides into a presentation.

MICROSOFT OFFICE

IV-168

    Hive: HKEY_CURRENT_USER
     Key: Software\Microsoft\Office\8.0\PowerPoint\Options
Value Name: NoEditTime
  Data Type: REG_DWORD
     Value: 0

Setting this value to 1 turns off Edit Time tracker. Setting this value to 0 enables the Edit Time tracker, and the total time shows up under Properties.

IV-169

    Hive: HKEY_CURRENT_USER
     Key: Software\Microsoft\Office\8.0\PowerPoint\Options
Value Name: NoStyledTitleBar
  Data Type: REG_DWORD
     Value: 0

Setting this value to 1 disables the styled text in the PowerPoint title bar.

IV-170

    Hive: HKEY_CURRENT_USER
     Key: Software\Microsoft\Office\8.0\PowerPoint\Options
Value Name: Number of Undos
  Data Type: REG_DWORD
     Value: 0x14 (20)

This value sets the number of times you can undo something. Increasing this value decreases the amount of memory available to PowerPoint.

IV-171

    Hive: HKEY_CURRENT_USER
     Key: Software\Microsoft\Office\8.0\PowerPoint\Options
Value Name: Options dialog current tab
  Data Type: REG_DWORD
     Value: 0

This value is an index to the last-used tab on the Options dialog box. Power-Point stores this value and displays the most recently used section of Options.

IV-172

    Hive: HKEY_CURRENT_USER
     Key: Software\Microsoft\Office\8.0\PowerPoint\Options
Value Name: Produce 8-bit metafiles
  Data Type: REG_DWORD
     Value: 0

Turning off this option displays metafiles better on 24-bit systems.

IV-173

> **Hive:** HKEY_CURRENT_USER
> **Key:** Software\Microsoft\Office\8.0\PowerPoint\Options
> **Value Name:** PromptForFileProperties
> **Data Type:** REG_DWORD
> **Value:** 0

Setting this value to 0 causes PowerPoint to open the Properties dialog box when you save a PowerPoint presentation for the first time.

IV-174

> **Hive:** HKEY_CURRENT_USER
> **Key:** Software\Microsoft\Office\8.0\PowerPoint\Options
> **Value Name:** Recolor imported Graph
> **Data Type:** REG_DWORD
> **Value:** 0

Setting this value to 0 causes PowerPoint to recolor imported graphs, which can slow down the display but makes imported graphs look better.

IV-175 Problem: You have users who want access to PowerPoint clip art, but you don't want to give them administrator access or have them log on as local users. In other words, you want domain users to have access to the clip art without giving away the farm. This registry entry helps you around this problem.

> **Hive:** HKEY_LOCAL_MACHINE
> **Key:** Software\Microsoft\ClipArt Gallery\2.0

With the 2.0 key highlighted, click Permissions. Give everyone full control to this key and the subkeys by clicking on the Change Existing Subkeys box in the dialog box. Now domain users have access to the clip art.

IV-176

> **Hive:** HKEY_CURRENT_USER
> **Key:** Software\Microsoft\Office\8.0\PowerPoint\Options
> **Value Name:** RulersVisible
> **Data Type:** REG_DWORD
> **Value:** 0

Setting this value to 1 enables the horizontal and vertical rulers, which appear on the top and left side of the slide window.

MICROSOFT OFFICE

IV-177

Hive: HKEY_CURRENT_USER
Key: Software\Microsoft\Office\8.0\PowerPoint\Options
Value Name: Save Text Content Stream
Data Type: REG_DWORD
Value: 0

Setting this value to 1 copies all slide text to a Text_Content index stream that the Find File uses. This feature corresponds to the "Save Full Text Search Information" option.

IV-178

Hive: HKEY_CURRENT_USER
Key: Software\Microsoft\Office\8.0\PowerPoint\Options
Value Name: SaveAutoRecoveryInfo
Data Type: REG_DWORD
Value: 1

Setting this value to 1 enables PowerPoint's AutoRecovery features.

IV-179

Hive: HKEY_CURRENT_USER
Key: Software\Microsoft\Office\8.0\PowerPoint\Options
Value Name: SaveFullTextSearchInfo
Data Type: REG_DWORD
Value: 1

Enabling this feature causes PowerPoint to save full text search information with your presentation.

IV-180

Hive: HKEY_CURRENT_USER
Key: Software\Microsoft\Office\8.0\PowerPoint\Options
Value Name: Send TrueType fonts as bitmaps
Data Type: REG_DWORD
Value: 0

Enabling this feature causes PowerPoint to print TrueType fonts as graphic images instead of downloading the TrueType font to your printer.

IV-181

Hive: HKEY_CURRENT_USER
Key: Software\Microsoft\Office\8.0\PowerPoint\Options
Value Name: Show Preview
Data Type: REG_DWORD
Value: 0

If this feature is enabled, the Slide Miniature window is visible under the File/Open dialog box.

IV-182

Hive: HKEY_CURRENT_USER
Key: Software\Microsoft\Office\8.0\PowerPoint\Options
Value Name: ShowStatusBar
Data Type: REG_DWORD
Value: 1

Disabling this registry key causes PowerPoint to hide the status bar. This feature is useful if you need more working room on the screen.

IV-183

Hive: HKEY_CURRENT_USER
Key: Software\Microsoft\Office\8.0\PowerPoint\Options
Value Name: SizeOfMRUList
Data Type: REG_DWORD
Value: 4

This value sets the number of Most Recently Used files PowerPoint tracks and displays at the bottom of the File menu. Acceptable values range from 1 to 9.

IV-184

Hive: HKEY_CURRENT_USER
Key: Software\Microsoft\Office\8.0\PowerPoint\Options
Value Name: SmartCutPaste
Data Type: REG_DWORD
Value: 1

Enabling this feature causes PowerPoint to remove extra spaces when you delete text and causes PowerPoint to add spaces when you insert text from the clipboard.

MICROSOFT OFFICE

IV-185

Hive: HKEY_CURRENT_USER
Key: Software\Microsoft\Office\8.0\PowerPoint\Options
Value Name: SmartQuotes
Data Type: REG_DWORD
Value: 1

If you enable this feature, PowerPoint changes straight quotation marks to smart quotation marks.

IV-186

Hive: HKEY_CURRENT_USER
Key: Software\Microsoft\Office\8.0\PowerPoint\Options
Value Name: SSEndOnBlankSlide
Data Type: REG_DWORD
Value: 0

If you enable this feature, PowerPoint displays a black slide as the last slide of your slide show.

IV-187

Hive: HKEY_CURRENT_USER
Key: Software\Microsoft\Office\8.0\PowerPoint\Options
Value Name: SSMenuButton
Data Type: REG_DWORD
Value: 1

If you enable this feature, PowerPoint displays the menu button on the bottom left during slide shows.

IV-188

Hive: HKEY_CURRENT_USER
Key: Software\Microsoft\Office\8.0\PowerPoint\Options
Value Name: SSRightMouse
Data Type: REG_DWORD
Value: 1

Setting this value to 1 displays a menu when you right-click during a Power-Point slide show.

`IV-189`

Hive: HKEY_CURRENT_USER
Key: Software\Microsoft\Office\8.0\PowerPoint\Options
Value Name: StartupDialog
Data Type: REG_DWORD
Value: 1

Setting this value to 1 causes PowerPoint to display its opening dialog box, which prompts you to create a blank presentation or run a PowerPoint creation wizard.

`IV-190`

Hive: HKEY_CURRENT_USER
Key: Software\Microsoft\Office\8.0\PowerPoint\Options
Value Name: StartupDialogDefault
Data Type: REG_DWORD
Value: 8

This value indicates the last setting chosen in the Startup dialog box. Acceptable values are

6   AutoContent Wizard (default)
7   Template
8   Blank Presentation
9   Open Existing Presentation

`IV-191`

Hive: HKEY_CURRENT_USER
Key: Software\Microsoft\Office\8.0\PowerPoint\Options
Value Name: SummaryInfo
Data Type: REG_DWORD
Value: 1

If this feature is enabled, PowerPoint displays the Summary Info dialog box when saving your presentation.

`IV-192`

Hive: HKEY_CURRENT_USER
Key: Software\Microsoft\Office\8.0\PowerPoint\Options
Value Name: TipOfDay
Data Type: REG_DWORD
Value: 0

If this feature is enabled, PowerPoint displays the Tip of the Day when you start it.

MICROSOFT OFFICE

IV-193

Hive: HKEY_CURRENT_USER
Key: Software\Microsoft\Office\8.0\PowerPoint\Options
Value Name: TipOfDayId
Data Type: REG_DWORD
Value: 0

This value is the ID Number of the last Tip of the Day PowerPoint displayed.

IV-194

Hive: HKEY_CURRENT_USER
Key: Software\Microsoft\Office\8.0\PowerPoint\Options
Value Name: True Inline Conversion
Data Type: REG_DWORD
Value: 1

This feature is available only in Far East versions of PowerPoint; it chooses the type of IME conversion that PowerPoint uses.

IV-195

Hive: HKEY_CURRENT_USER
Key: Software\Microsoft\Office\8.0\PowerPoint\Options
Value Name: Use Fast OLE Save
Data Type: REG_DWORD
Value: 1

Setting this value to 1 results in faster saves but slightly larger files.

IV-196

Hive: HKEY_CURRENT_USER
Key: Software\Microsoft\Office\8.0\PowerPoint\Options
Value Name: VerticalRuler
Data Type: REG_DWORD
Value: 1

If this feature is enabled, the vertical ruler is displayed on the left side of the PowerPoint window.

IV-197

Hive: HKEY_CURRENT_USER
Key: Software\Microsoft\Office\8.0\PowerPoint\Options
Value Name: WordSelection
Data Type: REG_DWORD
Value: 1

If this feature is enabled, PowerPoint automatically selects the entire word plus the space after the word when you select part of a word.

Section V

SECURITY

NT PERMISSIONS

Windows NT Security is a popular topic of discussion these days. Modifying these registry entries lets you set security as tightly or as loosely as you need to.

For each of the following keys, set the following permission.

Group: Permission

Everyone: QueryValue, Enumerate Subkeys, Notify, Read Control

To see the permissions that are already set, select the key in Regedt32.exe and go to the Security menu.

V-1

Hive: HKEY_LOCAL_MACHINE
Key: Software\

I strongly recommend setting this parameter. It determines who can install software. However, I don't recommend locking the entire subtree using this setting because that can render certain software unusable. Here is a list of each individual subtree. Changing each subtree lets you exert greater control over each individual software component.

V-2

Hive: HKEY_LOCAL_MACHINE
Key: Software\Microsoft\RPC

V-3

Hive: HKEY_LOCAL_MACHINE
Key: Software\Microsoft\WindowsNT\CurrentVersion

V-4

Hive: HKEY_LOCAL_MACHINE
Key: Software\Microsoft\WindowsNT\CurrentVersion\Profile List

V-5

Hive: HKEY_LOCAL_MACHINE
Key: Software\Microsoft\WindowsNT\CurrentVersion\AeDebug

V-6

Hive: HKEY_LOCAL_MACHINE
Key: Software\Microsoft\WindowsNT\CurrentVersion\Compatibility

V-7

Hive: HKEY_LOCAL_MACHINE
Key: Software\Microsoft\WindowsNT\CurrentVersion\Drivers

V-8

Hive: HKEY_LOCAL_MACHINE
Key: Software\Microsoft\WindowsNT\CurrentVersion\Embedding

V-9

Hive: HKEY_LOCAL_MACHINE
Key: Software\Microsoft\WindowsNT\CurrentVersion\Fonts

V-10

Hive: HKEY_LOCAL_MACHINE
Key: Software\Microsoft\WindowsNT\CurrentVersion\
FontSubstitutes

V-11

Hive: HKEY_LOCAL_MACHINE
Key: Software\Microsoft\WindowsNT\CurrentVersion\Font Drivers

V-12

Hive: HKEY_LOCAL_MACHINE
Key: Software\Microsoft\WindowsNT\CurrentVersion\Font Mapper

V-13

Hive: HKEY_LOCAL_MACHINE
Key: Software\Microsoft\WindowsNT\CurrentVersion\Font Cache

V-14

Hive: HKEY_LOCAL_MACHINE
Key: Software\Microsoft\WindowsNT\CurrentVersion\
GRE_Initialize

V-15

Hive: HKEY_LOCAL_MACHINE
Key: Software\Microsoft\WindowsNT\CurrentVersion\MCI

V-16

Hive: HKEY_LOCAL_MACHINE
Key: Software\Microsoft\WindowsNT\CurrentVersion\
MCI Extensions

V-17

Hive: HKEY_LOCAL_MACHINE
Key: Software\Microsoft\WindowsNT\CurrentVersion\PerfLib

If you remove the Read permissions for the Everyone group, remote users
cannot see performance data on the machine.

SECURITY

V-18

> **Hive:** HKEY_LOCAL_MACHINE
> **Key:** Software\Microsoft\WindowsNT\CurrentVersion\Port (and all subkeys)

V-19

> **Hive:** HKEY_LOCAL_MACHINE
> **Key:** Software\Microsoft\WindowsNT\CurrentVersion\Type1 Installer

V-20

> **Hive:** HKEY_LOCAL_MACHINE
> **Key:** Software\Microsoft\WindowsNT\CurrentVersion\WOW (and all subkeys)

V-21

> **Hive:** HKEY_LOCAL_MACHINE
> **Key:** Software\Microsoft\WindowsNT\CurrentVersion\ Windows3.1MigrationStatus (and all subkeys)

V-22

> **Hive:** HKEY_LOCAL_MACHINE
> **Key:** System\CurrentControlSet\Services\LanmanServer\Shares

V-23

> **Hive:** HKEY_LOCAL_MACHINE
> **Key:** System\CurrentControlSet\Services\UPS

Note that besides setting security on this key, you must also secure any batch or command file associated with the UPS service. Generally, if you allow administrators full control and system full control, everything should function normally.

EVENT LOG

By default, anyone can read your event logs; however, you might not want everyone reading some of the information in your logs. These registry entries let you restrict access to these logs from Guest and Null Logons accounts. A value of 1 restricts guest access and a value of 0 permits it. You must set these values for each log type: Application, Security, and System.

V-24

Hive: HKEY_LOCAL_MACHINE
Key: System\CurrentControlSet\Services\EventLog\Application
Value Name: RestrictGuessAccess
Data Type: Dword
Value: 1

This value controls guest access to the Application Log file.

V-25

Hive: HKEY_LOCAL_MACHINE
Key: System\CurrentControlSet\Services\EventLog\Security
Value Name: RestrictGuessAccess
Data Type: Dword
Value: 1

This value controls guest access to the Security Log file.

V-26

Hive: HKEY_LOCAL_MACHINE
Key: System\CurrentControlSet\Services\EventLog\System
Value Name: RestrictGuestAccess
Data Type: Dword
Value: 1

This value controls guest access to the System Log file. Make sure you change the security on this key to allow only Administrator and System access to these values.

SECURITY

PRINT DRIVER INSTALLATION

V-27

> **Hive:** HKEY_LOCAL_MACHINE
> **Key:** System\CurrentControlSet\Control\Print\Providers\
> LanMan Print Services
> **Value Name:** AddPrinterDrivers
> **Data Type:** Dword
> **Value:** 1

This value prevents users from adding printers on the local machine. It does not prevent additions from the network.

REMOVABLE MEDIA

V-28 This registry entry restricts access to the floppy disk drives on a system to only those users who are logged on interactively.
> **Hive:** HKEY_LOCAL_MACHINE
> **Key:** SOFTWARE\Microsoft\WindowsNT\CurrentVersion\
> Winlogon

Add the following value under the WinLogon key:
> **Value Name:** AllocateFloppies
> **Data Type:** REG_SZ
> **Value:** 1

V-29 You can restrict the CD-ROMs as well.
> **Hive:** HKEY_LOCAL_MACHINE
> **Key:** SOFTWARE\Microsoft\WindowsNT\CurrentVersion\
> Winlogon

Add the following value under the WinLogon key:
> **Value Name:** AllocateCDRoms
> **Data Type:** REG_SZ
> **Value:** 1

If either of these registry entries doesn't exist or is set to a value other than 1, all floppy and CD-ROM devices are available for shared use to all processes on the system.

AUDITING BASE SYSTEM OBJECTS

V-30 If you need to audit the base system objects on your Windows NT Server or Workstation, add the following registry value.

> **Hive:** HKEY_LOCAL_MACHINE
> **Key:** System\CurrentControlSet\Control\Lsa:

Add the following value under the Lsa key:
> **Value Name:** AuditBaseObjects
> **Data Type:** REG_DWORD
> **Value:** 1

You need to turn on auditing in User Manager for the "Object Access" category to actually begin auditing.

FULL PRIVILEGE AUDITING

V-31 Not all privileges are audited by Windows NT by default. Modifying this registry entry lets you audit these additional privileges.

> **Hive:** HKEY_LOCAL_MACHINE
> **Key:** System\CurrentControlSet\Control\Lsa:

Add the following value under the Lsa key:
> **Value Name:** FullPrivilegeAuditing
> **Data Type:** REG_BINARY
> **Value:** 1

The additional privileges audited are bypass traverse checking, debug programs, create a token object, replace process level token, generate security audits, back up files and directories, and restore files and directories.

SECURITY

SHUTDOWN ON FULL AUDIT LOG

V-32 If you monitor your logs closely, you may want to enable this feature. When the security log is full, Windows NT shuts down. The registry value is then set to 2, and when the system reboots, only administrators can log on. The administrator must clean out the log, reset the value to 1, and reboot the system before users can log on.

> **Hive:** HKEY_LOCAL_MACHINE
> **Key:** System\CurrentControlSet\Control\Lsa:

Add the following value under the Lsa key:

> **Value Name:** CrashOnAuditFail
> **Data Type:** REG_DWORD
> **Value:** 1

Section VI

PERFORMANCE

Improving the way parts of your system perform, particularly those parts
that affect your users, is a great way to make your life easier. However,
sometimes it's the subtle changes that can enhance system performance
the most. In this section, you'll find specific ways to improve the performance of your general system, your network (including special sections
on particular services), your file systems, and your printers.

GENERAL SYSTEM PERFORMANCE

The tuning parameters in this section tune the general performance of NT, rather than a specific aspect of NT such as file systems or memory. By our definition, these keys tune NT itself, not specific device drivers or user-level applications.

VI-1   Managing the number of threads can help you optimize performance. When NT boots, it creates a pool of worker threads that NT's kernel, Executive Subsystems, and device drivers use. When one of these components places a work item, such as the Cache Manager's lazy cache flusher or the Memory Manager's idle memory zero-filler, in a queue, a thread is assigned to process it. If too many threads are in the pool, they needlessly consume system resources. However, if not enough threads are in the pool, work items are not serviced in a timely manner. Adjust the following two registry keys to change the number of threads.

> **Hive:** HKEY_LOCAL_MACHINE
> **Key:** System\CurrentControlSet\Control\Session Manager\Executive
> **Value Name:** AdditionalCriticalWorkerThreads
> **Data Type:** REG_DWORD
> **Value:** <any number>

VI-2

> **Hive:** HKEY_LOCAL_MACHINE
> **Key:** System\CurrentControlSet\Control\Session Manager\Executive
> **Value Name:** AdditionalDelayedWorkerThreads
> **Data Type:** REG_DWORD
> **Value:** <any number>

The number you specify in the value increases the number of threads created for the specified work queue. NT has two thread queues. Threads in the Critical Work Queue execute in the low real-time priority range, so they have precedence over most system activity. Threads in the Delayed Work Queue have a slightly lower priority that results in higher latency — the threads that service it compete with other processing for CPU time. The number of threads created for each queue is based on two criteria: whether the system is a server or workstation and how much physical memory the system has. You can't tell directly whether more threads in a particular situation give you better performance, but you can experiment with benchmark workloads to see if they provide a benefit.

VI-3 To make your foreground windows more responsive than your background windows, in Windows 3.51 you could boost priorities. In NT 4.0 Workstation, instead of boosting priorities, you set quantums to boost foreground windows (Server treats foreground and background windows alike). Change this registry entry to set the boost value.

Hive: HKEY_LOCAL_MACHINE
Key: System\CurrentControlSet\Control
Value Name: PriorityControl
Data Type: REG_DWORD
Value: 0

You can also set the boost value with a slider in the Performance tab of the System Control Panel applet. Valid values are shown below.

0 No quantum boost for foreground windows
1 Foreground windows have quantums twice as long as other windows
2 Foreground windows have quantums three times as long as other windows

---

VI-4 Here's a tricky registry entry.

Hive: HKEY_LOCAL_MACHINE
Key: System\CurrentControlSet\Control\Session Manager\Executive
Value Name: PriorityQuantumMatrix
Data Type:
Value:

Although you can't use this value to enhance performance, its name implies that you can. This value actually encodes expiration data about NT Beta and Release Candidates.

PERFORMANCE

MEMORY PERFORMANCE

When you think of memory performance, fast SRAMs and multilevel caching come to mind. Although these hardware components play a critical role in the latency and throughput of a computer's memory subsystem, tweaking the Registry obviously cannot upgrade your machine's hardware. So in this section, improving memory performance means improving the way NT uses physical and virtual memory. You know you're experiencing memory problems that you can fix with registry entries, rather than additional hardware, when you get "not enough memory to complete task…" messages in the system Event Log or on the display monitor.

VI-5   The file system cache grows and shrinks as the applications' memory demands change. However, at system startup, the cache's minimum, maximum, and "ideal" sizes are calibrated based on the Registry value you set below.

> **Hive:** HKEY_LOCAL_MACHINE
> **Key:** System\CurrentControlSet\Control\Session Manager\ Memory Management
> **Value Name:** LargeSystemCache
> **Data Type:** REG_DWORD
> **Value:** 0

This value controls the size of the system's file system cache. A value of 0 indicates a small cache, which is the default setting for Workstation, while 1 indicates a large cache, which is the default setting for Server. Servers usually perform some file sharing and therefore require a larger cache.

VI-6 NT categorizes memory as either paged or nonpaged. Paged memory holds data that can temporarily be moved from physical memory to the system's paging file if space is needed for different data in physical memory. Nonpaged memory stores data that must be present in physical memory at all times. NT allocates a portion of physical memory for nonpaged memory when the system starts up, and this allocation can't grow. If drivers or NT exhaust this storage, the system may become unstable or operations may start to fail. Modifying these two registry entries lets you override the defaults set for the paged and nonpaged pools.

>   **Hive:** HKEY_LOCAL_MACHINE
>   **Key:** System\CurrentControlSet\Control\Session Manager\
>   Memory Management
>   **Value Name:** NonPagedPoolSize
>   **Data Type:** REG_DWORD
>   **Value:** < number in bytes >

This value is the number of bytes of physical memory you want to allocate for nonpaged memory. To monitor your memory, use Performance Monitor to watch the percentage of committed memory that's used. If more than 80 percent of memory is used consistently, you should increase this value. Likewise, if the system's nonpaged memory usage is low, reducing the amount allocated for it increases system performance.

VI-7

>   **Hive:** HKEY_LOCAL_MACHINE
>   **Key:** System\CurrentControlSet\Control\Session Manager\
>   Memory Management
>   **Value Name:** PagedPoolSize
>   **Data Type:** REG_DWORD
>   **Value:** < number in bytes >

This value is the number of bytes in the paged memory pool. It overrides the system's default calculation, which is roughly equal to the physical memory on Workstation and a minimum of 50 MB on Server. Paged pool is different from virtual memory size — the paged pool is space reserved in the system's virtual memory map for NT and device drivers to allocate pageable data.

You can monitor the amount of paged pool the system uses with the Performance Monitor, which also shows the maximum allocation possible. If the amount of memory used is consistently more than 80 percent, you should use this setting to override the default.

PERFORMANCE

NETWORKING PERFORMANCE

The registry gives you lots of control over Windows NT's various networking components. Because your system may not run every networking service, you should identify which components are active so that you can target them when evaluating networking performance with tools like Performance Monitor.

GENERAL NETWORKING

VI-8   This value controls the order in which your network redirectors are used. If you have more than one network redirector, such as Lanmanager Workstation or Client Services for NetWare, loaded on your system, you should consider changing this entry.

> **Hive:** HKEY_LOCAL_MACHINE
> **Key:** System\CurrentControlSet\Control\NetworkProvider
> **Value Name:** Order
> **Data Type:** REG_SZ
> **Value:** <redirector name,redirector name,redirector name>

In this value, you set the order in which the WNet API uses your network providers. When the WNet API is called, it processes requests by sending them to each network provider in the order listed. If it gets back a response that the provider doesn't process that type of request, the API calls the next provider listed. Thus, if most of your system's activity relates to accessing NetWare shares, you should move the NetWare provider name to the start of the list. This small modification can improve performance significantly.

REDIRECTOR

The Windows NT Redirector manages remote volume connections. When you access a volume across the network, Redirector takes the file system request and invokes the appropriate protocol to send the request to a file system server component on the other machine.

VI-9 The entry below switches the behavior of Redirector between write-through and write-behind. By default, Redirector delays sending the server write requests to a volume, which lets other operations proceed or complete. When you change this value, Redirector sends write operations immediately and waits for a response before proceeding with other operations.

> **Hive:** HKEY_LOCAL_MACHINE
> **Key:** System\CurrentControlSet\Services\Rdr\Parameters
> **Value Name:** UseWriteBehind
> **Data Type:** REG_DWORD
> **Value:** 0

To disable write-behind, change this value to 1; the default is 0. You may need to use this highly synchronous mode in specialized environments or when tracking down networking problems with a network monitoring tool; otherwise, you should use the write-behind value because write-through degrades performance.

VI-10 The value in the registry entry below is a hybrid between write-through and write-behind modes.

> **Hive:** HKEY_LOCAL_MACHINE
> **Key:** System\CurrentControlSet\Services\Rdr\Parameters
> **Value Name:** UseAsyncWriteBehind
> **Data Type:** REG_DWORD
> **Value:** 1

The default value of 1 enables asynchronous write-behind, which means that Redirector immediately sends write requests to the server but doesn't wait for a response before processing other requests. Changing the value to 0 disables asynchronous write-behind; you should disable it only when the network requires special coherency guarantees or when you're debugging.

PERFORMANCE

LANMANAGER WORKSTATION

Lanmanager Workstation is Microsoft's implementation of a Redirector. It speaks SMB (Server Message Block).

VI-11

> **Hive:** HKEY_LOCAL_MACHINE
> **Key:** System\CurrentControlSet\Services\LanmanWorkstation\Parameters
> **Value Name:** MaxCmds
> **Data Type:** REG_DWORD
> **Value:** 15

This value specifies the number of threads that the Workstation service creates during initialization to handle requests; the default value is 15. If Workstation has more requests than it has threads to service those requests, it holds up some requests until a thread finishes servicing a request. Therefore, if multiple users or applications are simultaneously accessing remote shares, increasing this value can improve network throughput.

VI-12

> **Hive:** HKEY_LOCAL_MACHINE
> **Key:** System\CurrentControlSet\Services\LanmanWorkstation\Parameters
> **Value Name:** SessTimeout
> **Data Type:** RED_DWORD
> **Value:** 45

This value sets the number of seconds after a request is queued before Lanmanager indicates that the request has failed (if it hasn't been processed). The default value is 45. Applications that access network shares may report not having enough memory to process a request — too many outstanding operations are on the volume and some requests are timing out. Raising this value lets more operations be serviced asynchronously and may cause the messages to go away.

VI-13

Hive: HKEY_LOCAL_MACHINE
Key: System\CurrentControlSet\Services\LanmanWorkstation\
Parameters
Value Name: CacheFileTimeout
Data Type: REG_DWORD
Value: 10

This value specifies the time after which Lanmanager Workstation purges its locally cached data after closing a file. Many applications open files, perform an operation, close them, and repeat this sequence to perform more operations. If you have a system with a dedicated application, you can adjust this value to improve performance. Increase the time if applications close and reopen the same files at intervals longer than 10 seconds, and reduce the time if applications access few files and do not open and close them regularly.

VI-14

Hive: HKEY_LOCAL_MACHINE
Key: System\CurrentControlSet\Services\LanmanWorkstation\
Parameters
Value Name: DormantFileLimit
Data Type: REG_DWORD
Value: 45

This value sets the number of files that Lanmanger leaves open in the file system cache after an application closes it. By default, Lanmanager Server allows only a certain number of open files from any one Lanmanager Redirector connection. Having a file open on the connection can improve performance if the application opens it again. However, keeping files open can also overload the server's limit, and in those cases you should reduce this value.

PERFORMANCE

`VI-15`   Normally, Lanmanager Workstation reads and stores data in the local file
cache before an application requests it. These read-aheads can cause network
degradation when applications rarely read files sequentially on shared volumes
or when the network's throughput is low. To better manage the read-ahead
function, change this registry entry.

       Hive: HKEY_LOCAL_MACHINE
       Key: System\CurrentControlSet\Services\LanmanWorkstation\
       Parameters
Value Name: ReadAheadThroughput
  Data Type: REG_DWORD
      Value: -1

This value sets the minimum network throughput, in kilobytes per second,
before Lanmanager Workstation enables the read-ahead function. The default
value is -1.

LANMANAGER SERVER

Lanmanger Server is Microsoft's implementation of an SMB (Server Message Block) file
server. It is a focal point of performance tuning for any file-sharing server.

`VI-16`   If you frequently get "server paged" or "server nonpaged" errors in Performance Monitor, you are seeing Lanmanager Server running out of memory that
it's allocated for itself. You may want to raise these values to give Lanmanager
Server more memory; however, giving these memory resources to Lanmanager
keeps other system drivers and applications from using them. To give Lanmanager more paged and nonpaged memory, change the registry entries below.

       Hive: HKEY_LOCAL_MACHINE
       Key: System\CurrentControlSet\Services\LanmanServer\
       Parameters
Value Name: MaxNonPagedMemoryUsage
  Data Type: REG_DWORD
      Value: 0

VI-17

> **Hive:** HKEY_LOCAL_MACHINE
> **Key:** System\CurrentControlSet\Services\LanmanServer\Parameters
> **Value Name:** MaxPagedMemoryUsage
> **Data Type:** REG_DWORD
> **Value:** 0

These values set the number of megabytes allocated by Lanmanager Server for nonpaged and paged memory. The default, which is determined internally, is 0.

VI-18 By default, Lanmanager Server's worker threads run at one priority level higher than typical application threads. If network throughput is low because the Server's threads are competing with other threads for processor time, you may want to change this registry entry to increase the priority boost.

> **Hive:** HKEY_LOCAL_MACHINE
> **Key:** System\CurrentControlSet\Services\LanmanServer\Parameters
> **Value Name:** ThreadPriority
> **Data Type:** REG_DWORD
> **Value:** 1

Valid values are 0, 1, or 2, which determine how many levels above normal priority Lanmanager's worker threads run; and 15, which makes Lanmanager Server's threads run at real-time priority. Increasing the priority may reduce the responsiveness of other applications and services on the machine, especially if you set it to real-time priority.

VI-19 When the server maintains extra pre-initialized end-points, establishing new connections takes less processing. This value sets the number of end-points the server maintains.

> **Hive:** HKEY_LOCAL_MACHINE
> **Key:** System\CurrentControlSet\Services\LanmanServer\Parameters
> **Value Name:** MinFreeConnections
> **Data Type:** RED_DWORD
> **Value:** 2

Valid values range from 2 to 5; the default is determined internally. You can reduce the value to minimize idle memory overhead when the memory resources on the system are in high demand.

PERFORMANCE

VI-20 If memory resources are scarce or if you want to limit the total number of users that can simultaneously log on to the server, change this registry entry.

> **Hive:** HKEY_LOCAL_MACHINE
> **Key:** System\CurrentControlSet\Services\LanmanServer\Parameters
> **Value Name:** Users
> **Data Type:** REG_DWORD
> **Value:** <number>

The value is the number of users who can long on to the server simultaneously.

VI-21 Every time a connection is made to Lanmanager Server, resources are allocated to service it. Sometimes idle connections tie up resources for a long time. To free resources sooner, change this registry entry.

> **Hive:** HKEY_LOCAL_MACHINE
> **Key:** System\CurrentControlSet\Services\LanmanServer\Parameters
> **Value Name:** AutoDisconnect
> **Data Type:** REG_DWORD
> **Value:** 15

This value specifies the number of minutes a connection can be idle before it is automatically disconnected and the resources associated with it are freed. The default value is 15. Reducing this value can keep resource usage to a minimum, but it's possible to incur additional overhead if clients reconnect after their connections are dropped.

VI-22 The registry entry below tells Lanmanager Server to allocate work items for processing raw SMBs (Server Message Blocks).

> **Hive:** HKEY_LOCAL_MACHINE
> **Key:** System\CurrentControlSet\Services\LanmanServer\Parameters
> **Value Name:** EnableRaw
> **Data Type:** REG_DWORD
> **Value:** 1

Setting this value to 1 (the default) enables support for raw SMBs, and performance improves. Setting this value to 0 disables support.

`VI-23` Opportunistic locking is a performance-enhancing protocol Windows NT file systems use to detect remote machines' modifications to shared files and directories. Enabling op-locks can cause you to lose cached data if the system fails.

Hive: HKEY_LOCAL_MACHINE
Key: System\CurrentControlSet\Services\LanmanServer\ Parameters
Value Name: EnableOpLocks
Data Type: REG_DWORD
Value: 1

The default value is 1, which enables op-locking. Change the value to 0 to disable this feature.

SERVICES FOR MACINTOSH

Services for Macintosh (SFM) lets Macintosh-based computers transparently access Windows NT network shares. You can tune the performance of these connections with registry entries. You should consider adjusting these values if you have a LAN that depends on the responsiveness of Windows NT share access from Macs.

`VI-24` The following entries' values control the amount of paged and nonpaged memory that SFM uses as it processes operations. Under heavy workloads, SFM memory requirements rise, and if it can allocate all the memory it requires in one request, its performance improves. However, raising these values can cause other applications, including Windows NT itself, to be unable to allocate memory when they need to.

Hive: HKEY_LOCAL_MACHINE
Key: System\CurrentControlSet\Services\MacFile\Parameters
Value Name: PagedMemLimit
Data Type: REG_DWORD
Value: 20,000

`VI-25`

Hive: HKEY_LOCAL_MACHINE
Key: System\CurrentControlSet\Services\MacFile\Parameters
Value Name: NonPagedMemLimit
Data Type: REG_DWORD
Value: 4,000

The value in the first key above sets the paged memory limit; the default is 20,000 K. The second key sets the limit of nonpaged memory; the default is 4,000 K.

PERFORMANCE

DYNAMIC HOST CONFIGURATION PROTOCOL

VI-26   Dynamic Host Configuration Protocol (DHCP) dynamically assigns IP addresses from a pool of allowable addresses to other machines on a LAN. This registry entry determines whether the DHCP server logs all IP address assignments to a database file. You can then use this database to track down problems in network configuration or behavior. However, logging each DHCP invocation can significantly reduce system performance. If your DHCP seems to be highly stable, you might consider turning off this flag to improve performance.

> **Hive:** HKEY_LOCAL_MACHINE
> **Key:** System\CurrentControlSet\Services\DhcpServer\Parameters
> **Value Name:** DatabaseLoggingFlag
> **Data Type:** REG_DWORD
> **Value:** 1

The default value of 1 enables DHCP logging; change the value to 0 to disable this feature.

NETBEUI

NetBEUI is a transport that has been migrated forward from LanManager and Windows for Workgroups 3.11. The NetBEUI transport is named NBF in Windows NT.

VI-27   This value controls the time NBF waits before resending Logical Link Control (LLC) messages if they are not acknowledged. You should change this registry entry to raise this value if NBF is running over a slow network.

> **Hive:** HKEY_LOCAL_MACHINE
> **Key:** System\CurrentControlSet\Services\NBF\Parameters
> **Value Name:** DefaultT1Timeout
> **Data Type:** REG_DWORD
> **Value:** <number>

The value specifies, in 100-nanosecond increments, the timeout period for unacknowledged LLC messages. The default is 600 milliseconds.

VI-28 This entry controls the number of LLC frames NBF sends before it stops sending and waits for acknowledgment. On a very reliable system, you can increase this number and improve performance. If your network is less reliable, raising the value is not wise because the performance benefit of raising the value is offset by retry operations.

Hive: HKEY_LOCAL_MACHINE
Key: System\CurrentControlSet\Services\NBF\Parameters
Value Name: LLCMaxWindowSize
Data Type: REG_DWORD
Value: 1

The value sets the number of frames NBF sends before waiting for acknowledgment. The default value is 1.

VI-29 This entry determines the number of times NBF retries a request when it gets a T1 timeout. If your NBF is running on a slow network, you might want to increase this value.

Hive: HKEY_LOCAL_MACHINE
Key: System\CurrentControlSet\Services\NBF\Parameters
Value Name: LLCRetries
Data Type: REG_DWORD
Value: 8

A value of 1 or more sets the number of times NBF retries a request; a value of 0 sets no limit on the number of NBF's retries. The default value is 8.

PERFORMANCE

NETLOGON

The NetLogon service manages the process of logging on to a domain. It interacts with the NT Local Security Authority (LSA) to validate account and password information. It also keeps all account information synchronized between the Primary Domain Controller (PDC) and the Backup Domain Controllers (BDCs).

VI-30   NetLogon collects account information for a specified period of time and sends it in one batch to each BDC that isn't already up-to-date. By default, NetLogon determines the interval based on the server's load, but you can tune the time period NetLogon collects account data to suit your environment or to minimize network traffic.

> **Hive:** HKEY_LOCAL_MACHINE
> **Key:** System\CurrentControlSet\Services\Netlogon\Parameters
> **Value Name:** Pulse
> **Data Type:** REG_DWORD
> **Value:** 300

The value is the number of seconds in the collection period. The default value is 300 seconds, or 5 minutes. Valid values range from 60 to 172,800 (48 hours).

VI-31   When a BDC receives a pulse from the PDC, it waits a specified time before returning a message. Changing this entry changes the wait period.

> **Hive:** HKEY_LOCAL_MACHINE
> **Key:** System\CurrentControlSet\Services\Netlogon\Parameters
> **Value Name:** Randomize
> **Data Type:** REG_DWORD
> **Value:** 1

The value is the number of seconds that a BDC waits before requesting updated information from a PDC after receiving a pulse. The default value is 1; valid values range from 0 to 120. Typically, you should keep this value small, less than the PulseTimeout1 value under the same key.

VI-32 The following entry specifies how many outstanding pulses the PDC has at any time. By adjusting this value you can control the load on a PDC — the higher the value, the higher the potential load when security or account information is updated. Decreasing the value increases the time required to propagate the information to all the BDCs. You can estimate the time it takes to replicate account or security database information with the formula ((Randomize/2) * NumberOfBdcsInDomain) / PulseConcurrency

        Hive: HKEY_LOCAL_MACHINE
        Key: System\CurrentControlSet\Services\Netlogon\Parameters
Value Name: PulseConcurrency
   Data Type: REG_DWORD
      Value: 20

The value is the number of outstanding pulse events the PDC allows. The default value is 20; valid values range from 0 to 500.

TCP/IP

VI-33 TCP/IP allows a certain number of bytes to be sent before the system waits for an acknowledgment. You can increase this number, also known as the Window Size, if your network is reliable and has high bandwidth. Ideally, it should be a multiple of the TCP Maximum Segment Size (MSS).

        Hive: HKEY_LOCAL_MACHINE
        Key: System\CurrentControlSet\Services\Tcpip\Parameters
Value Name: TcpWindowSize
   Data Type: REG_DWORD
      Value: 8760

The value is the size, in bytes, of the TCP/IP window. The default is 8760 in Ethernet networks; valid values range from 0 to 0xFFFF.

NWLINK

NWLink is an implementation of the IPX/SPX protocols popular in NetWare networks. The NWNBLink module provides support for the Novell implementation of the NetBIOS protocol.

VI-34 By default, the NWNBLink protocol allocates two frames to receive messages. When the frames are filled, it sends an acknowledgment to the sender. This entry is typically used as a clocking mechanism where the sender is on a fast part of the LAN but the receiver is on a slow link. You can set the value to 0 to prevent NWNBLink from sending any acknowledgments, which can improve performance. Note that you can direct NWNBLink to ignore the AckWindow if round-trip times are below a threshold indicated in the AckWindowThreshold value under the same key.

> **Hive:** HKEY_LOCAL_MACHINE
> **Key:** System\CurrentControlSet\Services\NWNBLink\Parameters
> **Value Name:** AckWindow
> **Data Type:** REG_DWORD
> **Value:** 2

VI-35

> **Hive:** HKEY_LOCAL_MACHINE
> **Key:** System\CurrentControlSet\Services\NWNBLink\Parameters
> **Value Name:** AckWindowThreshold
> **Data Type:** REG_DWORD
> **Value:** 2

The value determines the number of frames in the AckWindow that are filled with received messages before NWNBLink sends an acknowledgment. If the value is 0, not acknowledgments are sent. The default value is 2.

VI-36 While NWNBLink sessions are initialized, the maximum number of messages that the receiver can process at one time is transmitted to the sender. Increasing this value may increase performance on high-bandwidth networks.

> **Hive:** HKEY_LOCAL_MACHINE
> **Key:** System\CurrentControlSet\Services\NWNBLink\Parameters
> **Value Name:** RcvWindowMax
> **Data Type:** REG_DWORD
> **Value:** 4

The value sets the number of frames allocated for receiving message. The default value is 4. Valid values range from 0 to 49152.

VI-37   This entry determines how many messages can be received simultaneously; the value is sent to remote connections. Increasing this value could increase performance of IPX messaging on high-bandwidth networks.

> **Hive:** HKEY_LOCAL_MACHINE
> **Key:** System\CurrentControlSet\Services\NwLnkIpx\Parameters
> **Value Name:** WindowSize
> **Data Type:** REG_DWORD
> **Value:** 4

The value is the number of frames allocated for receiving SPX messages. The default value is 4; valid values range from 1 to 10.

VI-38   This value specifies how many messages can be received simultaneously; it is sent to remote connections. Increasing this value could increase performance of SPX messaging on high-bandwidth networks.

> **Hive:** HKEY_LOCAL_MACHINE
> **Key:** System\CurrentControlSet\Services\NwLnkSPX\Parameters
> **Value Name:** WindowSize
> **Data Type:** REG_DWORD
> **Value:** 4

The value is the number of frames allocated for receiving SPX messages. The default value is 4. Valid values range from 1 to 11.

PERFORMANCE

FILE SYSTEM PERFORMANCE

VI-39 This entry is the only performance-altering value related to file systems that you can control in the registry. By default, NTFS creates an MS-DOS-style "short file name" for every file created with a long file name; otherwise, these files won't be recognized by Windows 3.1 and MS-DOS programs running on NT. NTFS must therefore track two names for these files, which can cause performance to degrade, particularly the performance of directory-related operations such as file look-ups.

> **Hive:** HKEY_LOCAL_MACHINE
> **Key:** System\CurrentControlSet\Control\FileSystem
> **Value Name:** NtfsDisable8dot3NameCreation
> **Data Type:** REG_DWORD
> **Value:** 0

The value determines whether short names are generated for long file names. A value of 0 means that NTFS generates short names; a value of 1 means that NTFS doesn't generate the short names. If you don't run any Windows 3.1 or MS-DOS programs on your system, you don't need short file name compatibility; disable this value.

PRINTING PERFORMANCE

VI-40 The print spooler thread is responsible for feeding data to printers. By default, it runs in the NORMAL_PRIORITY_CLASS, along with most of the other threads in a system. However, you can reduce this value, which may enhance the responsiveness of other more important applications such as the file system server (LanmanServer).

> **Hive:** HKEY_LOCAL_MACHINE
> **Key:** System\CurrentControlSet\Control\Print
> **Value Name:** SpoolerPriority
> **Data Type:** REG_DWORD
> **Value:** 0x20

The value sets the class the print spooler thread runs in. The following three values are recognized; other values are ignored.

0x40 IDLE_PRIORITY_CLASS
0x20 NORMAL_PRIORITY_CLASS
0x80 HIGH_PRIORITY_CLASS

REGISTRY EDITOR PERFORMANCE

VI-41   Normally, when RegEdit processes a .reg file, it bring up a dialog box informing you that it added items to the registry. Using this feature is usually a good option, unless you want to add certain items automatically with a login script and you don't want users to have to click OK to close the window every time they log on. Luckily, Microsoft has provided an undocumented parameter for RegEdit that bypasses this option: the /y parameter. Use it like this:

```
Regedit /y <regfile.reg>
```

Note that this change only affects Regedit.exe, not Regedt32.exe or Regedt.exe.

Appendix A

ADMINISTERING THE REGISTRY

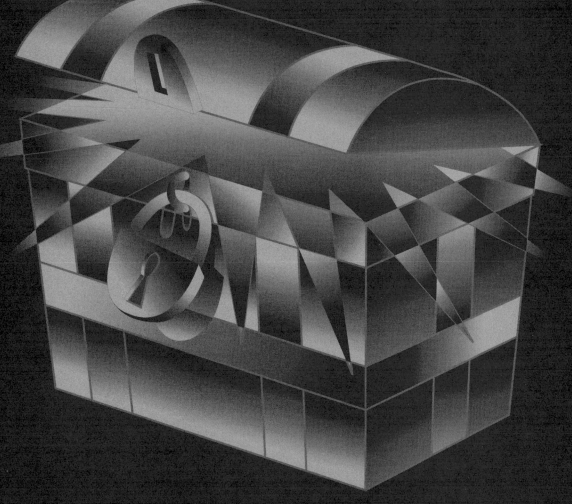

Windows NT and Windows 95 both let you administer the registry from remote locations. A simple way to change values on a system is to use Regedt32.exe to connect to a remote computer and modify the registry. This procedure works fine for small numbers of modifications or queries, but what if you have 20, 50, or 100 workstations to change?

You may decide that you want a way to automatically perform registry administration tasks on a remote computer. REGREM is a utility written in C that demonstrates remote registry administration; it queries the registry of a remote Windows NT computer. The program prints to the screen a copy of the network configuration settings for a remote Windows NT computer.

```c
// regrem.c
// Steve Scoggins 1997

#include <stdio.h>
#include <time.h>
#include <conio.h>
#include <ctype.h>
#include <windows.h>

#define OK ERROR_SUCCESS

main(int argc, char *argv[])
{
  static char lpszNIC_Description[80];
  static char lpszNIC_Manufacturer[80];
  static char lpszNIC_ProductName[80];
  static char lpszNIC_ServiceName[80];

  static char lpszTcpip_DefaultGateway[20];
  static char lpszTcpip_IPAddress[20];
  static char lpszTcpip_SubnetMask[20];

  static char lpszTcpip_Domain[80];
  static char lpszTcpip_Hostname[80];
  static char lpszTcpip_NameServer[80];
  static char lpszTcpip_SearchList[128];
  static char lpszComputerName[80];
  static char lpszDefaultDomainName[80];

  char szKeyPart1[] = "SYSTEM\\CurrentControlSet\\Services\\";
  char szKeyPart2[] = "\\Parameters";
  char szServiceKey[128];

  long InterruptNumber, IoBaseAddress;

  HKEY hkey, hNetKey ;
  DWORD lenKeyValue;
  unsigned long DataType;
  int err;

  char *name = argv[1];

    if ((err = RegConnectRegistry(name, HKEY_LOCAL_MACHINE, &hkey)) == OK)
    {

    // Open the Registry Key for the first instance of a Network Adapter in the Registry
    // Read the Description, Manufacturer, Product Name, and Service Name for this
    // instance of an installed Network Adapter.
```

```
if(RegOpenKey(hkey, "SOFTWARE\\Microsoft\\Windows NT\\CurrentVersion\\NetworkCards\\1",&hNetKey)
    == ERROR_SUCCESS)
{
  RegQueryValueEx(hNetKey, "Description", 0, &DataType, NULL, &lenKeyValue);
  RegQueryValueEx(hNetKey, "Description", 0, &DataType,(LPTSTR)lpszNIC_Description, &lenKeyValue);
  printf("Windows NT Network Adapter:\n");
  printf("Description: %s\n",lpszNIC_Description);

  RegQueryValueEx(hNetKey, "Manufacturer", 0, &DataType, NULL, &lenKeyValue);
  RegQueryValueEx(hNetKey, "Manufacturer", 0, &DataType,(LPTSTR)lpszNIC_Manufacturer, &lenKeyValue);
  printf("Manufacturer: %s\n",lpszNIC_Manufacturer);

  RegQueryValueEx(hNetKey, "ProductName", 0, &DataType, NULL, &lenKeyValue);
  RegQueryValueEx(hNetKey, "ProductName", 0, &DataType,(LPTSTR)lpszNIC_ProductName, &lenKeyValue);
  printf("Product Name: %s\n",lpszNIC_ProductName);

  RegQueryValueEx(hNetKey, "ServiceName", 0, &DataType, NULL, &lenKeyValue);
  RegQueryValueEx(hNetKey, "ServiceName", 0, &DataType,(LPTSTR)lpszNIC_ServiceName, &lenKeyValue);
  printf("Service Name: %s\n",lpszNIC_ServiceName);

  RegCloseKey(hNetKey);
}


// Now that we have the ServiceName for the Network Adapter from the NetworkCards key
// we will reconstruct the correct ServiceKey path based on the Service Name for this
// network adapter.

strcpy(szServiceKey, szKeyPart1);
strcat(szServiceKey, lpszNIC_ServiceName);
strcat(szServiceKey, szKeyPart2);

if(RegOpenKey(hkey, (LPCTSTR) szServiceKey, &hNetKey) == ERROR_SUCCESS)
{

  RegQueryValueEx(hNetKey, "InterruptNumber", 0, &DataType, NULL, &lenKeyValue);
  RegQueryValueEx(hNetKey, "InterruptNumber", 0, &DataType, (LPBYTE) &InterruptNumber, &lenKeyValue);
  printf("Interrupt Number: %x\n",InterruptNumber);

  RegQueryValueEx(hNetKey, "IoBaseAddress", 0, &DataType, NULL, &lenKeyValue);
  RegQueryValueEx(hNetKey, "IoBaseAddress", 0, &DataType, (LPBYTE) &IoBaseAddress, &lenKeyValue);
  printf("IO Base Address: %x\n",IoBaseAddress);
  RegCloseKey(hNetKey);
}


// Open the TCP/IP Key for this Network Adapter
// Read some of the key TCP/IP parameters for this Network Adapter

strcat(szServiceKey, "\\Tcpip");

if(RegOpenKey(hkey, (LPCTSTR) szServiceKey ,&hNetKey) == ERROR_SUCCESS)
{
  RegQueryValueEx(hNetKey, "DefaultGateway", 0, &DataType, NULL, &lenKeyValue);
  RegQueryValueEx(hNetKey, "DefaultGateway", 0, &DataType,(LPTSTR)lpszTcpip_DefaultGateway, &lenKeyValue);
  printf("TCP/IP DefaultGateway : %s\n",lpszTcpip_DefaultGateway);

  RegQueryValueEx(hNetKey, "IPAddress", 0, &DataType, NULL, &lenKeyValue);
  RegQueryValueEx(hNetKey, "IPAddress", 0, &DataType,(LPTSTR)lpszTcpip_IPAddress, &lenKeyValue);
  printf("TCP/IP IPAddress : %s\n",lpszTcpip_IPAddress);

  RegQueryValueEx(hNetKey, "SubnetMask", 0, &DataType, NULL, &lenKeyValue);
  RegQueryValueEx(hNetKey, "SubnetMask", 0, &DataType,(LPTSTR)lpszTcpip_SubnetMask, &lenKeyValue);
  printf("TCP/IP Subnet Mask : %s\n",lpszTcpip_SubnetMask);
  RegCloseKey(hNetKey);
```

```
    }


    // Read the global TCP/IP paramters

    if(RegOpenKey(hkey, "SYSTEM\\CurrentControlSet\\Services\\Tcpip\\Parameters",&hNetKey) == ERROR_SUCCESS)
    {
      RegQueryValueEx(hNetKey, "Domain", 0, &DataType, NULL, &lenKeyValue);
      RegQueryValueEx(hNetKey, "Domain", 0, &DataType,(LPTSTR)lpszTcpip_Domain, &lenKeyValue);
      printf("TCP/IP Domain Name: %s\n",lpszTcpip_Domain);

      RegQueryValueEx(hNetKey, "Hostname", 0, &DataType, NULL, &lenKeyValue);
      RegQueryValueEx(hNetKey, "Hostname", 0, &DataType,(LPTSTR)lpszTcpip_Hostname, &lenKeyValue);
      printf("TCP/IP Hostname: %s\n",lpszTcpip_Hostname);

      RegQueryValueEx(hNetKey, "NameServer", 0, &DataType, NULL, &lenKeyValue);
      RegQueryValueEx(hNetKey, "NameServer", 0, &DataType,(LPTSTR)lpszTcpip_NameServer, &lenKeyValue);
      printf("TCP/IP DNS Name Servers: %s\n",lpszTcpip_NameServer);

      RegQueryValueEx(hNetKey, "SearchList", 0, &DataType, NULL, &lenKeyValue);
      RegQueryValueEx(hNetKey, "SearchList", 0, &DataType,(LPTSTR)lpszTcpip_SearchList, &lenKeyValue);
      printf("TCP/IP Domain Name Search List: %s\n",lpszTcpip_SearchList);

      RegCloseKey(hNetKey);
    }


    // Read the Computer Name and Domain Name for this Windows NT Computer

    if(RegOpenKey(hkey, "SYSTEM\\CurrentControlSet\\Control\\ComputerName\\ActiveComputerName", &hNetKey)
         == ERROR_SUCCESS)
    {
      RegQueryValueEx(hNetKey, "ComputerName", 0, &DataType, NULL, &lenKeyValue);
      RegQueryValueEx(hNetKey, "ComputerName", 0, &DataType,(LPTSTR)lpszComputerName, &lenKeyValue);
      printf("Windows NT Computer Name: %s\n",lpszComputerName);

      RegCloseKey(hNetKey);
    }

    if(RegOpenKey(hkey, "SOFTWARE\\Microsoft\\Windows NT\\CurrentVersion\\Winlogon", &hNetKey) == ERROR_SUCCESS)
    {
      RegQueryValueEx(hNetKey, "DefaultDomainName", 0, &DataType, NULL, &lenKeyValue);
      RegQueryValueEx(hNetKey, "DefaultDomainName", 0, &DataType,(LPTSTR)lpszDefaultDomainName, &lenKeyValue);
      printf("Windows NT DomainName: %s\n",lpszDefaultDomainName);

      RegCloseKey(hNetKey);
    }

    RegCloseKey(hkey);
    }

    else
    {
        switch (err)
        {
            #define MSG(x) case x : printf("%s\t\t\t\n", #x)
            MSG(ERROR_OPERATION_ABORTED); break;
            MSG(ERROR_BAD_NETPATH); break;
            MSG(ERROR_ACCESS_DENIED); break;
            default: printf("Error #%u (look in WINERROR.H)\n", err);
            break;
        }
        printf("failed to connect to remote registry");
    }
    printf("bye!\n");
    return 0;
}
```

The source and the compiled executable are available on the CD-ROM that comes with this book. To run REGREM, you must be logged on as an administrator of the Windows NT Domain for the remote computer.

A network administrator could use this type of software utility to query the network configuration for all the Windows NT computers on the local network. The results are printed to the screen. If you want a file containing this information, you can redirect the screen printout to a file using the following form of the command:

```
REGREM ComputerName > FileName
```

Sample output from REGREM is shown below.

```
Windows NT Network Adapter:
Description: 3Com Etherlink III PCI Bus-Master Adapter (3C590)
Manufacturer: 3Com
Product Name: EL59x
Service Name: EL59x1
Interrupt Number: 12ff8c
IO Base Address: 3
TCP/IP DefaultGateway : 200.200.200.254
TCP/IP IPAddress : 200.200.200.200
TCP/IP Subnet Mask : 255.255.255.0
TCP/IP Domain Name: test.com
TCP/IP Hostname: bigdog
TCP/IP DNS Name Servers:
TCP/IP Domain Name Search List:
Windows NT Computer Name: BIGDOG
Windows NT DomainName: BIGDOG
bye!
```

You can also run the Regrem.exe client on any Windows 95 or Windows NT workstation that is logged on to your Windows NT Domain. To run this utility on a Windows 95 computer, install the Microsoft Remote Registry Services. The REGREM client utility uses Winreg.dll as an RPC client that communicates with the RPC server on the remote Windows NT computer. The RPC service on the remote computer uses Regserv.exe.

You must enable user-level access before you can run remote registry software on a Windows 95 computer. You also must be authenticated by the Windows NT Domain server before you are allowed to connect to a remote registry on a Windows NT computer in the Windows NT Domain.

INSTALLING REMOTE REGISTRY SERVICES
ON A WINDOWS 95 COMPUTER

1. Open My Computer.
2. Open Control Panel.
3. Open the Network applet.
4. Click Add.
5. Double-click Service.
6. Click Have Disk.
7. When the install dialog box opens, type **Admin\NetTools\RemoteReg** for the directory path.
8. Click OK.
9. When the network service dialog box opens, select the Microsoft Remote Registry service.
10. Click OK.
11. Click the Access Control Tab in the Network setup dialog box.
12. Check the "User-level access control" option.
13. Click OK.
14. Type your Windows NT Domain name in the "Obtain list of users and groups from" box and click OK.

ENABLING REMOTE ADMINISTRATION
FOR A WINDOWS 95 COMPUTER

Note: for remote registry administration to work, you must enable remote registration on the remote Windows 95 computers.

1. Open My Computer.
2. Open the Control Panel.
3. Open the Passwords applet.
4. Click the Remote Administration tab.
5. Check "Enable Remote Administration of this server."
6. The Domain Administrators are listed in the list box of users allowed to use Remote Administration. Click the Add button to add other NT Domain users authorized to use Remote Administration.
7. Click OK to finish.

This program is meant as a demonstration of what is possible. Make sure you visit this book's Web site frequently for updates and other programming examples.

USING WINDOWS 95-STYLE INF FILES
TO MODIFY REGISTRY SETTINGS

Another way to modify the Windows NT registry automatically without writing code is to use .inf files. You can change multiple workstations and servers remotely and automatically. To avoid having to fire up Regedt32.exe for each change, you can simply tell the Logon.bat file to run your .inf file, which can perform any sort command or registry modification.

The following command line runs an .inf file on a Windows NT computer:

```
RUNDLL32 syssetup,SetupInfObjectInstallAction DefaultInstall 128 E:\NT Registry\cdautoff.inf
```

It is very important that you provide the fully qualified path to the .inf file. If you just supply the filename, this procedure will not work. You can place this command line in a logon batch file if you want to make this modification for multiple users. You can then edit the users' profiles and specify this batch file.

Listed below is an INF file that turns off CD-ROM Autorun via the registry.

```
; CDAUTOFF.INF
;
; This is an example INF setup information file to turn OFF CD-ROM Autorun


[Version]
Signature="$Windows NT$"
Provider=%Provider%

[Strings]
Provider="Steve Scoggins"

[DefaultInstall]
AddReg = add.reg

[add.reg]
HKLM,SYSTEM\CurrentControlSet\Services\Cdrom,"Autorun",0x10001,0
```

You can automatically roll out any number of modifications to the registry using this technique. The trick is learning what the bit fields for each key does.

For more information about using INF files to automate installing applications or making registry changes, I recommend the references cited below:

* *Microsoft Windows NT Workstation Resource Kit,* Microsoft Press ISBN 1-57231-343-9, Chapter 2, Customizing Setup; "Creating .inf files", page 59

* *Microsoft Visual C++ 5.0 Professional Edition,* Microsoft Developer Studio Infoviewer

Appendix B

HOW TO USE THE CD-ROM

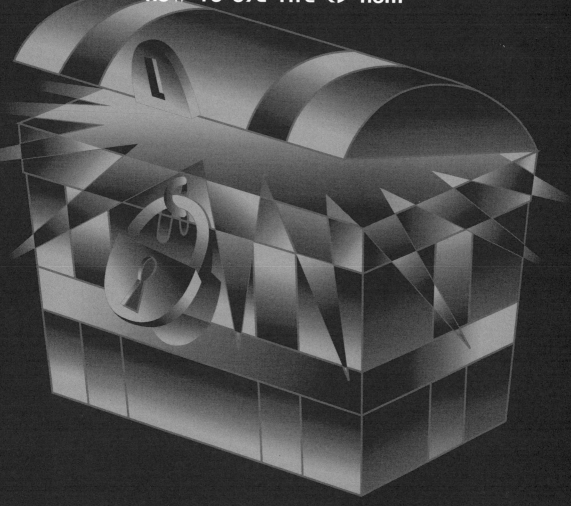

The CD-ROM is set up to run automatically under Windows 95 and Windows NT 4.0. If Autorun is enabled on your machine, you should be able to insert the disk into your CD-ROM drive, and it will start automatically. If Autorun is disabled on your machine, you can launch a Web browser and open Index.html, which is located at the root level of the CD-ROM. We have provided Microsoft Internet Explorer 3.02 on the CD-ROM for you to install if you don't have a Web browser.

CD-ROM CONTENTS

The disk is organized in HTML and can be navigated with any Web browser. It includes separate pages with information and links to Windows NT registry Web sites, listservers, and newsgroups. In addition, the CD includes source code and programs

SOURCE CODE

- Regrem.zip — The REGREM is an example utility written in C that demonstrates remote registry administration. This utility queries the registry of a remote Windows NT computer. The program prints (to the screen) a copy of the network configuration settings for a remote Windows NT computer. Regrem.zip contains all the files you need to compile Regrem.exe

- CDAutoff.zip — This zip file contains files that show you how to use batch files to configure the registry automatically. It lets you avoid manually changing the registry using a registry editor. The good news is you can run an INF-type install from the logon.bat file.

PROGRAMS

- RegAdmin — RegAdmin Pro is a part of Administrator Assistant Tool Kit (A2NT), a set of tools that substantially facilitates security administration of NT-based networks. It gives an administrator functions that native NT tools lack. A2NT currently consists of FileAdmin, RegAdmin and ScanNT.

- Ini2Reg — The purpose of Ini2Reg is to migrate existing applications from 16-bit Windows (most of which used INI files to save user settings) to the 32-bit Windows (Windows 95 and NT) registry.

- Ntdure — A small program that allows an NT administrator to change the settings easily for the following default items: Screen Saver File, Screen Saver Active, Screen Saver Timeout, Wallpaper file, Wallpaper tiled, Allow a shutdown at the login prompt, Legal Notice Prompt text, Legal Notice Prompt caption.

- NTRegmon — NTRegmon is a GUI/device driver combination that monitors and displays all Registry activity on a system. It has advanced filtering and search capabilities that make it a powerful tool for exploring the way NT works, seeing how applications use the Registry, and tracking down problems in system or application configurations.

- RegeditX — The Registry Editor extensions "extend" the Registry Editor included with Windows 95 and Windows NT 4.0. A combo box is inserted into the Registry Editor; the box remembers the keys you have edited and lets you return to them quickly.

- RegSrch — Registry Search + Replace (Regsrch.exe) is a Win32 utility that simplifies maintenance of the Windows NT and Windows 95 registration databases. For more complete information on what this utility offers, how to use it, or about its author, see the product's support site at http://www.iserv.net/~sjhswdev.

DISCLAIMER

All software on the CD is provided on an "as is" basis. Duke Press makes no claims for it nor accepts any responsibility for any damage it may do to an individual user's computer. Support for the CD by Duke Press is limited to the workings of the shell structure only. For support of the software provided on the CD, please contact the individual software vendors.

APPENDIX B

INDEX

Index entries in **boldface** refer to specific registry values.

P

Packets
  data queue memory, 88
  keep-alive
    frequency of, 90
    interval, 103
    number of, 115
    NWLink wait time, 114
    NWNBLink sending, 109
  lost, minimizing, 88
  router queue memory, 88
  SPX, allocation field, 113
  type, setting, 111
Palm Computing, Pilot Desktop, 158
Parameters
  /:, 188
  /iisadmin, 188
  /Scripts, 188
  /srchadm, 188
  AcceptDefaultRoutes, 120
  AcceptHostRoutes, 120
  AcceptVJCompression, 118
  AccessDeniedMessage, 187
  AckDelayTime, 105
  AckWindow, 105, 290
  AckWindowThreshold, 106, 290
  AdminEmail, 176, 181, 186
  AdminName, 175, 181, 185
  AlertSched, 79
  AllowSessionState, 191
  AnnotateDirectories, 178
  AnnounceDefaultRoutes, 121
  AnnounceHostRoutes, 121
  AnonymousUserName, 190
  Application, 69, 70
  AppParameters, 69, 70
  AutoDisconnect, 76, 78, 79, 284
  BcastNameQueryCount, 100
  BcastQueryTimeout, 101
  BroadcastCount, 107
  BroadcastTimeout, 107
  BusMaster, 77
  CachedOpenLimit, 214
  CacheFileTimeout, 281
  CacheSecurityDescriptor, 192
  CacheTimeout, 102
  ChangeLogSize, 51
  Circular Logging, 150
  Configuration, 104
  ConnectionCount, 108, 114
  ConnectionlessAutoDisc, 81
  ConnectionTimeout, 108, 114
  Database Log Files Path, 151
  DatabaseLoggingFlag, 286

DatabasePath, 86
DB Path, 152
Default1Timeout, 286
DefaultLogonDomain, 182, 189
DefaultMaxPacketSize, 9
DefaultTTL, 85
DhcpServer, 96
DisableMemoryCache, 189
DisableOtherSourcePackets, 78
DisableOtherSrcPackets, 119
DiskSpaceThreshold, 83
DormantFileLimt, 281
DriverParameter, 138
DSA Database File, 151
DSA Hierarchy Table File, 151
DSA Temporary File, 151
DSA Working Directory, 152
EnableDeadGWDetect, 87
EnableDns, 99
EnableLmhosts, 98
EnableOpLocks, 285
EnablePiggyBackAck, 106
EnablePMTUDiscovery, 87
EnableProxyRegCheck, 102
EnableRaw, 284
EnableSecurityFilters, 91
EnableTriggeredUpdates, 121
EnableWFW311DirectIpx, 81
ErrorControl, 129
ExitMessage, 178
Extensions, 105
ForwardBufferMemory, 88
GarbageTimeout, 122
GreetingMessage, 178
HelpLocation, 190
Hidden, 80
Hostname, 93
IGMPLevel, 89
IgnoreBroadcastFlag, 95
InitialRefreshTimeout, 103
InitialRetransmissionTime, 108
Internet, 107
IPAddress, 93
KeepAliveCount, 109, 115
KeepAliveInterval, 90
KeepAliveTime, 89
KeepAliveTimeout, 109, 114
KeyboardDataQueSize, 126
ListenBackLog, 189
LLCMaxWindowSize, 287
LLCRetries, 287
Lmannounce, 80
LmhostTimeout, 101
LogFileBatchSize, 192
LogFilePeriod, 176, 182, 186

LogFileTruncateSize, 176, 183, 186
Logging, 118
LoggingLevel, 123
LogNonAnonymous, 180
LowercaseFiles, 180
MailDuplicateTimeout, 84
MaintainServerList, 77
MaxClientsMessage, 182
MaxCmds, 280
MaxConnections, 177, 181, 187
MaxDgramBuffering, 100
MaxFrameSize, 9
MaxFreeConnections, 78
MaxGlobalOpenSearch, 82
MaximumMailslotMessages, 83
MaximumMailslotTimeout, 84
MaximumSGList, 138
MaxNonPagedMemoryUsage, 282
MaxPagedMemoryUsage, 283
MaxTriggeredUpdateFrequency, 122
MaxUserPort, 90
MaxWorkItems, 78
MemoryCacheSize, 192
MimeMap, 187
MinFileKbSec, 191
MinFreeConnections, 60, 62, 283
MinFreeWorkItems, 61
MinKeepSearch, 61
MinLinkThroughPut, 61
MinRcvQueues, 62
MouseDataQueSize, 126
NameServerBackup, 100
NameServerPort, 102
NameSrvQueryCount, 103
NetworkErrorThreshold, 81
NodeType, 101
NonPagedMemLimit, 285
NumberOfRings, 115
ObjectCacheTTL, 193
OptionNames, 99
PagedMemLimit, 285
PersistentRoutes, 85
Ports, 129
PPTPTcpMaxDataRetransmissions, 86
Pulse, 51, 288
PulseConcurrency, 51, 289
PulseMaximum, 52
PulseTimeout1, 52
PulseTimeout2, 52
Randomize, 53, 288
RcvWindowMax, 106, 290
ReadAheadThroughput, 282
ReplicationGovernor, 53
RequestVJCompression, 117

INDEX

New Books in the Duke Press Library

THE ADMINISTRATOR'S GUIDE TO MICROSOFT SQL SERVER 6.5

By Kevin Cox and William Jones

This book guides database managers and administrators into a thorough understanding of the client/server aspects of the SQL Server 6.5 product, and includes many useful tips for managing security, troubleshooting, and improving performance. 469 pages.

BUILDING AS/400 CLIENT/SERVER APPLICATIONS

Put ODBC and Client Access APIs to Work

By Mike Otey

Mike Otey, a leading client/server authority with extensive practical client/server application development experience, gives you the why, what, and how-to of AS/400 client/server computing, which matches the strengths of the AS/400 with the PC GUIs that users want. This book's clear and easy-to-understand style guides you through all the important aspects of AS/400 client/server applications. Mike covers APPC and TCP/IP communications, as well as the underlying architectures for each of the major AS/400 client/server APIs. CD with complete source code for several working applications included. 505 pages.

CONTROL LANGUAGE PROGRAMMING FOR THE AS/400, SECOND EDITION

By Bryan Meyers and Dan Riehl, NEWS/400 technical editors

This comprehensive CL programming textbook offers students up-to-the-minute knowledge of the skills they will need in today's MIS environment. Chapters progress methodically from CL basics to more complex processes and concepts, guiding students toward a professional grasp of CL programming techniques and style. In this second edition, the authors have updated the text to include discussion of the Integrated Language Environment (ILE) and the fundamental changes ILE introduces to the AS/400's execution model. 522 pages.

DEVELOPING YOUR AS/400 INTERNET STRATEGY

By Alan Arnold

This book addresses the issues unique to deploying your AS/400 on the Internet. It includes procedures for configuring AS/400 TCP/IP and information about which client and server technologies the AS/400 supports natively. This enterprise-class tutorial evaluates the AS/400 as an Internet server and teaches you how to design, program, and manage your Web home page. 248 pages.

INSIDE THE AS/400, SECOND EDITION

Featuring the AS/400e series

By Frank G. Soltis

Learn from the architect of the AS/400 about the new generation of AS/400e systems and servers, and about the latest system features and capabilities introduced in Version 4 of OS/400. Dr. Frank Soltis demystifies the system, shedding light on how it came to be, how it can do the things it does, and what its future may hold. 402 pages.

INTERNET SECURITY WITH WINDOWS NT

By Mark Joseph Edwards

Security expert and *Windows NT Magazine* news editor Mark Edwards provides the quintessential guide to Internet and intranet security from the Windows NT platform. Security is the number one concern of NT users, and this comprehensive book covers network security basics as well as IIS and MPS, and includes specific advice about selecting NT tools and security devices. The accompanying CD-ROM includes security-related utilities, tools, and software packages — firewalls, port scanners, network-monitoring software, and virus detection and prevention utilities. These tools, combined with the tips and techniques in the book, are powerful weapons in your security efforts. 520 pages.

The Microsoft Exchange Server Internet Mail Connector
By Spyros Sakellariadis
Achieve Internet connectivity using Exchange Server 4.0 and 5.0. This book presents four Internet connectivity models, shows how to set up the Internet Mail Connector with an Internet Service Provider, and illustrates how to monitor Internet traffic. It also includes troubleshooting and reference guides. 234 pages.

The Microsoft Exchange User's Handbook
By Sue Mosher
Microsoft Exchange is all about making connections — connections to a Microsoft Mail server, to Exchange Server, to a fax machine, or to online services. Here's the must-have, complete guide for users who need to know how to set up and use all the features of the Microsoft Exchange client product. Includes chapters about Microsoft Exchange Server 5.0 and Microsoft Outlook. 692 pages. CD included.

The Microsoft Outlook E-Mail and Fax Guide
By Sue Mosher
Here's a book for Microsoft Outlook 97 end users and the administrators who support them. This easy to read volume will expand your knowledge of Outlook's e-mail functions and explain the real world tasks that you are likely to encounter. Sue Mosher explains the setup of individual e-mail services and components, e-mail options and when you might want to use them, and many time-saving techniques that take you beyond the basics. Users at all levels will learn from this comprehensive introduction to Microsoft's next generation of messaging software. The book includes coverage of the Internet Mail Enhancement Patch, Rules Wizard, and special features for Microsoft Exchange Server users. 600 pages.

Migrating to Windows NT 4.0
By Sean Daily
This book is a comprehensive yet concise guide to the significant changes users will encounter as they make the move to Windows NT 4.0. The author, a Microsoft Certified Systems Engineer (MCSE), eases the transition with his enthusiastic presentation of a wealth of tips and techniques that give readers the sense they're receiving "insider information." 475 pages.

Powering Your Web Site with Windows NT Server
By Nik Simpson
Powering Your Web Site with Windows NT Server explores the tools necessary to establish a presence on the Internet or on an internal corporate intranet using Web technology and Windows NT Server. The author helps readers navigate the process of creating a new information infrastructure, from the basics of justifying the decision to management through the complete implementation cycle. 640 pages. CD included.

The Technology Guide to Accounting Software
A Handbook for Evaluating Vendor Applications
By Stewart McKie
If you are involved in recommending or selecting financial software for your department or company, this book is must reading! It is designed to help managers evaluate accounting software, with an emphasis on the issues in a client/server environment. McKie provides a range of useful checklists for shortlisting products to evaluate in more detail. More than 50 vendors are profiled, and a resource guide and a glossary are included. 225 pages.

Also Published by Duke Press

The A to Z of EDI
By Nahid M. Jilovec
Electronic Data Interchange (EDI) can help reduce administrative costs, accelerate information processing, ensure data accuracy, and streamline business procedures. Here's a comprehensive guide to EDI to help in planning, startup, and

implementation. The author reveals all the benefits, challenges, standards, and implementation secrets gained through extensive experience. 263 pages.

APPLICATION DEVELOPER'S HANDBOOK FOR THE AS/400

Edited by Mike Otey, a NEWS/400 *technical editor*

Learn how to effectively use the AS/400 to build reliable, flexible, and efficient business applications. The book contains RPG/400 and CL coding examples and tips, and provides both step-by-step instructions and handy reference material. Includes diskette. 768 pages.

AS/400 DISK SAVING TIPS & TECHNIQUES

By James R. Plunkett

Want specific help for cleaning up and maintaining your disks? Here are more than 50 tips, plus design techniques for minimizing your disk usage. Each tip is completely explained with the "symptom," the problem, and the technique or code you need to correct it. 72 pages.

AS/400 SUBFILES IN RPG

Edited by Catherine T. Rivera

On the AS/400, subfiles are powerful and easy to use, and with this book you can start working with subfiles in just a few hours — no need to wade through page after page of technical jargon. You'll start with the concept behind subfiles, then discover how easy they are to program. The book contains all of the DDS subfile keywords announced in V2R3 of OS/400. Five complete RPG subfile programs are included, and the book comes complete with a 3.5" PC diskette containing all those programs plus DDS. The book is an updated version of the popular *Programming Subfiles in RPG/400.* 200 pages.

C FOR RPG PROGRAMMERS

By Jennifer Hamilton, a NEWS/400 *author*

Written from the perspective of an RPG programmer, this book includes side-by-side coding examples written in both C and RPG, clear identification of unique C constructs, and a comparison of RPG op-codes to equivalent C concepts. Includes many tips and examples covering the use of C/400. 292 pages.

CLIENT ACCESS TOKEN-RING CONNECTIVITY

By Chris Patterson

Client Access Token-Ring Connectivity details all that is required to successfully maintain and troubleshoot a Token-Ring network. The first half of the book introduces the Token-Ring and describes the Client Access communications architecture, the Token-Ring connection from both the PC side and the AS/400 side, and the Client Access applications. The second half provides a useful guide to Token-Ring management, strategies for Token-Ring error identification and recovery, and tactics for resolving Client Access error messages. 125 pages.

COMMON-SENSE C
Advice and Warnings for C and C++ Programmers

By Paul Conte, a NEWS/400 *technical editor*

C programming language has its risks; this book shows how C programmers get themselves into trouble, includes tips to help you avoid C's pitfalls, and suggests how to manage C and C++ application development. 100 pages.

DDS PROGRAMMING FOR DISPLAY & PRINTER FILES

By James Coolbaugh

Offers a thorough, straightforward explanation of how to use Data Description Specifications (DDS) to program display files and printer files. Covers basic to complex tasks using DDS functions. The author uses DDS programming examples for CL and RPG extensively throughout the book, and you can put these examples to use immediately. A complimentary diskette includes all the source code presented in the book. 446 pages.

DATABASE DESIGN AND PROGRAMMING FOR DB2/400

By Paul Conte

This textbook is the most complete guide to DB2/400 design and programming available anywhere. The author shows you everything you need to know about physical and logical file DDS, SQL/400, and RPG IV and COBOL/400 database programming. Clear explanations illustrated by a wealth of examples demonstrate efficient database programming and error handling with both DDS and SQL/400. Each programming chapter includes a specific list of "Coding Suggestions" that will help you write faster and more maintainable code. In addition, the author provides an extensive section on practical database design for DB2/400. 772 pages.

DESKTOP GUIDE TO THE S/36

By Mel Beckman, Gary Kratzer, and Roger Pence, NEWS/400 technical editors

This definitive S/36 survival manual includes practical techniques to supercharge your S/36, including ready-to-use information for maximum system performance tuning, effective application development, and smart Disk Data Management. Includes a review of two popular Unix-based S/36 work-alike migration alternatives. Diskette contains ready-to-run utilities to help you save machine time and implement power programming techniques such as External Program Calls. 387 pages.

THE ESSENTIAL GUIDE TO CLIENT ACCESS FOR DOS EXTENDED

By John Enck, Robert E. Anderson, and Michael Otey

The Essential Guide to Client Access for DOS Extended contains key insights and need-to-know technical information about Client Access for DOS Extended, IBM's strategic AS/400 product for DOS and Windows client/server connectivity. This book provides background information about the history and architecture of Client Access for DOS Extended; fundamental information about how to install and configure Client Access; and advanced information about integrating Client Access with other types of networks, managing how Client Access for DOS Extended operates under Windows, and developing client/server applications with Client Access. Written by industry experts based on their personal and professional experiences with Client Access, this book can help you avoid time-consuming pitfalls that litter the path of AS/400 client/ server computing. 430 pages.

ILE: A FIRST LOOK

By George Farr and Shailan Topiwala

This book begins by showing the differences between ILE and its predecessors, then goes on to explain the essentials of an ILE program — using concepts such as modules, binding, service programs, and binding directories. You'll discover how ILE program activation works and how ILE works with its predecessor environments. The book covers the new APIs and new debugging facilities and explains the benefits of ILE's new exception-handling model. You also get answers to the most commonly asked questions about ILE. 183 pages.

IMPLEMENTING AS/400 SECURITY, SECOND EDITION

A practical guide to implementing, evaluating, and auditing your AS/400 security strategy

By Wayne Madden, NEWS/400 publisher and editor in chief

Concise and practical, this second edition brings together in one place the fundamental AS/400 security tools and experience-based recommendations that you need and also includes specifics on the latest security enhancements available in OS/400 Version 3 Release 1. Completely updated from the first edition, this is the only source for the latest information about how to protect your system against attack from its increasing exposure to hackers. 389 pages.

INTRODUCTION TO AS/400 SYSTEM OPERATIONS

By Patrice Gapen and Heidi Rothenbuehler

Here's the textbook that covers what you need to know to become a successful AS/400 system operator. System operators typically help users resolve problems, manage printed reports, and perform regularly scheduled procedures. *Introduction to AS/400 System Operations* covers a broad range of topics, including system architecture; DB2/400 and Query; user interface and Operational Assistant; managing jobs and printed reports; backup and restore; system configuration and networks; performance; security; and Client Access (PC Support). 233 pages.

An Introduction to Communications for the AS/400, Second Edition

By John Enck and Ruggero Adinolfi

This second edition has been revised to address the sweeping communications changes introduced with V3R1 of OS/400. As a result, this book now covers the broad range of AS/400 communications technology topics, ranging from Ethernet to X.25, and from APPN to AnyNet. The book presents an introduction to data communications and then covers communications fundamentals, types of networks, OSI, SNA, APPN, networking roles, the AS/400 as host and server, TCP/IP, and the AS/400-DEC connection. 210 pages.

Jim Sloan's CL Tips & Techniques

By Jim Sloan, developer of QUSRTOOL's TAA Tools

Written for those who understand CL, this book draws from Jim Sloan's knowledge and experience as a developer for the S/38 and the AS/400, and his creation of QUSRTOOL's TAA tools, to give you tips that can help you write better CL programs and become more productive. Includes more than 200 field-tested techniques, plus exercises to help you understand and apply many of the techniques presented. 564 pages.

Mastering AS/400 Performance

By Alan Arnold, Charly Jones, Jim Stewart, and Rick Turner

If you want more from your AS/400 — faster interactive response time, more batch jobs completed on time, and maximum use of your expensive resources — this book is for you. In *Mastering AS/400 Performance*, the experts tell you how to measure, evaluate, and tune your AS/400's performance. From the authors' experience in the field, they give you techniques for improving performance beyond simply buying additional hardware. Learn the techniques, gain the insight, and help your company profit from the experience of the top AS/400 performance professionals in the country. 259 pages.

Mastering the AS/400
A Practical, Hands-On Guide

By Jerry Fottral

This introductory textbook to AS/400 concepts and facilities has a utilitarian approach that stresses student participation. A natural prerequisite to programming and database management courses, it emphasizes mastery of system/user interface, member-object-library relationship, utilization of CL commands, and basic database and program development utilities. Also includes labs focusing on essential topics such as printer spooling; library lists; creating and maintaining physical files; using logical files; using CL and DDS; working in the PDM environment; and using SEU, DFU, Query, and SDA. 484 pages.

Object-Oriented Programming for AS/400 Programmers

By Jennifer Hamilton, a NEWS/400 author

Explains basic OOP concepts such as classes and inheritance in simple, easy-to-understand terminology. The OS/400 object-oriented architecture serves as the basis for the discussion throughout, and concepts presented are reinforced through an introduction to the C++ object-oriented programming language, using examples based on the OS/400 object model. 114 pages.

Performance Programming — Making RPG Sizzle

By Mike Dawson, CDP

Mike Dawson spent more than two years preparing this book — evaluating programming options, comparing techniques, and establishing benchmarks on thousands of programs. "Using the techniques in this book," he says, "I have made program after program run 30%, 40%, even 50% faster." To help you do the same, Mike gives you code and benchmark results for initializing and clearing arrays, performing string manipulation, using validation arrays with lookup techniques, using arrays in arithmetic routines, and a lot more. 257 pages.

Power Tools for the AS/400, Volumes I and II

Edited by Frederick L. Dick and Dan Riehl

NEWS 3X/400's Power Tools for the AS/400 is a two-volume reference series for people who work with the AS/400. *Volume I* (originally titled *AS/400 Power Tools*) is a collection of the best tools, tips, and techniques published in

NEWS/34-38 (pre-August 1988) and *NEWS 3X/400* (August 1988 through October 1991) that are applicable to the AS/400. *Volume II* extends this original collection by including material that appeared through 1994. Each book includes a diskette that provides load-and-go code for easy-to-use solutions to many everyday problems. *Volume I:* 709 pages; *Volume II:* 702 pages.

PROGRAMMING IN RPG IV, REVISED EDITION
By Judy Yaeger, Ph.D., a NEWS/400 *technical editor*
This textbook provides a strong foundation in the essentials of business programming, featuring the newest version of the RPG language: RPG IV. Focusing on real-world problems and down-to-earth solutions using the latest techniques and features of RPG, this book provides everything you need to know to write a well-designed RPG IV program. This revised edition includes a new section about subprocedures and an addition about using the RPG ILE source debugger. Each chapter includes informative, easy-to-read explanations and examples as well as a section of thought-provoking questions, exercises, and programming assignments. Four appendices and a handy, comprehensive glossary support the topics presented throughout the book. An instructor's kit is available. 436 pages.

PROGRAMMING IN RPG/400, SECOND EDITION
By Judy Yaeger, Ph.D., a NEWS/400 *technical editor*
This second edition refines and extends the comprehensive instructional material contained in the original textbook and features a new section that introduces externally described printer files, a new chapter that highlights the fundamentals of RPG IV, and a new appendix that correlates the key concepts from each chapter with their RPG IV counterparts. Includes everything you need to learn how to write a well-designed RPG program, from the most basic to the more complex, and each chapter includes a section of questions, exercises, and programming assignments that reinforce the knowledge you have gained from the chapter and strengthen the groundwork for succeeding chapters. An instructor's kit is available. 464 pages.

PROGRAMMING SUBFILES IN COBOL/400
By Jerry Goldson
Learn how to program subfiles in COBOL/400 in a matter of hours! This powerful and flexible programming technique no longer needs to elude you. You can begin programming with subfiles the same day you get the book. You don't have to wade through page after page, chapter after chapter of rules and parameters and keywords. Instead, you get solid, helpful information and working examples that you can apply to your application programs right away. 204 pages.

THE QUINTESSENTIAL GUIDE TO PC SUPPORT
By John Enck, Robert E. Anderson, Michael Otey, and Michael Ryan
This comprehensive book about IBM's AS/400 PC Support connectivity product defines the architecture of PC Support and its role in midrange networks, describes PC Support's installation and configuration procedures, and shows you how you can configure and use PC Support to solve real-life problems. 345 pages.

RPG ERROR HANDLING TECHNIQUE
Bulletproofing Your Applications
By Russell Popeil
RPG Error Handling Technique teaches you the skills you need to use the powerful tools provided by OS/400 and RPG to handle almost any error from within your programs. The book explains the INFSR, INFDS, PSSR, and SDS in programming terms, with examples that show you how all these tools work together and which tools are most appropriate for which kind of error or exception situation. It continues by presenting a robust suite of error/exception handling techniques within RPG programs. Each technique is explained in an application setting, using both RPG III and RPG IV code. 164 pages.

RPG IV BY EXAMPLE
By George Farr and Shailan Topiwala
RPG IV by Example addresses the needs and concerns of RPG programmers at any level of experience. The focus is on RPG IV in a practical context that lets AS/400 professionals quickly grasp what's new without dwelling on the old.

Beginning with an overview of RPG IV specifications, the authors prepare the way for examining all the features of the new version of the language. The chapters that follow explore RPG IV further with practical, easy-to-use applications. 500 pages.

RPG IV Jump Start, Second Edition
Moving Ahead With the New RPG
By Bryan Meyers, a NEWS/400 *technical editor*

In this second edition of *RPG IV Jump Start*, Bryan Meyers has added coverage for new releases of the RPG IV compiler (V3R2, V3R6, and V3R7) and amplified the coverage of RPG IV's participation in the integrated language environment (ILE). As in the first edition, he covers RPG IV's changed and new specifications and data types. He presents the new RPG from the perspective of a programmer who already knows the old RPG, pointing out the differences between the two and demonstrating how to take advantage of the new syntax and function. 204 pages.

RPG/400 Interactive Template Technique
By Carson Soule, CDP, CCP, CSP

Here's an updated version of Carson Soule's *Interactive RPG/400 Programming*. The book shows you time-saving, program-sharpening concepts behind the template approach, and includes all the code you need to build one perfect program after another. These templates include code for cursor-sensitive prompting in DDS, for handling messages in resident RPG programs, for using the CLEAR opcode to eliminate hard-coded field initialization, and much more. There's even a new select template with a pop-up window. 258 pages.

S/36 Power Tools
Edited by Chuck Lundgren, a NEWS/400 *technical editor*

Winner of an STC Award of Achievement in 1992, this book contains five years' worth of articles, tips, and programs published in *NEWS 3X/400* from 1986 to October 1990, including more than 280 programs and procedures. Extensively cross-referenced for fast and easy problem solving, and complete with diskette containing all the programming code. 738 pages.

Starter Kit for the AS/400, Second Edition
An indispensable guide for novice to intermediate AS/400 programmers and system operators
By Wayne Madden, NEWS/400 *publisher and editor in chief,*
with contributions by Bryan Meyers, Andrew Smith, and Peter Rowley

This second edition contains updates of the material in the first edition and incorporates new material to enhance its value as a resource to help you learn important basic concepts and nuances of the AS/400 system. New material focuses on installing a new release, working with PTFs, AS/400 message handling, working with and securing printed output, using operational assistant to manage disk space, job scheduling, save and restore basics, and more basic CL programming concepts. Optional diskette available. 429 pages.

Subfile Technique for RPG/400 Programmers
By Jonathan Yergin, CDP, and Wayne Madden

Here's the code you need for a complete library of shell subfile programs: RPG/400 code, DDS, CL, and sample data files. There's even an example for programming windows. You even get some "whiz bang" techniques that add punch to your applications. This book explains the code in simple, straightforward style and tells you when each technique should be used for best results. 326 pages, 3.5" PC diskette included.

TECHNICAL REFERENCE SERIES: DESKTOP GUIDES

Edited by Bryan Meyers, a NEWS/400 *technical editor*

Written by experts, these unique desktop guides put the latest AS/400 applications and techniques at your fingertips. These "just-do-it" books are priced so you can keep your personal set handy. Optional online Windows help diskette available for each book.

Desktop Guide to AS/400 Programmers' Tools

By Dan Riehl, a NEWS/400 *technical editor*

This second book of the NEWS/400 *Technical Reference Series* gives you the "how-to" behind all the tools included in *Application Development ToolSet/400* (ADTS/400), IBM's Licensed Program Product for Version 3 of OS/400; includes Source Entry Utility (SEU), Programming Development Manager (PDM), Screen Design Aid (SDA), Report Layout Utility (RLU), File Compare/Merge Utility (FCMU), and Interactive Source Debugger. Highlights topics and functions specific to Version 3 of OS/400. 266 pages.

Desktop Guide to CL Programming

By Bryan Meyers, a NEWS/400 *technical editor*

This first book of the NEWS/400 *Technical Reference Series* is packed with easy-to-find notes, short explanations, practical tips, answers to most of your everyday questions about CL, and CL code segments you can use in your own CL programming. Complete "short reference" lists every command and explains the most-often-used ones, along with names of the files they use and the MONMSG messages to use with them. 205 pages.

Desktop Guide to Creating CL Commands

By Lynn Nelson

In *Desktop Guide to Creating CL Commands*, author Lynn Nelson shows you how to create your own CL commands with the same functionality and power as the IBM commands you use every day, including automatic parameter editing, all the function keys, F4 prompt for values, expanding lists of values, and conditional prompting. After you have read this book, you can write macros for the operations you do over and over every day or write application commands that prompt users for essential information. Whether you're in operations or programming, don't miss this opportunity to enhance your career-building skills. 164 pages.

Desktop Guide to DDS

By James Coolbaugh

This third book of the NEWS/400 *Technical Reference Series* provides a complete reference to all DDS keywords for physical, logical, display, printer, and ICF files. Each keyword is briefly explained, with syntax rules and examples showing how to code the keyword. All basic and pertinent information is provided for quick and easy access. While this guide explains every parameter for a keyword, it doesn't explain every possible exception that might exist. Rather, the guide includes the basics about what each keyword is designed to accomplish. The *Desktop Guide to DDS* is designed to give quick, "at your fingertips" information about every keyword — with this in hand, you won't need to refer to IBM's bulky *DDS Reference* manual. 132 pages.

Desktop Guide to OPNQRYF

By Mike Dawson and Mike Manto

The OPNQRYF command is the single most dynamic and versatile command on the AS/400. But unless you understand just what it is and what it does, it can seem mysterious. Our new Desktop Guide leads you through the details with lots of examples to bring you up to speed quickly. 150 pages.

Desktop Guide to RPG/400

By Roger Pence and Julian Monypenny, NEWS/400 *technical editors*

This fourth book in the *Technical Reference Series* provides a variety of RPG templates, subroutines, and copy modules, sprinkled with evangelical advice that will help you write robust and effective RPG/400 programs. Highlights of the information provided include string-handling routines, numeric editing routines, date routines, error-handling modules, tips for using OS/400 APIs with RPG/400, and interactive programming techniques. For all types of RPG projects, this book's tested and ready-to-run building blocks will easily snap into your RPG. The programming solutions provided here would otherwise take you days or even weeks to write and test. 211 pages.

DESKTOP GUIDE TO SQL
By James Coolbaugh
The *Desktop Guide to SQL* is an invaluable reference guide for any programmer looking to gain a better understanding of SQL syntax and rules. For the novice SQL user, the book features plenty of introductory-level explanatory text and examples. More experienced users will appreciate the in-depth treatment of key SQL concepts, including using SQL on distributive databases, accessing a database with SQL's powerful data manipulation language, and much more. 210 pages.

UNDERSTANDING BAR CODES
By James R. Plunkett
One of the most important waves of technology sweeping American industry is the use of bar coding to capture and track data. With so many leading-edge technologies, it can be difficult for IS professionals to keep up with the concepts and applications they need to make solid decisions. This book gives you an overview of bar code technology including a discussion of the bar codes themselves, the hardware that supports bar coding, how and when to justify and then implement a bar code application, plus examples of many different applications and how bar coding can be used to solve problems. 70 pages.

USING QUERY/400
By Patrice Gapen and Catherine Stoughton
This textbook, designed for any AS/400 user from student to professional with or without prior programming knowledge, presents Query as an easy and fast tool for creating reports and files from AS/400 databases. Topics are ordered from simple to complex and emphasize hands-on AS/400 use; they include defining database files to Query, selecting and sequencing fields, generating new numeric and character fields, sorting within Query, joining database files, defining custom headings, creating new database files, and more. Instructor's kit available. 92 pages.

USING VISUAL BASIC WITH CLIENT ACCESS APIs
By Ron Jones
This book is for programmers who want to develop client/server solutions on the AS/400 and the personal computer. Whether you are a VB novice or a VB expert, you will gain by reading this book because it provides a thorough overview of the principles and requirements for programming in Windows using VB. Companion diskettes contain source code for all the programming projects referenced in the book, as well as for numerous other utilities and programs. All the projects are compatible with Windows 95 and VB 4.0. 680 pages.

FOR A COMPLETE CATALOG OR TO PLACE AN ORDER, CONTACT

NEWS/400 and Duke Press
Duke Communications International
221 E. 29th Street • Loveland, CO 80538-2727
(800) 621-1544 • (970) 663-4700 • Fax: (970) 669-3016

OR SHOP OUR WEB SITE: **www.dukepress.com**